Frederic P. Miller, Agnes F. Vandome,
John McBrewster (Ed.)

Dance

AF010957

Frederic P. Miller, Agnes F. Vandome,
John McBrewster (Ed.)

Dance

Motion (physics). Performance, History of dance, Choreography, Dance therapy, Health risks of professional dance, Dance in India, Dances of Sri Lanka, Concert dance,Ballet

Alphascript Publishing

Imprint

Permission is granted to copy, distribute and/or modify this document under the terms of the GNU Free Documentation License, Version 1.2 or any later version published by the Free Software Foundation; with no Invariant Sections, with the Front-Cover Texts, and with the Back-Cover Texts. A copy of the license is included in the section entitled "GNU Free Documentation License".

All parts of this book are extracted from Wikipedia, the free encyclopedia (www.wikipedia.org).

You can get detailed informations about the authors of this collection of articles at the end of this book. The editors (Ed.) of this book are no authors. They have not modified or extended the original texts.

Pictures published in this book can be under different licences than the GNU Free Documentation License. You can get detailed informations about the authors and licences of pictures at the end of this book.

The content of this book was generated collaboratively by volunteers. Please be advised that nothing found here has necessarily been reviewed by people with the expertise required to provide you with complete, accurate or reliable information. Some information in this book maybe misleading or wrong. The Publisher does not guarantee the validity of the information found here. If you need specific advice (f.e. in fields of medical, legal, financial, or risk management questions) please contact a professional who is licensed or knowledgeable in that area.

Any brand names and product names mentioned in this book are subject to trademark, brand or patent protection and are trademarks or registered trademarks of their respective holders. The use of brand names, product names, common names, trade names, product descriptions etc. even without a particular marking in this works is in no way to be construed to mean that such names may be regarded as unrestricted in respect of trademark and brand protection legislation and could thus be used by anyone.

Cover image: www.PureStockX.com
Concerning the licence of the cover image please contact PureStockX.

Publisher:
Alphascript Publishing is a trademark of
VDM Publishing House Ltd.,17 Rue Meldrum, Beau Bassin,1713-01 Mauritius
Email: info@vdm-publishing-house.com
Website: www.vdm-publishing-house.com

Published in 2009

Printed in: U.S.A., U.K., Germany. This book was not produced in Mauritius.

ISBN: 978-613-0-09308-2

Contents

Articles

Dance	1
Motion (physics)	8
Performance	14
History of dance	16
Choreography	20
Dance therapy	22
Health risks of professional dance	26
Dance in India	28
Dances of Sri Lanka	30
Concert dance	34
Ballet	37
20th century concert dance	41
African-American dance	44
Ballroom dance	50
B-boying	55
Dancesport	61
Krumping	63
Kandyan dance	65
Irish dance	69
Indian classical dance	74
Modern dance	76
Rock and Roll (dance)	83
Dance squad	86
Dancing with the Stars	88

References

Article Sources and Contributors	118
Image Sources, Licenses and Contributors	121

Dance

Dance (from French *danser*, perhaps from Frankish) is a sport and art form that generally refers to → movement of the body, usually rhythmic and to music,[1] used as a form of expression, social interaction or presented in a spiritual or → performance setting.

Dance may also to regarded as a form of nonverbal communication between humans, and is also performed by other animals (bee dance, patterns of behaviour such as a mating dance). Gymnastics, figure skating and synchronized swimming are sports dance disciplines, while martial arts kata are often compared to dances. → Motion in inanimate objects may also be described as dances (*the leaves danced in the wind*), and certain musical forms or genres.

→ Modern dance

Definitions of what constitutes dance are dependent on social, cultural, aesthetic, artistic and moral constraints and range from functional movement (such as folk dance) to virtuoso techniques such as → ballet. Dance can be participatory, social or → performed for an audience. It can also be ceremonial, competitive or erotic. Dance movements may be without significance in themselves, such as in → ballet or European folk dance, or have a gestural vocabulary/symbolic system as in many Asian dances. Dance can embody or express ideas, emotions or tell a story.

Dancing has evolved many styles. Breakdancing and → Krumping are related to the hip hop culture. African dance is interpretive. Ballet, Ballroom, Waltz, and Tango are classical styles of dance while Square and the Electric Slide are forms of step dances.

Every dance, no matter what style, has something in common. It not only involves flexibility and body movement, but also physics. If the proper physics is not taken into consideration, injuries may occur.

→ Choreography is the art of creating dances. The person who creates (i.e., choreographs) a dance is known as the choreographer.

Origins and history of dance

Dance does not leave behind clearly identifiable physical artifacts such as stone tools, hunting implements or cave paintings. It is not possible to say when dance became part of human culture. Dance has certainly been an important part of ceremony, rituals, celebrations and entertainment since before the birth of the earliest human civilizations. Archeology delivers traces of dance from prehistoric times such as the 9,000 year old Rock Shelters of Bhimbetka paintings in India and Egyptian tomb paintings depicting dancing figures from circa 3300 BC.

Eighteenth century social dance. Translated caption: *A cheerful dance awakens love and feeds hope with lively joy*, (Florence, 1790).

One of the earliest structured uses of dances may have been in the performance and in the telling of myths. It was also sometimes used to show feelings for one of the opposite gender. It is also linked to the origin of "love making." Before the production of written languages, dance was one of the methods of passing these stories down from generation to generation. [2]

Another early use of dance may have been as a precursor to ecstatic trance states in healing rituals. Dance is still used for this purpose by many cultures from the Brazilian rainforest to the Kalahari Desert.[3]

Sri Lankan dances goes back to the mythological times of aboriginal yingyang twins and "yakkas" (devils). According to a Sinhalese legend, → Kandyan dances originate, 250 years ago, from a magic ritual that broke the spell on a bewitched king. Many contemporary dance forms can be traced back to historical, traditional, ceremonial, and ethnic dance.

Dance classification and genres

Dancing

Dance categories by number of interacting dancers are mainly solo dance, partner dance and group dance. Dance is performed for various purposes like ceremonial dance, erotic dance, performance dance, social dance etc.

Dancing and music

Many early forms of music and dance were created and performed together. This paired development has continued through the ages with dance/music forms such as: jig, waltz, tango, disco, salsa, electronica and hip-hop. Some musical genres also have a parallel dance form such as baroque music and baroque dance whereas others developed separately: classical music and classical ballet.

Although dance is often accompanied by music, it can also be presented independently or provide its own accompaniment (tap dance). Dance presented with music may or may not be performed *in time* to the music depending on the style of dance. Dance performed without music is said to be *danced to its own rhythm.*

Ballroom dancing is an art although it may incorporates many fitness components using an artistic state of mind.

Dance studies and techniques

In the early 1920s, dance studies (dance practice, critical theory, Musical analysis and history) began to be considered an academic discipline. Today these studies are an integral part of many universities' arts and humanities programs. By the late 20th century the recognition of practical knowledge as equal to academic knowledge lead to the emergence of *practice research* and *practice as research*. A large range of dance courses are available including:

- Professional practice: performance and technical skills
- Practice research: choreography and performance
- Ethnochoreology, encompassing the dance-related aspects of anthropology, cultural studies, gender studies, area studies, postcolonial theory, ethnography, etc.

Partner dance.

- → Dance therapy or dance-movement therapy.
- Dance and technology: new media and performance technologies.
- Laban Movement Analysis and somatic studies

Academic degrees are available from BA (Hons) to PhD and other postdoctoral fellowships, with some dance scholars taking up their studies as *mature students* after a professional dance career.

Dance competitions

A **dance competition** is an organized event in which contestants perform dances before a judge or judges for awards and, in some cases, monetary prizes. There are several major types of dance competitions, distinguished primarily by the style or styles of dances performed. Major types of dance competitions include:

- **Competitive dance**, in which a variety of theater dance styles—such as acro, → ballet, jazz, hip-hop, lyrical, and tap—are permitted.

An amateur dancesport competition at MIT.

- **Open** competitions, which permit a wide variety of dance styles. A popular example of this is the TV program So You Think You Can Dance.
- → **Dancesport**, which is focused exclusively on → ballroom and latin dance. Popular examples of this are TV programs → Dancing with the Stars and Strictly Come Dancing.
- **Single-style** competitions, such as highland dance, → dance team, and → Irish dance, which only permit a single dance style.

Today, there are various dances and dance show competitions on Television and the Internet.

Dance occupations

There are different careers connected with dancing: Dancer, dance teacher, dance sport coach, → dance therapist and choreographer.

Dancer

Dance training differs depending on the dance form. There are university programs and schools associated with professional dance companies for specialised training in classical dance (e.g. Ballet) and modern dance. There are also smaller, privately owned dance studios where students may train in a variety of dance forms including competitive dance forms (e.g. Latin dance, ballroom dance, etc.) as well as ethnic/traditional dance forms.

Professional dancers are usually employed on contract or for particular performances/productions. The professional life of a dancer is generally one of constantly changing work situations, strong competition pressure and low pay. Professional dancers often need to supplement their income, either in dance related roles (e.g., dance teaching, dance sport coaches, yoga) or Pilates instruction to achieve financial stability.

Professional dancers at the Tropicana Club, Havana, Cuba, in 2008

In the U.S. many professional dancers are members of unions such as the American Guild of Musical Artists, the Screen Actors Guild and Actors' Equity Association. The unions help determine working conditions and minimum salaries for their members.

Dance teachers

Dance teacher and operators of dance schools rely on reputation and marketing. For dance forms without an association structure such as Salsa or Tango Argentino they may not have formal training. Most dance teachers are self employed.

Dancesport coaches

Dancesport coaches are tournament dancers or former dancesports people, and may be recognised by a dance sport federation.

Choreographer

Choreographers are generally university trained and are typically employed for particular projects or, more rarely may work on contract as the resident choreographer for a specific dance company. A choreographic work is protected intellectual property. Dancers may undertake their own choreography.

Dance by ethnicity or region

Dance in South Asia

India

During the first millennium BCE in India, many texts were composed which attempted to codify aspects of daily life. In the matter of dance, Bharata Muni's *Natyashastra* (literally *"the text of dramaturgy"*) is the one of the earlier texts. Though the main theme of *Natyashastra* deals with drama, dance is also widely featured, and indeed the two concepts have ever since been linked in Indian culture. The text elaborates various hand-gestures or mudras and classifies movements of the various limbs of the body, gait, and so on. The Natyashastra categorised dance into four groups and into four regional varieties, naming the groups: secular, ritual, abstract, and, interpretive. However, concepts of regional geography has altered and so have regional varieties of Indian dances. Dances like *"Odra Magadhi"*, which after decades long debate, has been traced to present day Mithila-Orissa region's dance form of Odissi, indicate influence of dances in cultural interactions between different regions.[4]

South indian traditional Dance like a horse known as Poi Kal Kudirai

From these beginnings rose the various classical styles which are recognised today. Therefore, all Indian classical dances are to varying degrees rooted in the Natyashastra and therefore share common features: for example, the mudras, some body positions, and the inclusion of dramatic or expressive acting or abhinaya. The Indian classical music tradition provides the accompaniment for the dance, and as percussion is such an integral part of the tradition, the dancers of nearly all the styles wear bells around their ankles to counterpoint and complement the percussion.

Bhangra in the Punjab

The Punjab area overlapping India and Pakistan is the place of origin of Bhangra. It is widely known both as a style of music and a dance. It is mostly related to ancient harvest celebrations, love, patriotism or social issues. Its music is coordinated by a musical instrument called the 'Dhol'. Bhangra is not just music but a dance, a celebration of the harvest where people beat the dhol (drum), sing Boliyaan (lyrics) and dance.It developed further with the Vaisakhi festival of the Sikhs.

Dances of Sri Lanka

The devil dances of Sri Lanka or "yakun natima" are a carefully crafted ritual with a history reaching far back into Sri Lanka's pre-Buddhist past. It combines ancient "Ayurvedic" concepts of disease causation with psychological manipulation. The dance combines many aspects including Sinhalese cosmology, the dances also has an impact on the classical dances of Sri Lanka.[5]

Morris dancing in the grounds of Wells Cathedral, Wells, England

In Europe and North America

Concert (or performance) dance

Ballet

→ Ballet developed first in Italy and then in France from lavish court spectacles that combined music, drama, poetry, song, costumes and dance. Members of the court nobility took part as performers. During the reign of Louis XIV, himself a dancer, dance became more codified. Professional dancers began to take the place of court amateurs, and ballet masters were licensed by the French government. The first ballet dance academy was the Académie Royale de Danse (Royal Dance Academy), opened in Paris in 1661. Shortly thereafter, the first institutionalized ballet troupe, associated with the Academy, was formed; this troupe began as an all-male ensemble but by 1681 opened to include women as well.[2]

Harlequin and Columbine from the mime theater at *Tivoli*, Denmark.

20th century concert dance

At the beginning of the 20th century, there was an explosion of innovation in dance style characterized by an exploration of freer technique. Early pioneers of what became known as → modern dance include Loie Fuller, Isadora Duncan, Mary Wigman and Ruth St. Denis. The relationship of music to dance serves as the basis for Eurhythmics, devised by Emile Jaques-Dalcroze, which was influential to the development of Modern dance and modern ballet through artists such as Marie Rambert. Eurythmy, developed by Rudolf Steiner and Marie Steiner-von Sivers, combines formal elements reminiscent of traditional dance with the new freer style, and introduced a complex new vocabulary to dance. In the 1920s, important founders of the new style such as Martha Graham and Doris Humphrey began their work. Since this time, a wide variety of dance styles have been developed; see → Modern dance.

The influence of African American dance

African American dances are those dances which have developed within African American communities in everyday spaces, rather than in dance studios, schools or companies and its derivatives, tap dance, disco, jazz dance, swing dance, hip hop dance and breakdance. Other dances, such as the lindy hop with its relationship to rock and roll music and rock and roll dance have also had a global influence.

See also

Lists

- List of choreographers
- List of dance style categories
- List of dance topics
- List of dance wikibooks

Related topics

- African American dance
- *An American Ballroom Companion*
- Backup dancer

Dancers in a city square

- → Ballroom dance
- Cheerleading

- Entrainment (Biomusicology)
- Dance costumes
- Dance criticism
- Dance theory
- Majorettes

Further reading

- Adshead-Lansdale, J. (Ed) (1994) *Dance History: An Introduction*. Routledge. ISBN 0-415-09030-X
- Carter, A. (1998) *The Routledge Dance Studies Reader*. Routledge. ISBN 0-415-16447-8
- Cohen, S, J. (1992) *Dance As a Theatre Art: Source Readings in Dance History from 1581 to the Present*. Princeton Book Co. ISBN 0-87127-173-7
- Charman, S. Kraus, R, G. Chapman, S. and Dixon-Stowall, B. (1990) *History of the Dance in Art and Education*. Pearson Education. ISBN 0-13-389362-6
- Daly, A. (2002) *Critical Gestures: Writings on Dance and Culture*. Wesleyan University Press. ISBN 0-8195-6566-0
- Dils, A. (2001) *Moving History/Dancing Cultures: A Dance History Reader*. Wesleyan University Press. ISBN 0-8195-6413-3
- Miller, James, L. (1986) *Measures of Wisdom: The Cosmic Dance in Classical and Christian Antiquity*, University of Toronto Press. ISBN 0802025536

External links

- Historic illustrations of dancing from 3300 B.C. to 1911 A.D. [6] from Project Gutenberg
- United States National Museum of Dance and Hall of Fame [7]

ckb:ھە‌ڵپەركێ

References

[1] britannica (http://www.britannica.com/eb/article-9110116/dance)
[2] Nathalie Comte. "Europe, 1450 to 1789: Encyclopedia of the Early Modern World". Ed. Jonathan Dewald. Vol. 2. New York: Charles Scribner's Sons, 2004. pp 94–108.
[3] Guenther, Mathias Georg. 'The San Trance Dance: Ritual and Revitalization Among the Farm Bushmen of the Ghanzi District, Republic of Botswana.' Journal, South West Africa Scientific Society, v30, 1975–76.
[4] Dance: The Living Spirit of Indian Arts (http://www.exoticindiaart.com/article/dance), by Prof. P. C. Jain and Dr. Daljeet.
[5] "The yakun natima — devil dance ritual of Sri Lanka" (http://www.lankalibrary.com/rit/yakun natuma.htm) at the "Virtual Library of Sri Lanka"
[6] http://www.gutenberg.org/etext/17289
[7] http://www.dancemuseum.org/

Motion (physics)

In physics, **motion** means a change in the location of a body. Change in motion is the result of applied force. Motion is typically described in terms of velocity, acceleration, displacement, and time.[1] An object's velocity cannot change unless it is acted upon by a force, as described by Newton's first law also known as Inertia. An object's momentum is directly related to the object's mass and velocity, and the total momentum of all objects in a closed system (one not affected by external forces) does not change with time, as described by the law of conservation of momentum.

A body which does not move is said to be *at rest*, *motionless*, *immobile*, *stationary*, or to have constant (time-invariant) position.

Motion involves change in position, such as in this perspective of rapidly leaving Yongsan Station

Motion is always observed and measured relative to a frame of reference. As there is no absolute reference frame, *absolute motion* cannot be determined; this is emphasised by the term *relative motion*.[2] A body which is motionless relative to a given reference frame, moves relative to infinitely many other frames. Thus, everything in the universe is moving.[3]

More generally, the term **motion** signifies any spatial and/or temporal change in a physical system. For example, one can talk about motion of a wave or a quantum particle (or any other field) where the concept **location** does not apply.

Laws of Motion

In physics, motion in the universe is described through two sets of apparently incompatible laws of mechanics. Motions of all large scale and familiar objects in the universe (such as projectiles, planets, cells, and humans) are described by classical mechanics. Whereas the motion of very small atomic and sub-atomic sized objects is described by quantum mechanics.

Classical mechanics

Classical mechanics is used for describing the motion of macroscopic objects, from projectiles to parts of machinery, as well as astronomical objects, such as spacecraft, planets, stars, and galaxies. It produces very accurate results within these domains, and is one of the oldest and largest subjects in science, engineering and technology.

Classical mechanics is fundamentally based on Newton's Laws of Motion. These laws describe the relationship between the forces acting on a body and the → motion of that body. They were first compiled by Sir Isaac Newton in his work *Philosophiæ Naturalis Principia Mathematica*, first published on July 5, 1687. His three laws are:

1. In the absence of a net external force, a body either is at rest or moves with constant velocity.
2. The net external force on a body is equal to the mass of that body times its acceleration; $F = ma$. Alternatively, force is proportional to the time derivative of momentum.
3. Whenever a first body exerts a force F on a second body, the second body exerts a force $-F$ on the first body. F and $-F$ are equal in magnitude and opposite in direction.[4]

Newton's three laws of motion, along with his law of universal gravitation, explain Kepler's laws of planetary motion, which were the first to accurately provide a mathematical model or understanding orbiting bodies in outer space. This explanation unified the motion of celestial bodies and motion of objects on earth.

Classical mechanics was later further enhanced by Albert Einstein's special relativity and general relativity. Special relativity explains the motion of objects with a high velocity, approaching the speed of light; general relativity is employed to handle gravitation motion at a deeper level.

Quantum mechanics

Quantum mechanics is a set of principles describing physical reality at the atomic level of matter (molecules and atoms) and the subatomic (electrons, protons, and even smaller particles). These descriptions include the simultaneous wave-like and particle-like behavior of both matter and radiation energy, this described in the wave–particle duality.

In contrast to classical mechanics, where accurate measurements and predictions can be calculated about location and velocity, in the quantum mechanics of a subatomic particle, one can never specify its state, such as its simultaneous location and velocity, with complete certainty (this is called the Heisenberg uncertainty principle).

In addition to describing the motion of atomic level phenomenon, quantum mechanics is useful in understanding some large scale phenomenon such as superfluidity, superconductivity, and biological systems, including the function of smell receptors and the structures of proteins.

List of "imperceptible" human motions

Humans, like all things in the universe are in constant motion,[5] however, aside from obvious movements of the various external body parts and locomotion, humans are in motion in a variety of ways which are more difficult to perceive. Many of these "imperceptible motions" are only perceivable with the help of special tools and careful observation. The larger scales of "imperceptible motions" are difficult for humans to perceive for two reasons: 1) Newton's laws of motion (particularly Inertia) which prevent humans from feeling motions of a mass to which they are connected, and 2) the lack of an obvious frame of reference which would allow individuals to easily see that they are moving.[6] The smaller scales of these motions are too small for humans to sense.

Universe

- Spacetime (the fabric of the universe) is actually expanding. Essentially, everything in the universe is stretching like a rubber band. This motion is the most obscure as it is not physical motion as such, but rather a change in the very nature of the universe. The primary source of verification of this expansion was provided by Edwin Hubble who demonstrated that all galaxies and distant astronomical objects were moving away from us (*"Hubble's law"*) as predicted by a universal expansion.[7]

Galaxy

- The Milky Way Galaxy, is hurtling through space at an incredible speed. It is powered by the force left over from the Big Bang. Many astronomers believe the Milky Way is moving at approximately 600 km/s relative to the observed locations of other nearby galaxies. Another reference frame is provided by the Cosmic microwave background. This frame of reference indicates that The Milky Way is moving at around 552 km/s.[8]

Solar System

- The Milky Way is rotating around its dense galactic center, thus the solar system is moving in a circle within the galaxy's gravity. Away from the central bulge or outer rim, the typical stellar velocity is between 210 and 240 km/s.[9]

Earth

- The Earth is rotating or spinning around its axis, this is evidenced by day and night, at the equator the earth has an eastward velocity of 0.4651 km/s (or 1040 mi/h).[10]
- The Earth is orbiting around the Sun in an orbital revolution. A complete orbit around the sun takes one year or about 365 days; it averages a speed of about 30 km/s (or 67,000 mi/h).[11]

Continents

- The Theory of Plate tectonics tells us that the continents are drifting on convection currents within the mantle causing them to move across the surface of the planet at the slow speed of approximately 1 inch (2.54 cm) per year.[12][13] However, the velocities of plates range widely. The fastest-moving plates are the oceanic plates, with the Cocos Plate advancing at a rate of 75 mm/yr[14] (3.0 in/yr) and the Pacific Plate moving 52–69 mm/yr (2.1–2.7 in/yr). At the other extreme, the slowest-moving plate is the Eurasian Plate, progressing at a typical rate of about 21 mm/yr (0.8 in/yr).

Internal body

- The human heart is constantly contracting to move blood throughout the body. Through larger veins and arteries in the body blood has been found to travel at approximately 0.33 m/s.[15] Though considerable variation exists, and peak flows in the venae cavae have been found to range between 0.1 m/s and 0.45 m/s.[16]
- The smooth muscles of hollow internal organs are moving. The most familiar would be peristalsis which is where digested food is forced throughout the digestive tract. Though different foods travel through the body at rates, an average speed through the human small intestine is 2.16 m/h or 0.036 m/s.[17]
- Typically some sound is audible at any given moment, when the vibration of these sound waves reaches the ear drum it moves in response and allows the sense of hearing.
- The human lymphatic system is constantly moving excess fluids, lipids, and immune system related products around the body. The lymph fluid has been found to move through a lymph capillary of the skin at approximately 0.0000097 m/s.[18]

Cells

The cells of the human body have many structures which move throughout them.

- Cytoplasmic streaming is a way which cells move molecular substances throughout the cytoplasm.[19]
- Various motor proteins work as molecular motors within a cell and move along the surface of various cellulars substrate such as microtubules. Motor proteins are typically powered by the hydrolysis of adenosine triphosphate, (ATP), and convert chemical energy into mechanical work.[20] Vesicles propelled by motor proteins have been found to have a velocity of approximately 0.00000152 m/s.[21]

Particles

- According to the laws of thermodynamics all particles of matter are in constant random motion as long as the temperature is above absolute zero. Thus the molecules and atoms which make you up are vibrating, colliding, and moving. This motion can be detected as temperature; high temperatures (which represent greater kinetic energy in the particles) feel warmer to humans, whereas lower temperatures feel colder.[22]

Subatomic particles

- Within each atom the electrons are speeding around the nucleus so fast that they are not actually in one location, but rather smeared across a region of the electron cloud. Electrons have a high velocity, and the larger the nucleus they are orbiting the faster they move. In a hydrogen atom, electrons have been calculated to be orbiting at a speed of approximately 2,420,000 m/s[23]
- Inside the atomic nucleus the protons and neutrons are also probably moving around due the electrical repulsion of the protons and the presence of angular momentum of both particles.[24]

Light

Light propagates at 299,792,458 m/s (about 186,282.397 mi/s). According to the theory of relativity, nothing can move faster than the speed of light.

Types

- Simple harmonic motion – pendulum).
- Linear motion – motion which follows a straight linear path, and whose displacement is exactly the same as its trajectory.
- Reciprocating (i.e. vibration)
- Brownian Motion (i.e. the random movement of particles)
- Circular motion (e.g. the orbits of planets)
- Rotary motion – a motion about a fixed point ex. the wheel of a bicycle

See also

- Equation of motion
- Molecular dynamics
- Motion perception
- Newton's laws of motion
- Trajectory of a projectile
- Rigid body motion

References

[1] Nave, R. 2005. Motion. HyperPhysics. Georgia State University (http://hyperphysics.phy-astr.gsu.edu/hbase/hframe.html)
[2] Wåhlin, L. 1997. "THE DEADBEAT UNIVERSE" (http://www.colutron.com/download_files/chapt9.pdf), Chapter 9. Colutron Research Corporation ISBN 0 933407 03 3
[3] De Grasse Tyson, N., Liu, C., & Irion, R. 2000. One Universe: At home in the cosmos. p.20–21. Joseph Henry Press. ISBN 0-309-06488-0 (http://www.nap.edu/html/oneuniverse/motion_20-21.html)
[4] Newton's "Axioms or Laws of Motion" can be found in the "Principia" on page 19 of volume 1 of the 1729 translation (http://books.google.com/books?id=Tm0FAAAAQAAJ&pg=PA19#v=onepage&q=&f=false).
[5] De Grasse Tyson, N., Liu, C., & Irion, R. 2000. One Universe: At home in the cosmos. p.8–9. Joseph Henry Press. ISBN 0-309-06488-0 (http://www.nap.edu/html/oneuniverse/motion_8-9.html)
[6] Safkan, Y. 2007 (http://www.physlink.com/education/askexperts/ae118.cfm) "f the term 'absolute motion' has no meaning, then why do we say that the earth moves around the sun and not vice versa?" Ask the Experts. PhysicsLink
[7] Hubble, Edwin, " A Relation between Distance and Radial Velocity among Extra-Galactic Nebulae (http://adsabs.harvard.edu/cgi-bin/nph-bib_query?bibcode=1929PNAS...15..168H&db_key=AST&data_type=HTML&format=&high=42ca922c9c30954)" (1929) *Proceedings of the National Academy of Sciences of the United States of America*, Volume 15, Issue 3, pp. 168–173 (Full article (http://www.pnas.org/cgi/reprint/15/3/168), PDF)
[8] Kogut, A.; Lineweaver, C.; Smoot, G. F.; Bennett, C. L.; Banday, A.; Boggess, N. W.; Cheng, E. S.; de Amici, G.; Fixsen, D. J.; Hinshaw, G.; Jackson, P. D.; Janssen, M.; Keegstra, P.; Loewenstein, K.; Lubin, P.; Mather, J. C.; Tenorio, L.; Weiss, R.; Wilkinson, D. T.; Wright, E. L. (1993). " Dipole Anisotropy in the COBE Differential Microwave Radiometers First-Year Sky Maps (http://adsabs.harvard.edu/cgi-bin/nph-bib_query?bibcode=1993ApJ...419....1K)". *Astrophysical Journal* **419**: 1. doi: 10.1086/173453 (http://dx.doi.org/10.1086/173453). . Retrieved 2007-05-10.
[9] Imamura, Jim (August 10 2006). " Mass of the Milky Way Galaxy (http://zebu.uoregon.edu/~imamura/123/lecture-2/mass.html)". University of Oregon. . Retrieved 2007-05-10.
[10] Ask and Astrophysicist (http://imagine.gsfc.nasa.gov/docs/ask_astro/answers/970401c.html). NASA Goodard Space Flight Center.
[11] Williams, David R. (September 1, 2004). " Earth Fact Sheet (http://nssdc.gsfc.nasa.gov/planetary/factsheet/earthfact.html)". NASA. . Retrieved 2007-03-17.
[12] Staff. " GPS Time Series (http://sideshow.jpl.nasa.gov/mbh/series.html)". NASA JPL. . Retrieved 2007-04-02.
[13] Huang, Zhen Shao. " Speed of the Continental Plates (http://hypertextbook.com/facts/ZhenHuang.shtml)". *The Physics Factbook*. . Retrieved 2007-11-09.
[14] Meschede, M.; Udo Barckhausen, U. (November 20, 2000). " Plate Tectonic Evolution of the Cocos-Nazca Spreading Center (http://www-odp.tamu.edu/publications/170_SR/chap_07/chap_07.htm)". *Proceedings of the Ocean Drilling Program*. Texas A&M University. . Retrieved 2007-04-02.
[15] Penny, P. (http://www.coheadquarters.com/PennLibr/MyPhysiology/lect5/xpen5.01.htm) 2003. Hemodynamic: Blood Velocity
[16] LEWIS WEXLER, DEREK H. BERGEL, IVOR T. GABE, GEOFFREY S. MAKIN, & CHRISTOPHER J. MILLS (01 Sep 1968). " Velocity of Blood Flow in Normal Human Venae Cavae (http://circres.ahajournals.org/cgi/content/abstract/circresaha;23/3/349)". *Circulation Research*. **23** (3): 349. PMID 5676450. . Retrieved 2007-11-14.
[17] Bowen, R. (http://www.vivo.colostate.edu/hbooks/pathphys/digestion/basics/transit.html) 2006. Gastrointestinal Transit: How Long Does It Take? Colorado State University.
[18] M. Fischer, U. K. Franzeck, I. Herrig, U. Costanzo, S. Wen, M. Schiesser, U. Hoffmann and A. Bollinger (01 Jan 1996). " Flow velocity of single lymphatic capillaries in human skin (http://ajpheart.physiology.org/cgi/content/abstract/270/1/H358)". *Am J Physiol Heart Circ Physiology* **270** (1): H358–H363. PMID 8769772. . Retrieved 2007-11-14.
[19] Cytoplasmic Streaming: Encyclopedia Britannica (http://www.britannica.com/eb/article-9028448/cytoplasmic-streaming)
[20] Microtubule Motors: Rensselaer Polytechnic Institute. (http://www.rpi.edu/dept/bcbp/molbiochem/MBWeb/mb2/part1/kinesin.htm)
[21] Hill, David; Holzwarth, George; Bonin, Keith (2002). " Velocity and Drag Forces on motor-protein-driven Vesicles in Cells (http://adsabs.harvard.edu/abs/2002APS..SES.EA002H)". *American Physical Society, the 69th Annual Meeting of the Southeastern* **abstract #EA.002**. . Retrieved 2007-11-14.
[22] Temperature and BEC. (http://www.colorado.edu/UCB/AcademicAffairs/ArtsSciences/physics/PhysicsInitiative/Physics2000/bec/temperature.html) Physics 2000: Colorado State University Physics Department

[23] Ask a scientist archive. Argonne National Laboratory, United States Department of Energy (http://www.newton.dep.anl.gov/newton/askasci/1993/physics/PHY112.HTM)
[24] Chapter 2, Nuclear Science- A guide to the nuclear science wall chart. Berkley National Laboratory. (http://www.lbl.gov/abc/wallchart/teachersguide/pdf/Chap02.pdf)

ckb:جووڵە (فیزیک)

Performance

Performing arts
Major forms
→ Dance · Music · Opera · Theatre · Circus Arts
Minor forms
Magic · Puppetry
Genres
Drama · Tragedy · Comedy · Tragicomedy · Romance · Satire · Epic · Lyric

A **performance**, in performing arts, generally comprises an event in which one group of people (the performer or performers) behave in a particular way for another group of people (the audience). Sometimes the dividing line between performer and the audience may become blurred, as in the example of "participatory theatre" where audience members might get involved in the production. Singing choral music, and performing in a → ballet are examples. Usually the performers participate in rehearsals beforehand. Afterwards audience members often clap, indicating appreciation. However, sometimes this rule is reversed. In Japan, the greatest compliment is complete silence.

Performances, for example in theatre, can take place daily, or at some other regular interval. Performances can take place at someone's house, in a subway, or even at a dollar store. Talent, on the other hand, is subjective.

Performance genres

Examples of performance genres include:
- musical genres:
  - concert
  - recital
  - music competition
- theatrical genres:
  - play
  - opera
  - operetta
  - → ballet and other types of dance
  - musical theater
- other genres:
  - circus acts
  - performance art
  - performance poetry
  - busking
  - magic (illusion)
  - storytelling

Music performance (a concert or a recital) may take place indoors in a concert hall or outdoors in a field, and may require the audience to remain very quiet, or encourage them to sing and → dance along with the music.

A performance may also describe the way in which an actor performs. In a solo capacity, it may also refer to a mime artist, comedian, conjurer, or other entertainer.

Kanye West performing in December 2008

A U.S. Navy sailor singing on a stage at a sporting event.

Buskers perform in San Francisco

Bibliography

- Philip V. Bohlman, Marcello Sorce Keller, and Loris Azzaroni (eds.), *Musical Anthropology of the Mediterranean: Interpretation, Performance, Identity*, Bologna, Edizioni Clueb – Cooperativa Libraria Universitaria Editrice, 2009.

History of dance

→ Dance does not often leave behind clearly identifiable physical artifacts that last over millennia, such as stone tools, hunting implements or cave paintings. It is not possible to say when dance became part of human culture. Dance has certainly been an important part of ceremony, rituals, celebrations and entertainment since before the birth of the earliest human civilizations. Archeology delivers traces of dance from prehistoric times such as the 9,000 year old Bhimbetka rock shelters paintings in India and Egyptian tomb paintings depicting dancing figures from circa 3300 BC.

One of the earliest structured uses of dances may have been in the performance and in the telling of myths. It was also sometimes used to show feelings for one of the opposite gender. It is also linked to the origin of "love making." Before the production of written languages, dance was one of the methods of passing these stories down from generation to generation.[1]

Another early use of dance may have been as a precursor to ecstatic trance states in healing rituals. Dance is still used for this purpose by many cultures from the Brazilian rainforest to the Kalahari Desert.[2]

Sri Lankan dances goes back to the mythological times of aboriginal yingyang twins and "yakkas" (devils). According to a Sinhalese legend, → Kandyan dances originate, 2500 years ago, from a magic ritual that broke the spell on a bewitched king.

Veiled dancer, terracotta figurine from Myrina, ca. 150–100 BC. Louvre Museum

Many contemporary dance forms can be traced back to historical, traditional, ceremonial, and ethnic dances.

An early manuscript describing dance is the Natya Shastra on which is based the *modern* interpretation of classical Indian dance (e.g. Bharathanatyam).

The ancient chronicle, the Sinhalese (Sri Lankans), the Mahavamsa states when King Vijaya landed in Sri Lanka in 543 BCE he heard sounds of music and dancing from a wedding ceremony. Origins of the → Dances of Sri Lanka are dated back to the aboriginal tribes. The Classical dances of Sri Lanka, Kandyan Dances features a highly developed system of tala (rhythm), provided by cymbals called thalampataa.

In European culture, one of the earliest records of dancing is by Homer, whose "Iliad"; describes chorea (*khoreia*). The early Greeks made the art of dancing into a system, expressive of all the different passions. For example, the dance of the Furies, so represented, would create complete terror among those who witnessed them. The Greek philosopher, Aristotle, ranked dancing with poetry, and said that certain dancers, with rhythm applied to gesture, could express manners, passions, and actions. The most eminent Greek sculptors studied the attitude of the dancers for their art of imitating the passions.

Asia

Drawing of 'urddhakeshin' Shiva at Nawda Todo, forms of monkeys at Gupteshvara and a number of human figures at Pahadgarh, Tikla and Abachand present evidence of dance. These drawings belong to the period from 5000 to 2000 B.C. As revealed by the stone statuette of a male dancer from Harappa and the bronze figurine of a dancing girl from Mohenjodaro, the Indus Valley civilization had a well-evolved dance culture.

→ Indian classical dance in the 20th Century

During the reign of the last Mughals and Nawabs of Oudh dance fell down to the status of 'nautch', an unethical sensuous thing of courtesans.

Dancing is historically entwined with many cultures around the world. Here, 17th century PersiansPersian women dance in a ceremony in Iran.

Later, linking dance with immoral trafficking and prostitution, British rule prohibited public performance of dance. Many disapproved it. In 1947, India won her freedom and for dance an ambience where it could regain its past glory. Classical forms and regional distinctions were re-discovered, ethnic specialties were honored and by synthesizing them with the individual talents of the masters in the line and fresh innovations emerged dance with a new face but with classicism of the past.

European dance

18th and 19th centuries: from court dancing to Romanticism

By the 1700s → ballet had migrated from the royal court to the Paris Opera, and the director Lully 'preserved the ballet du cour's basic concept of a composite form, in which the dance was an essential and important element.' During this century the ballet was to develop throughout Europe, from a courtly arrangement of moving images used as part of a larger spectacle, to a performance art in its own right, the ballet d'action. This new form swept away much of the artificiality of the court dance and strove towards 'the concept that art should aspire to imitate nature'. This ultimately resulted in costuming and choreography that was much more liberating to the dancer, and conducive to a fuller use of the expressive capacity of the body. It also opened the door to pointework, for this acceptance of more naturalistic costuming allowed the development of the heel-less shoe, which led to the dancer being able to make more use of the rise onto demi-pointe.

Pietro Longhi, "La lezione di danza" (The Dancing Lesson), ca 1741, Venezia, Gallerie dell'Accademia.

The era of Romanticism in the early 1800s, with ballets that focused more on the emotions, the fantasy and the spiritual worlds, heralded the beginning of true pointe-work. Now, on her toes, the deified ballerina (embodied in this period by the legendary ballerina Marie Taglioni) seemed to magically skim the surface of the stage, an ethereal being never quite touching the ground. It was during this period that the ascending star of the ballerina quite eclipsed the presence of the poor male dancer, who was in many cases reduced to the status of a moving statue, present only in order to lift the ballerina. This sad state was really only redressed by the rise of the male ballet star Nijinsky, with the Ballets Russes, in the early twentieth century. Ballet as we know it had well and truly evolved by this time, with all the familiar conventions of costume, choreographic form, plot, pomp, and circumstance firmly fixed in place.

Early 20th century: from ballet to contemporary dance

Since the Ballets Russes began revolutionising ballet in the early 20th century, there have been continued attempts to break the mold of classical ballet. Currently the artistic scope of ballet technique (and its accompanying music, jumper, and multimedia) is more all-encompassing than ever. The boundaries that classify a work of classical ballet are constantly being stretched, muddied and blurred until perhaps all that remains today are traces of technique idioms such as 'turn-out'.

It was during the explosion of new thinking and exploration in the early 20th century that dance artists began to appreciate the qualities of the individual, the necessities of ritual and religion, the primitive, the expressive and the emotional. In this atmosphere → modern dance began an explosion of growth. There was suddenly a new freedom in what was considered acceptable, what was considered art, and what people wanted to create. All kinds of other things were suddenly valued as much as, or beyond, the costumes and tricks of the ballet.

Most of the early 20th century modern choreographers and dancers saw ballet in the most negative light. Isadora Duncan thought it most ugly, nothing more than meaningless gymnastics. Martha Graham saw it as European and Imperialistic, having nothing to do with the modern American people. Merce Cunningham, while using some of the foundations of the ballet technique in his teaching, approached choreography and performance from a totally radical standpoint compared to the traditional balletic format.

The twentieth century was indeed a period of breaking away from everything that ballet stood for. It was a time of unprecedented creative growth, for dancers and choreographers. It was also a time of shock, surprise and broadening of minds for the public, in terms of their definitions of what dance was. It was a revolution in the truest sense.

Late 20th century / Early 21st century

After the explosion of modern dance in the early 20th century, the 1960s saw the growth of postmodernism. Postmodernism veered towards simplicity, the beauty of small things, the beauty of untrained bodies, and unsophisticated movement. The famous 'No' manifesto rejecting all costumes, stories and outer trappings in favour of raw and unpolished movement was perhaps the extreme of this wave of thinking. Unfortunately lack of costumes, stories and outer trappings do not make a good dance show, and it was not long before sets, décor and shock value re-entered the vocabulary of modern choreographers.

By the 1980s dance had come full circle and modern dance (or, by this time, 'contemporary dance') was clearly still a highly technical and political vehicle for many practitioners. Existing alongside classical ballet, the two art-forms were by now living peacefully next door to one another with little of the rivalry and antipathy of previous eras. In a cleverly designed comment on this ongoing rivalry the brilliant collaboration of Twyla Tharp (one of the 20th Century's cutting edge Dance avant-gardist/contemporary) and Ballet dance was ultimately achieved. The present time sees us still in the very competitive artistic atmosphere where choreographers compete to produce the most shocking work, however, there are still glimpses of beauty to be had, and much incredible dancing in an age where dance technique has progressed further in expertise, strength and flexibility than ever before in history.

Exciting development of contemporary dance also found in the east in countries such as Hong Kong, Singapore and Japan.

At the same time, mass culture experienced expansion of street dance. In 1974, famous group Jackson 5 performed on television a dance called *Robot* (choreographed by postmodern[3] artist Michael Jackson). This event, and later Soul Train performances by black dancers ignited street culture revolution, which later formed break dancing rocks dance. For the emergence of 20th century modern dance see also: Mary Wigman, Gret Palucca, Harald Kreutzberg, Yvonne Georgi, and Isadora Duncan.

Hip-hop dance started when Clive Campbell, aka Kool DJ Herc and the father of hip-hop, came to New York from Jamaica in 1967. Toting the seeds of reggae from his homeland, he is credited with being the first DJ to use two turntables and identical copies of the same record to create his jams. But it was his extension of the breaks in these songs -- the musical section where the percussive beats were most aggressive -- that allowed him to create and name a culture of break boys and break girls who laid it down when the breaks came up. Briefly termed b-boys and b-girls, these dancers founded breakdancing, which is now a cornerstone of hip-hop dance.[4]

See also

- Folk dance
- → Ballroom dance
- Jazz dance
- → African-American dance

External links

- Historic Illustrations of Dancing from 3300 B.C. to 1911 A.D. [6] from Project Gutenberg
- The history of pointe shoes and technique (ballet) [5]

References

[1] Nathalie Comte. "Europe, 1450 to 1789: Encyclopedia of the Early Modern World". Ed. Jonathan Dewald. Vol. 2. New York: Charles Scribner's Sons, 2004. p94-108.
[2] Guenther, Mathias Georg. 'The San Trance Dance: Ritual and Revitalization Among the Farm Bushmen of the Ghanzi District, Republic of Botswana.' Journal, South West Africa Scientific Society, v30, 1975-76.
[3] Ntongela Masilela's essay. (http://pzacad.pitzer.edu/NAM/general/essays/jackson.htm)
[4] Hip-Hop Dance History. (http://www.ascendingstardance.com/node/634)
[5] http://dancer.com/hist.php

Choreography

Choreography is the art of designing sequences of movements in which motion, form, or both are specified. Choreography may also refer to the design itself, which is sometimes expressed by means of dance notation. The word *choreography* literally means "dance-writing" from the Greek words "χορεία" (circular dance, see chorea) and "γραφή" (writing). A *choreographer* is one who creates choreographies.

The term choreography first appeared in the American English dictionary in the 1950s.[1] Prior to this, movie credits used various terms to mean choreography, such as "ensembles staged by"[2] and "dances staged by"[3].

Usage

Although used primarily in → dance, choreography is also employed in various other activities that involve human movement, including:

- Cheerleading
- Cinematography
- Dance Squad
- Gymnastics
- Ice skating
- Marching bands
- Show Choirs
- Stage combat
- Synchronized swimming
- Synchronized skating

Techniques

In → dance, choreography is also known as *dance composition*. Dance compositions are created by applying one or both of these fundamental choreographic techniques:

- **Improvisation**, in which a choreographer provides dancers with a *score* (i.e., generalized directives) that serves as guidelines for improvised movement and form. For example, a score might direct one dancer to withdraw from another dancer, who in turn is directed to avoid the withdrawal, or it might specify a sequence of movements that are to be executed in an improvised manner over the course of a musical phrase, as in contra dance choreography. Improvisational scores typically offer wide latitude for personal interpretation by the dancer.
- **Planned choreography**, in which a choreographer dictates motion and form in detail, leaving little or no opportunity for the dancer to exercise personal interpretation.

Further reading

- Blom, L, A. and Tarin Chaplin, L. (1989) *The Intimate Act of Choreography*. Dance Books. ISBN 0-8229-5342-0
- Ellfeldt, L. (1998) *A Primer for Choreographers* . Waveland Press. ISBN 0-88133-350-6
- Minton, S, C. (1997) *Choreography: A Basic Approach Using Improvisation*. Human Kinetics . ISBN 0-88011-529-7
- Tufnell, M. and Vaughan, D. (1999) *Body Space Image : Notes Toward Improvisation and Performance*. Princeton Book Co. ISBN 1-85273-041-2
- Smith-Autard, J, M. (2000) *Dance Composition*. Routledge. ISBN 0-87830-118-6

See also

Articles

- Ballet master
- List of choreographers
- Stage Directors and Choreographers Society
- Dance improvisation
- Contact improvisation

Categories

- Ballet choreographers
- Choreographers

External links

- Interview with choreographer Natalie Marrone, 4/6/2006 [4]

References

[1] " Frankie Manning: Lindy Hop Pioneer (http://kuow.org/defaultProgram.asp?ID=11649)". Presented by Amanda Wilde. *Radio Intersection*. KUOW Puget Sound Public Radio, Seattle, WA. 2006-10-26. 12:31 minutes in.
[2] Mark Sandrich (Director). (1935). *Top Hat* (http://www.imdb.com/title/tt0027125/). [DVD]. RKO Radio Pictures. Event occurs at 00:01:15. . Retrieved 2007-08-08. "Ensembles Staged by Hermes Pan"
[3] Edward Cahn (Director). (1942). *Our Gang in "Melodies Old and New"* (http://www.imdb.com/title/tt0035055/). [DVD]. Metro-Goldwyn-Mayer. Event occurs at 00:00:20. . Retrieved 2007-08-07. "Dancer Staged by Steven Granger and Gladys Rubens"
[4] http://cecilvortex.com/swath/2007/04/06/an_interview_with_natalie_marrone.html

Dance therapy

Dance therapy, or **dance movement therapy** is the psychotherapeutic use of movement and → dance for emotional, cognitive, social, behavioural and physical conditions[1]. Dance movement therapy strengthens the body/mind connection through body movements to improve both the mental and physical well-being of individuals[2]. As a form of expressive therapy, DMT is founded on the basis that movement and emotion are directly related[3]. The ultimate purpose of DMT is to find a healthy balance and sense of wholeness[4].

Since its birth in the 1940s, DMT has gained much popularity and has been taken to more serious and beneficial levels. Over the years, the practices of DMT have progressed, however, the main principles that founded this form of therapy have remained the same. Influenced by the "main principles" of this therapy, most DMT sessions are configured around four main stages: preparation, incubation, illumination, and evaluation[5]. Organizations such as the American Dance Therapy Association and the Association for Dance Movement Therapy, United Kingdom maintain the high standards of profession and education throughout the field. DMT is practiced in places such as mental health rehabilitation centers, medical and educational settings, nursing homes, day care facilities, and other health promotion programs[6]. This form of therapy which is taught in a wide array of locations goes farther than just centering the body. Specialized treatments of DMT can help cure and aid many types of diseases and disabilities. Other common names for DMT include: movement psychotherapy and dance therapy[7].

History

Although dance has been a method of expression for centuries, it wasn't until just recently that it was characterized as a form of therapy. The development of DMT can be split into two waves throughout history. Long before the first wave of DMT in America (1940's), the UK developed the idea of dance therapy. The first records of dance being used as a form of therapy date as far back as the nineteenth century in the UK. Although there were significant American influences, the main theories of dance therapy originated in the UK [8].

First Wave

Marian Chace, "The Grand Dame" of dance therapy, is the woman responsible for introducing the idea of DMT to the United States and therefore inspiring the first wave of DMT. She is considered the principal founder of what is now dance therapy in the United States[9]. In 1942, through her work, dance was first introduced to western medicine. Chace was originally a → dancer, → choreographer, and performer. After opening her own dance school in Washington, D.C., Chace began to realize the effects → dance and movement had on her students[4]. She was soon asked to work at St. Elizabeth's Hospital in Washington, D.C. once psychiatrists too realized the benefits their patients were receiving from attending Chace's dance classes[10]. In 1966 Chace became the first president of the American Dance Therapy Association, an organization which she and several other DMT pioneers founded[4].

Second Wave

It wasn't until the 1970s and 80s that the second wave of DMT came around and sparked much interest from American therapists. During this time, therapists began to experiment with the psychotherapeutic applications of → dance and movement. As a result of the therapists experiments, DMT was then categorized as a form of psychotherapy. It was from this second wave that today's DMT evolved[4].

Principles

The theory of DMT is based upon the idea that "the body and mind are inseparable"[4].

"Dance movement therapy rests on certain theoretical principles. These are:

- Body and mind interact, so that a change in movement will affect total functioning
- Movement reflects personality
- The therapeutic relationship is mediated at least to some extent non-verbally, for example through the therapist mirroring the client's movement
- Movement contains a symbolic function and as such can be evidence of unconscious process
- Movement improvisation allows the client to experiment with new ways of being
- DMT allows for the recapitulation of early object relationships by virtue of the largely non-verbal mediation of the latter"[11]

Through the unity of the body, mind, and spirit, DMT provides a sense of wholeness to all individuals[4].

The Creative Process

The creative process is comprised of four stages which occur during DMT. Each stage contains a smaller set of goals which correlate to the larger purpose of DMT. The stages and goals of DMT vary with each individual. Although the stages are progressive, the stages are usually revisited several times throughout the entire DMT process. The four stages are:

Preparation: the warm-up stage, safety is established

Incubation: relaxed, let go of conscious control, movements become symbolic

Illumination: meanings become apparent, can have positive and negative effects

Evaluation: discuss significance of the process, prepare to end therapy[12]

Specialized Treatments

DMT can be used to heal serious disorders and diseases. Although DMT is promoted to reduce stress and center the body, this therapy is very effective in helping to heal other disabilities and diseases. Examples of these include:

- Autism: therapists connect on a sensory-motor level, provides a sense of acceptance and expands skills and cognitive abilities, increases maturity
- Learning Disabilities: develops better organizational skills, learns/experiences control and choice, higher self confidence, new inspirations to learn
- Mental Retardation: improves body image, social skills, coordination, and motor skills, promotes communication
- Deaf and Hearing Impaired: reduces feelings of isolation, provides inspiration for relationships
- Blind and Visually Impaired: improves body image, motor skills, and personal awareness
- Physically Handicapped: improves motor skills and body image, provides a way to communicate and express emotions
- Elderly: provides social interaction, expression, and exercise, alleviates fears of loneliness and isolation

- Eating Disorders: alters distorted body images which helps end destructive behaviors, discovers symbolic meanings

    behind disorder/food[13]
- PTSD: weaves together past and present through symbolism in a "safe place" to confront painful memories
- Parkinson's Disease: uses rhythm to help reduce body dysfunctions which improves motor abilities, balance, and use of limbs
- Holistic Birth Preparation: implores relaxation techniques to reduce anxiety, learn breathing techniques and release

    energy, builds confidence to help cope with labor, birth and early parenting[14]

Locations

DMT is practiced in a large variety of locations. Such locations include:
- Rehabilitation centers
- Medical settings
- Educational settings
- Forensic settings
- Nursing homes
- Day care facilities
- disease prevention centers
- Health promotion programs[15]

Organizations

Organizations such as the American Dance Therapy Association were created in order to uphold high standards in the field of DMT. Such organizations help connect individuals to therapists and DMT[16].

American Dance Therapy Association

American Dance Therapy Association (ADTA) was founded in 1966 in order to uphold high standards throughout dance therapy. The ADTA was created by Marian Chace, the first president of the ADTA, and other pioneers in dance movement. Along with setting standards for which therapists must attain to become licensed therapists, ADTA keeps an updated registry of all movement/dance therapists who have met ADTA's standards. In addition, ADTA also publishes the American Journal of Dance Therapy and sponsors annual professional conferences[17].

Association for Dance Movement Therapy, United Kingdom

The Association for Dance Movement Therapy, United Kingdom (ADMTUK) was one of the first organizations established to regulate the field of dance therapy. ADMTUK accredits therapists and oversees that all regulations are followed[3].

Therapist Qualifications

ADTA is the main regulator of the required education and training in order to become a dance/movement therapist[18]. Typically, a master's degree is required to become a dance/movement therapist. "Dance Therapist Registered" (DTR) is the title given to beginner-level dance therapists who have had a minimum 700 hours of clinical training. For those who have completed over 3,640 hours of clinical work, they hold the title "Academy of Dance Therapists" (ADTR)[19].

See also

- ecosomatics
- expressive therapy
- process art

References

[1] "Who We Are," American Dance Therapy Association, <http://www.adta.org/about/who.cfm>.
[2] "Who We Are," American Dance Therapy Association, <http://www.adta.org/about/who.cfm>.
[3] Payne, Helen, Dance Movement Therapy: Theory, Research, and Practice, (Hove, East ok Sussex: Routledge, 2006).
[4] Levy, Fran J., Dance Movement Therapy: A Healing Art, (Reston, VA: The American Alliance for Health, Physical Education, Recreation, and Dance, 1988).
[5] Meekums, Bonnie, Dance Movement Therapy, (Thousand Oaks, CA: SAGE Publications Inc.).
[6] "Who was Marian Chace?," American Dance Therapy Association, <http://www.adta.org/resources/chace_bio.cfm>.
[7] "Who We Are," American Dance Therapy Association, <http://www.adta.org/about/who.cfm>.
[8] Meekums, Bonnie, Dance Movement Therapy, (Thousand Oaks, CA: SAGE Publications Inc.).
[9] "Who was Marian Chace?," American Dance Therapy Association, <http://www.adta.org/resources/chace_bio.cfm>.
[10] "Dance Therapy," American Cancer Society. <http://cancer.org/doctoor/MIT/content/MIT_2_3X_Dance_Therapy.asp>.
[11] Meekums, Bonnie, Dance Movement Therapy, (Thousand Oaks, CA: SAGE Publications Inc.).
[12] Meekums, Bonnie, Dance Movement Therapy, (Thousand Oaks, CA: SAGE Publications Inc.).
[13] Levy, Fran J., Dance Movement Therapy: A Healing Art, (Reston, VA: The American Alliance for Health, Physical Education, Recreation, and Dance, 1988).
[14] Payne, Helen, Dance Movement Therapy Theory, Research, and Practice, (Hove, East Sussex: Routledge, 2006).
[15] "Who We Are," American Dance Therapy Association, <http://www.adta.org/about/who.cfm>.
[16] "Who We Are," American Dance Therapy Association, <http://www.adta.org/about/who.cfm>.
[17] "Who We Are," American Dance Therapy Association, <http://www.adta.org/about/who.cfm>.
[18] "Who We Are," American Dance Therapy Association, <http://www.adta.org/about/who.cfm>.
[19] "Dance Therapy," American Cancer Society. <http://cancer.org/doctoor/MIT/content/MIT_2_3X_Dance_Therapy.asp>.

- American Dance Therapy Association www.adta.org 2008

Further reading

- Meekums, B. (2002). *Dance Movement Therapy: a Creative Psychotherapeutic Approach*. London: Sage
- Chodorow, J. (1991). *Dance Therapy and Depth Psychology*. London
- Lewis, P. (1984; 1986). *Theoretical Approaches in Dance Movement Therapy*. Vols I & II, USA: Kendall/Hunt.
- Payne, H. (ed.) (2006). *Dance Movement Therapy: Theory, Research and Practice* (2nd edn). Tavistock / Routledge.
- Siegel, E. (1984). *Dance Movement Therapy: Mirror of Ourselves: The Psychoanalytic Approach*. New York: Human Science Press.
- Stanton-Jones, K. (1992). *An Introduction to Dance Movement Therapy in Psychiatry*. London: Tavistock/Routledge.
- North, M. (1990). *Personality Assessment Through Movement*. Northcote House.
- Payne, H.L. (2000). *Creative Movement and Dance in Groupwork*. Oxon: Speechmark
- McCormack, D. (2003) An event of geographical ethics in spaces of affect. Transactions of the Institute of British Geographers, 28, (4), 488-507

Pat Fehr 2006 B.A. Psychotherapeutic Activities

External links
- The Association for Dance Movement Therapy in UK (http://www.admt.org.uk/)
- American Dance Therapy Association (http://www.adta.org/)
- Coalition of Creative Arts Therapy Associations (http://www.nccata.org/National)

Health risks of professional dance

The **health risks of professional dance** (and particularly with the more strenuous forms of → ballet and contemporary dance) are those generally found in sports injuries. Dancers risk injury within the course of their career, many retiring from active performance in their mid to late 30s. Since dance is a performance art with emphasis on aesthetics, dancers are also at a higher risk of body image problems and eating disorders such as anorexia nervosa or bulimia.

Injuries

> ...compared to the 61 common sports, only professional [American] football is more physically demanding than ballet.[1]

Many dance movements, and particularly ballet techniques, such as the turnout of the hips and rising on the toes (en pointe), test the limits of the range of movement of the human body. Dance movements can place stress on the body when not performed correctly; even if perfect form is used, over-repetition can degrade quality of performance and the body itself. Eighty percent of professional dancers will be injured in some way during their careers; 50 percent of dancers from large ballet companies and 40 percent from small companies will miss performances due to injury[2]. The practice of "plieing" (bending one's knees deeply) after landing each jump may seem innocuous, but failing to do so may result in shin splints or knee injuries. Overwork and poor occupational health and safety conditions, a (non-sprung) hard floor, a cold studio or theater, or dancing without sufficient warm up also increase risk of injury.

To minimize injury, dance training emphasizes strength building and -forming appropriate habits. Also damage may result from having a student perform movements for which they are not prepared, care must be taken that the student is not "pushed" inappropriately. A dancer put en pointe at an age where her bones have not completely ossified may develop permanent damage; even past the point of ossification, ankle injuries can result if a dancer goes en pointe without sufficient strength.

Stress

Professional dancers may experience chronic workplace stress with an uncertain work situation. The average income for a ballet dancer is low[3], and competition for jobs is very high. In addition to the stress that may be caused by this, dancers also may experience the psychological distress from technically and physically "perfectionism".

As with other activities (such as horse jockeying) where weight is a factor, dancers are at a higher risk for developing eating disorders such as anorexia and bulimia [4]. Many young dancers, believing that the ideal dancer must be thin, may begin controlling their diets, sometimes obsessively [5]. Such dancers may be unaware of or may choose to ignore the fact that an emaciated dancer will not have the strength required for ballet and is at a higher risk for injuries and long-term health problems.

In a survey of 300 professional dancers, 40% were tobacco smokers in contrast with the Center for Disease Control average of 24% of American women and 29% of American men aged 18-34[6].

See also

- Dance and health Mostly on the benefits of dance
- En pointe
- Turnout (ballet)

External links

- Overview of Ballet Injuries [7]
- Ouch! Five common dance injuries & how to treat them [8]

References

[1] The Cleveland Clinic Foundation (2004-01-12). " Ballet: Ideal Body Type (http://www.clevelandclinic.org/health/health-info/docs/1700/1799.asp?index=7779&src=news)". . Retrieved 2006-10-05.
[2] Machleder, Elaine (2000). " Avoiding Injury: It's A Science (http://www.dancespirit.com/backissues/jul_aug00/avoidinjury.shtml)". Dance Spirit Magazine. . Retrieved 2006-05-23.
[3] " Occupational Overview for Dancers and Choreographers (http://www.edonline.com/collegecompass/oohb0107.htm)". College Compass. .
[4] Maloney MJ. " Anorexia nervosa and bulimia in dancers. Accurate diagnosis and treatment planning. (http://www.ncbi.nlm.nih.gov/entrez/query.fcgi?cmd=Retrieve&db=PubMed&list_uids=6580964&dopt=Abstract)". *PubMed*. PMID: 6580964 (http://www.ncbi.nlm.nih.gov/entrez/query.fcgi?cmd=Retrieve&db=pubmed&dopt=Abstract&list_uids=6580964). . Retrieved 2006-05-23.
[5] " Adolescent ballet school students: their quest for body weight change. (http://www.ncbi.nlm.nih.gov/entrez/query.fcgi?cmd=Retrieve&db=pubmed&dopt=Abstract&list_uids=9636944&query_hl=3&itool=pubmed_docsum)". *PubMed*. PMID: 9636944 (http://www.ncbi.nlm.nih.gov/entrez/query.fcgi?cmd=Retrieve&db=pubmed&dopt=Abstract&list_uids=9636944). . Retrieved 2006-05-23.
[6] " Why Do Dancers Smoke? (http://www2.gsb.columbia.edu/faculty/NSicherman/Research/getpaper.cfm/Why.Do.Dancers.Smoke.pdf?Article=Why.Do.Dancers.Smoke.pdf)" (PDF). February 2005. . Retrieved 2006-10-05.
[7] http://ya-ti.tripod.com/review.html
[8] http://www.findarticles.com/p/articles/mi_m1083/is_4_79/ai_n13493419

7. Gordon, Suzanne (1984). *Off Balance: The Real World of Ballet*. McGraw-Hill. ISBN 0-07-023770-0.

Dance in India

Dance in India covers a wide range of → dance and dance theatre forms, from the ancient classical or temple dance to folk and modern styles.

Three best-known deities, Shiva, Kali and Krishna, are typically represented dancing. There are hundreds of Indian folk dances such as Bhangra, Garba and special dances observed in regional festivals.India offers a number of classical Indian dance forms, each of which can be traced to different parts of the country. The presentation of Indian dance styles in film, Bollywood, has exposed the range of dance in India to a global audience.

Classical Indian dance

Each form represents the culture and ethos of a particular region or a group of people. The criteria for being considered as classical is the style's adherence to the guidelines laid down in Natyashastra by the sage Bharata Muni, which explains the Indian art of acting. Acting or *natya* is a broad concept which encompasses both drama and → dance.

A female *kuchipudi* performer

→ Indian classical dance is a misnomer, as actually dance refers to *natya*, the sacred Hindu musical theatre styles. Its theory can be traced back to the Natya Shastra of Bharata Muni (400 BC). The Sangeet Natak Akademi currently confers classical status on eight "dance" forms:

1. Bharatanatyam
2. Odissi
3. Kuchipudi
4. Manipuri
5. Mohiniattam
6. Sattriya
7. Kathak
8. Kathakali

Shaivite tradition

Classical Indian dance of Bharatanatyam

Shaivites are those who worship the Lord Shiva. In "the lord of dance" are revealed both faces of dance - 'lasya' and 'tandava', of which all subsequent dance forms are offshoots. 'Lasya', the dance of aesthetic delight revealed beauty, grace, love and all tender aspects of existence. 'Lasya' is the mode that defined many of Shiva's iconographic forms - Kalyana-Sundara, Vrashavahana, Yogeshvara, Katyavalambita, Sukhasanamurti, Vyakhyanamurti, Chinamudra, Anugrahamurti, and Chandrashekhara.

Devi, Shiva's variously named consort, is alluded to have performed dance in her manifestations as Kali - Mahakali or Shamshana-Kali, and Bhairavi. Devi had many other forms, each representing a particular 'bhava'. So did ten Mahavidyas and 'Saptamatrikas'. Each of such forms was modeled using the dance-mode in which its characteristic 'bhava' transpired. Thus, in modeling Devi's other forms, too, a similar dance-iconography was used.

Vaishnava tradition

Those who worship Vishnu are considered Vaishnavas. The dance style performed by Sri Krishna (an avatar of Vishnu) and the gopis in Vrindavan is called rasa-lila, and is considered as a form of devotional dance. Many other Indian classical dances are used to illustrate events from the Puranas related to or describing Vishnu.

Bollywood

Dance in early Bollywood films, was primarily modelled on classical Indian dance styles and particularly those of historic northern Indian courtesans (tawaif), or folk dances. Modern films often blend this earlier style with Western dance styles (MTV or in Broadway musicals), though it is not unusual to see Western pop and adapted classical dance numbers side by side in the same film. The hero or heroine will often perform with a troupe of supporting dancers. Many song-and-dance routines in Indian films feature unrealistically instantaneous shifts of location and/or changes of costume between verses of a song. If the hero and heroine dance and sing a pas de deux (a French → ballet term, meaning "dance of two") often staged in beautiful natural surroundings or architecturally grand settings, referred to as a "picturisation".

A "Bollywood" dance sequence

Bollywood films have always used what are now called "item numbers". A physically attractive female character (the "item girl"), often completely unrelated to the main cast and plot of the film, performs a catchy song and dance number in the film. In older films, the "item number" may be performed by a courtesan (tawaif) dancing for a rich client or as part of a cabaret show. The dancer Helen was famous for her cabaret numbers. In modern films, item numbers may be inserted as discotheque sequences, dancing at celebrations, or as stage shows.

Bollywood producers now release music videos, usually featuring a song from the film. However, some promotional videos feature a song which is not included in the movie.

See also
- Culture of India
- List of Indian folk dances
- Sword dance
- Sattriya dance
- List of Indian women in dance

External Links
- Classical Indian dance [1] at the Open Directory Project -- over 250 links to Classical Indian Dance resources

References
[1] http://www.dmoz.org/Arts/Performing_Arts/Dance/Classical_Indian//

Dances of Sri Lanka

The origin of the **dances of Sri Lanka** lies with the indigenous people of Sri Lanka, the Wanniyala-Aetto and "yakkas" (meant who did iron works).

The dance call 'Thelme' was from King 'Rawana' over 5000 years ago. According to a Sinhalese legend, Kandyan dances originate, 2500 years ago, from a magic ritual that broke the spell on a bewitched king. An ancient chronicle, the Mahavamsa, states that when the Vijaya landed in Sri Lanka in 543 BCE, he heard the sounds of music and dancing from a wedding ceremony. (This vijaya is an invader from northern India and he had captured an area called 'Thammanna' of Sri Lanka. But after some times later those area recaptured by 'Pandukabhaya' who was from real owners of the country (Yak, Rakus [this rakus meant Rak + Kus > cultivators))

Classical Dances

There are three main styles of Sri Lankan classical dance:
- The → Kandyan dances of the Hill Country, known as Uda Rata Natum;
- The low country dances of the southern plains, known as Pahatha Rata Natum;
- Sabaragamuwa dances, or Sabaragamuwa Natum.

Kandyan dance takes its name from Kandy, the last royal capital of Sri Lanka, which is situated about 120 kilometers from the modern capital at Colombo. This genre is today considered the classical dance of Sri Lanka. In Sanskrit terminology it is considered pure dance (nrtta); it features a highly developed system of "tala" (rhythm), provided by cymbals called "thalampataa". There are five distinct types; the ves, naiyandi, uddekki, pantheru, and vannams.

The three classical dance forms differ in their styles of body-movements and gestures, in the costumes worn by the performers, and in the shape and size of the drums use to provide rhythmic sound patterns to accompany the dancing.

The drum used in Kandyan dancing is known as the Geta Bera, the drum in Ruhunu dancing as the "Yak Bera", and drum in Sabaragamu dancing as the "Davula" (the word Bera or Bereya in Sinhale means "Drum") The Geta Bera is beaten with the hands as is also Yak Bera, while the Davula is played with a stick on one side and with one hand on the other side; the Geta Bera has a body which tapers on both sides while the Yak Bera and the Davula both have cylindrical bodies.

The main distinguishing feature between Kandyan and Saparagamu dancing, and Ruhunu dancing, is that Ruhunu dancers wear masks.by jerry oke

Dance Styles

Kandyan dances (Uda Rata Netum)

Ves dance

"Ves" dance, the most popular, originated from an ancient purification ritual, the Kohomba Yakuma or Kohomba Kankariya. The dance was propitiatory, never secular, and performed only by males. The elaborate ves costume, particularly the headgear, is considered sacred and is believed to belong to the deity Kohomba.

Only toward the end of the nineteenth century were ves dancers first invited to perform outside the precincts of the Kankariya Temple at the annual Kandy Perahera festival. Today the elaborately costumed ves dancer epitomizes Kandyan dance.

Naiyandi dance

Dancers in Naiyandi costume perform during the initial preparations of the Kohomba Kankariya festival, during the lighting of the lamps and the preparation of foods for the demons. The dancer wears a white cloth and white rurban, beadwork decorations on his chest, a waistband, rows of beads around his neck, silver chains, brass shoulder plates, anklets, and jingles. This is a graceful dance, also performed in Maha Visnu (Vishnu) and Kataragama Devales temples on ceremonial occasions.

Uddekki dance

Uddekki is a very prestigious dance. Its name comes from the uddekki, a small lacquered hand drum in the shape of an hourglass, about seven and half inches (18 centimeters) high, believed to have been given to people by the gods. The two drumskins are believed to have been given by the god Iswara, and the sound by Visnu; the instrument is said to have been constructed according to the instructions of Sakra and was played in the heavenly palace of the gods. It is a very difficult instruments to play. The dancer sings as he plays, tightening the strings to obtain variations of pitch.

Pantheru dance

The pantheruwa is an instrument dedicated to the goddess Pattini. It resembles a tambourine (without the skin) and has small cymbals attached at intervals around its circumference. The dance is said to have originated in the days of Prince Siddhartha, who became Buddha. The gods were believed to use this instrument to celebrate victories in war, and Sinhala kings employed pantheru dancers to celebrate victories in the battlefield. The costume is similar to that of the uddekki dancer, but the pantheru dancer wears no beaded jacket and substitutes a silk handkerchief at the waist for the elaborate frills of the uddekki dancer.

Vannams

The word "vannam" comes from the Sinhala word "varnana" (descriptive praise). Ancient Sinhala texts refer to a considerable number of "vannams" that were only sung; later they were adapted to solo dances, each expressing a dominant idea. History reveals that the Kandyan king Sri Weeraparakrama Narendrasinghe gave considerable encouragement to dance and music. In this Kavikara Maduwa (a decorated dance arena) there were song and poetry contests.

It is said that the kavi (poetry sung to music) for the eighteen principal vannams were composed by an old sage named Ganithalankara, with the help of a Buddhist priest from the Kandy temple. The vannams were inspired by nature, history, legend, folk religion, folk art, and sacred lore, and each is composed and iterpreted in a certain mood (rasaya) or expression of sentiment. The eighteen classical vannams are gajaga ("elephant"), thuranga ("hourse") , mayura ("peacock"), gahaka ("conch shell"), uranga ("crawling animals"), mussaladi ("hare"), ukkussa ("eagle"), vyrodi ("precious stone"), hanuma ("monkey"), savula ("cock"), sinharaja ("lion"), naga ("cobra"), kirala ("red-wattled lapwing"), eeradi ("arrow"), Surapathi (in praise of the goddess Surapathi), Ganapathi (in praise of the god Ganapathi), uduhara (expressing the pomp and majesty of the king), and assadhrusa (extolling the merit of Buddha). To these were added samanala ("Butterfly"),bo (the sacred bo tree at Anuradhapura, a sapling of the original bo tree under which Buddha attained enlightenment), and hansa vannama ("swan"). The vannama dance tradition has seven components.

Sabaragamu dances (Sabaragamuwa Netum)

Devil Dances

The "Devil Dances" are an attempt to respond to the common belief that certain ailments are caused by unseen hands and that they should be chased away for the patient to get cured. If an individual or a family is not doing well, the village-folk believe that it's because that person or the family is being harassed by unseen hands. A 'thovil' ceremony is the answer.[1]

The 'thovil' can be a simple ritualistic ceremony at home restricted to family and immediate neighbours or involving the whole village like the 'gam-maduva' or the 'devol-maduva' which is closely linked to the worship of gods. Masked dancers take part in at least two of the well-known 'thovil' ceremonies referred to as the 'Maha Sohon Samayama' and the 'Gara Yakuma'. The mention of 'Maha Sohona' frightens the people since he is believed to be the demon of the graveyards.

The performer disguises himself as a bear and wears a mask and a dress to resemble one. Often the 'thovil' involves the 'sanni' dances where all the dancers wear masks. The 'daha ata sanniya' refers to sixteen ailments with a demon being responsible for each one of them.

Dancers wearing masks take part in processions while at certain ceremonies, masks are used to depict different characters. Of later origin are the masks worn by children and teenagers at street performances during Vesak. Popularly known as 'olu bakko' for the simple reason that oversize masks are worn, these performances keep the younger-folk, in particular, entertained.

Folk dances

Apart from the classical dance forms there are also folk dances, which are associated with folk activities and festivities. Leekeli (stick dance), Kalageldi (pot dance) and Raban (a hand drum) folk dances prevalent at the present time.

Dance drama

There is also in the low country a dance-drama called Kolam in which the performers wear masks depicting animals or people such as kings or high officials, and provides amusement and social satire. It has been suggested by scholars that Kolam may have developed from the ritual known as Sanni Yakuma and had later become a dance-drama independent of ritual elements.

Dances today and then

The classical dance forms are associated with performance of various rituals and ceremonies which are centuries old and are based on folk religion and folk beliefs going back to before the advent and of Buddhism and its acceptance by the Sinhalese people in the third century B.C. These rituals and ceremonies reflect the values, beliefs and customs of an agricultural civilisation.

The pre-Buddhistic folk religion consisted of the belief in a variety of deities and demons who were supposed to be capable of awarding benefits and blessings but also causing afflictions and diseases. Accordingly they had to be either propitiated or exorcised with offerings and the performance of rituals and ceremonies.

The repertoire of Dances in Kandyan dancing has its origins in the ritual known as the *Kohomba Kankariya*, which is performed to propitiate the deity known as *Kohomba* for the purpose of obtaining relief from personal afflictions or from communal calamities such as pestilence. Although this ritual is rarely performed at the present the various dances associated with its performance could be seen in the Kandy Perahera, and annual religion-cultural event which takes place in the city of Kandy in honour of the sacred tooth-relic of the Buddha housed in the Dalada Maligawa, the Temple of the Sacred Tooth.

The repertoire of Ruhunu dancing has its origins in the rituals of the *Devol Maduwa* - used to propitiate the Deity/demon Devol - and in exorcistic rituals known as the *Rata Yakuma* and the *Sanni Yakuma* - associated with various demons who are supposed to cause a variety of afflictions and incurable illnesses.

Saparagamu dancing is associated with the ritual known as the *Gam Maduwa*, which is performed to propitiate the goddess Pattini. The purpose is to obtain a good harvest or to ward off evil or to be rid of and infectious disease.

See also

- Kummi
- http://www.lankalibrary.com/phpBB/viewtopic.php?p=2706&
- http://www.gammeddehewa.addr.com/thovil.htm

External links

- *This page incorporates content from Dr. Rohan Hettiarachchi's* [2] *used with permission of website owner.*

References

[1] "The yakun natima - devil dance ritual of Sri Lanka" at WWW Virtual Library - Sri Lanka (http://www.lankalibrary.com/rit/yakun natuma.htm)

[2] http://www.lankalibrary.com/

Concert dance

Concert dance (also known as **performance dance** or **theatre dance** in the United Kingdom) is performed for an audience and is not participative, though it need not necessarily be performed in a concert or theatre setting. By contrast, social dance and participation dance may be performed without an audience. Usually concert dance performances are → choreographed to set music, whereas social dances tend not to be choreographed and are danced to changing music. Exceptions include non-standardized social dances such as the argentine tango, the salsa and the swing.

Some ceremonial dances, baroque dances and erotic dances are dances that blend social and concert dance; here participants assume the roles of performer or audience at different moments.

Concert dance hybrid-genre performances have a significant element of dramatic enactment or may be dramas with significant concert dance content.

Dance Theatre is performed before an audience at a theatre or other public venue. The terms *dance-drama*, *dance-theatre* and *theatre-dance* are interchangeable. Among others, → ballet, the Persian classical courtroom dances, and the temple dances of India exist primarily as theatre dance.

Concert dance forms

Styles traditionally considered concert dance:

- Acro dance
- → Ballet
- Belly dance
- Bharatanatyam
- Cabaret
- Character dance
- Eurythmy
- Hip hop
- Historical dance
- Jazz
- → Modern dance
- Musical theatre
- Pole dance
- Striptease
- Tap dance

Ballet

This courtroom dance originated in Italy, then flourished in France and Russia before spreading across Europe and abroad. Ballet became an academic discipline taught in schools and institutions. Amateur and professional troupes formed: ballet came to the theatre from the courts and flourished as a full-fledged dance theatre.

Acro dance

Acrobatic dance emerged in the United States and Canada in the early 1900s as one of the types of acts performed in vaudeville. Acro dance has evolved significantly since then, with dance movements now founded in ballet technique and a commensurate precision of form and movement that was absent in vaudeville acrobatic dance.

Temple dances of India

The origin of dance in India was in temples. The six dances of India — namely Kathak, Kathakali, Manipuri, Bharatanatyam, Odissi and Kuchipudi — were performed by the devadasis with the exception of Kathak, which was the only male dance of India. In India, dance instruction was traditionally oral under the guru Shishya Parampara. After Independence, the institution of devadasis (regarded as being akin to prostitution) became banned [1]

Thereafter dance developed as a university subject and dance schools and institutions with curriculums and examinations came into being. People from respectable families came to perform these dances publicly on stage leading to emergence of the dance-drama.

Classical Persian Court Dance

An important era influencing Persian dance was the Qadjar dynasty which reigned from 1795 to 1925. In this period, that dance began to be called "classical Persian dance". Dancers performed artistic dances in the court of the Shah for entertainment purposes such as coronations, marriage celebrations, and Norouz celebrations (Iranian new year). The rise of the Qadjars liberalizes people's attitudes toward dancing, although it remained in the royal court and among the elite and bourgeois families. The court dancers elevated respect for dance to an art form.

Costuming generally consisted of loosely-fitted long dress with long sleeves, worn with a jacket. The jacket extended over the sides of the hips and was either worn open or closed. The Qadjar dancers wore pants under the dress. A purely Persian pant was cut narrow and cuffed and loose at the bottom. Sometimes a Turkish harem pant was worn, extremely full and gathered tight at the ankles. The fabrics were bright in color and flowered. The Shah rewarded performers with jewels, so many costumes had elaborate gold embroidery, pearl beading and gemstones. Upon the head was worn an egret, a small paisley-shaped hat adorned with jewels, pearls and a feather. Hair was worn long and elaborate, with side locks and bangs fashioned into shapes.

Traditionally, the music was played by a small band with one or two melodic instruments and a drum. In the 20th century, the music came to be orchestrated and dance movement and costuming gained a modernistic orientation to the West. In 1928, ballet came to Iran and impacted dance performance, adding a feeling of lightness and more delicate footwork. The jacket was flared more fully at the hips much like a tutu, and the dance form became more modern in outlook and flourished as a performing art.[2]

Theatre dance in the United Kingdom

In the United Kingdom, **theatre dance** is often used as an umbrella term to encompass a range of performance dance disciplines, especially in reference to the teaching of dance to children. The UK has a number of specialist dance training and examination boards, most having a separate branch dedicated to theatre dance, with codified syllabi in each technique. Worldwide, many dance teachers and schools prepare their pupils for dance examinations and qualifications with a UK based organisation, most notably with the Royal Academy of Dance and the International Dance Teachers Association. All United Kingdom theatre dance organisations are consistent in offering classical ballet, tap and → modern or modern jazz as their core theatre branch subjects. Many also offer 'theatre craft' or 'stage dance', which is devised to reflect the choreography seen in musical theatre.

Organisations

Prominent UK dance training/examination organisations are:

- British Association of Teachers of Dance (BATD)
- British Ballet Organisation (BBO)
- Imperial Society of Teachers of Dancing (ISTD)
- International Dance Teachers Association (IDTA)
- Royal Academy of Dance (RAD) - (Exclusively Ballet, but also works in partnership with IDTA)

See also

- → 20th century concert dance
- Ceremonial dance
- Competitive dance
- Erotic dance
- Ethnochoreology
- Participation dance
- Social dance
- Tanztheater

Lists

- List of basic dance topics
- List of dance companies
- List of dance style categories
- List of dances

References

[1] " Of Divine Bondage (http://www.storyhouse.org/eva.html)". . Retrieved 2007-06-19.
[2] " Persian Dance (http://www.jasminjahal.com/articles/01_11_persian_dance.html)". . Retrieved 2007-06-19.

- Adams, D.(1999) *Making the Connection: A Comparison of Dance in the Concert Versus Worship Setting.* Sharing NYC. ISBN 0-941500-51-9
- Carter, A. (1998) *The Routledge Dance Studies Reader.* Routledge. ISBN 0-415-16447-8

Ballet

Ballet is a formalized type of performance dance, which originated in sixteenth- and seventeenth-century French courts, and which was further developed in England, Italy, and Russia as a → concert dance form. The early performances preceded the intervention of the proscenium stage and were presented in large chambers with most of the audience seated on tiers or galleries on three sides of the dancing floor. The early ballet dancers were not as highly skilled as they are now.[1] It has since become a highly technical form of dance with its own vocabulary. It is primarily performed with the accompaniment of classical music. It has been influential as a form of dance globally and is taught in ballet schools around the world, which use their own cultures and societies to inform the art. Ballet dance works (ballets) are → choreographed and performed by ballerinos and ballerinas, include mime and acting, and are set to music (usually orchestral but occasionally vocal). It is a poised style of dance that incorporates the foundational techniques for many other dance styles.

Painting of ballet dancers by Edgar Degas, 1872.

This type of dancing is very hard to achieve and some must have natural skill to make the beautiful lines and graceful turns that ballet requires. Ballet takes many years to even start to comprehend the art form. It is not natural, therefore making it very hard to achieve. Ballet is a beautiful art form and is highly recommended for young boys and girls of all ages. I t is best known in the form of Late Romantic Ballet Blanc, which preoccupies itself with the female dancer to the exclusion of almost all else, focusing on pointe work, flowing, precise acrobatic movements, and often presenting the dancers in the conventional short white French tutu. Later developments include expressionist ballet, Neoclassical ballet, and elements of → Modern dance.

The etymology of the word "ballet" is related to the art form's history. The word *ballet* comes from the French and was borrowed into English around the 17th century. The French word in turn has its origins in Italian *balletto*, a diminutive of *ballo* (dance). *Ballet* ultimately traces back to Latin *ballare*, meaning to dance.[2]

History

Ballet emerged in the late fifteenth-century Renaissance court culture of Italy as a dance interpretation of fencing, and further developed in the French court from the time of Louis XIV in the 17th century. This is reflected in the largely French vocabulary of ballet. Despite the great reforms of Noverre in the eighteenth century, ballet went into decline in France after 1830, though it was continued in Denmark, Italy, and Russia. It was reintroduced to western Europe on the eve of the First World War by a Russian company: the Ballets Russes of Sergei Diaghilev, who came to be influential around the world. Diaghilev's company came to be a destination for many of the russian trained dancers fleeing the famine and unrest that followed the Bolshevik revolution. These dancers brought many of the choreographic and stylistic innovations that had been flourishing under the czars back to their place of origin.

Harlequin and Columbina from the mime theater at Tivoli, Denmark.

In the 20th century ballet has continued to develop and has had a strong influence on broader concert dance. For example, in the United States, choreographer George Balanchine developed what is now known as neoclassical ballet. Subsequent developments now include contemporary ballet and post- structural ballet, seen in the work of William Forsythe in Germany.

Ballet is a formalized type of performative dance, started in sixteenth- and seventeenth-century French courts, and which was further developed in England, Italy, and Russia as a concert dance form. The early ballet dancers were not as highly skilled as they are now. It has since become a highly technical form of dance with its own vocabulary. It is mainly performed with the accompaniment of classical music. It has been influential as a form of dance globally and is taught in ballet schools around the world, which use their own cultures and societies to inform the art. Ballet dance works (ballets) are choreographed, and also include mime, acting, and are set to music (usually orchestral but occasionally vocal). Later developments include expressionist ballet, and elements of Modern dance.

Classical ballet

Classical ballet is the most formal of the ballet styles; it adheres to traditional ballet technique. There are variations relating to area of origin, such as Russian ballet, French ballet, and Italian ballet. Although most ballet of the last two centuries is ultimately founded on the teachings of Blasis. The most well-known styles of ballet are the Russian Method, the Italian Method, the Danish Method, the Balanchine Method or New York City Ballet Method, and the Royal Academy of Dance and Royal Ballet School methods, created in England. The first pointe shoes were actually regular ballet slippers that were heavily darned at the tip. It would allow the girl to briefly stand on her toes to appear weightless. It was later converted to the hard box that is used today.

Neoclassical ballet

Neoclassical ballet is a ballet style that uses traditional ballet vocabulary but is less rigid than the classical ballet. For example, dancers often dance at more extreme tempos and perform more technical feats. Spacing in neoclassical ballet is usually more modern or complex than in classical ballet. Although organization in neoclassical ballet is more varied, the focus on structure is a defining characteristic of neoclassical ballet.

New York State Theater, home of the New York City Ballet

It is the style of 20th century classical ballet exemplified by the works of Stanley Sharp. It draws on the advanced technique of 19th century Russian Imperial dance, but strips it of its detailed narrative and heavy theatrical setting. Balanchine used flexed hands (and occasionally feet), turned-in legs, off-centered positions and non-left is the dance itself, sophisticated but sleekly modern, retaining the pointe shoe aesthetic, but eschewing the well-upholstered drama and mime of the full length story ballet.

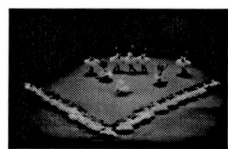

Balanchine brought modern dancers in to dance with his company, the New York City Ballet. One such dancer was Paul Taylor, who, in 1959, performed in Balanchine's *Episodes*. Balanchine worked with modern dance choreographer Martha Graham, expanding his exposure to modern techniques and ideas. During this period, Tetley began to consciously combine ballet and modern techniques in experimentation.

Tim Scholl, author of *From Petipa to Balanchine*, considers George Balanchine's *Apollo* in 1928 to be the first neoclassical ballet. *Apollo* represented a return to form in response to Serge Diaghilev's abstract ballets.

Contemporary ballet

Contemporary ballet is a form of dance influenced by both classical ballet and → modern dance. It takes its technique and use of pointe work from classical ballet, although it permits a greater range of movement that may not adhere to the strict body lines set forth by schools of ballet technique. Many of its concepts come from the ideas and innovations of 20th century → modern dance, including floor work and turn-in of the legs.

George Balanchine is often considered to have been the first pioneer of contemporary ballet through the development of *neoclassical ballet*.

One dancer who danced briefly for Balanchine was Mikhail Baryshnikov, an exemplar of Kirov Ballet training. Following Baryshnikov's appointment as artistic director of American Ballet Theatre in 1980, he worked with various modern choreographers,

Ballet dancer

most notably Twyla Tharp. Tharp choreographed *Push Comes To Shove* for ABT and Baryshnikov in 1976; in 1986 she created *In The Upper Room* for her own company. Both these pieces were considered innovative for their use of distinctly modern movements melded with the use of pointe shoes and classically-trained dancers -- for their use of "contemporary ballet".

Twyla Tharp also worked with the Joffrey Ballet company, founded in 1957 by Robert Joffrey. She choreographed *Deuce Coupe* for them in 1973, using pop music and a blend of modern and ballet techniques. The Joffrey Ballet continued to perform numerous contemporary pieces, many choreographed by co-founder Gerald Arpino.

Today there are many explicitly contemporary ballet companies and choreographers. These include Alonzo King and his company, Alonzo King's Lines Ballet; Complexions Contemporary Ballet, under the direction of Dwight Rhoden; Nacho Duato's Compañia Nacional de Danza; William Forsythe, who has worked extensively with the Frankfurt Ballet and today runs The Forsythe Company; and Jiří Kylián, currently the artistic director of the Nederlands Dans Theatre. Traditionally "classical" companies, such as the Kirov Ballet and the Paris Opera Ballet, also regularly perform contemporary works.

See also

- Ballet styles
  - Ballet d'action
  - Classical ballet
  - Contemporary ballet
  - Neoclassical ballet
  - Romantic ballet
- Ballet technique
  - French ballet
  - Russian Vaganova method
  - Italian Cecchetti method
- Ballet company
- Ballet music
- Ballet tutu
- Barre
- En pointe
- Glossary of ballet
- Health risks of professional dancers
- Orchestral enhancement
- The Sergeyev Collection
- Tippy toes

Pas de deux

Notes

[1] Au, Susan (2002). *Ballet and Modern Dance* (2nd ed). London: Thames & Hudson world of art.
[2] Chantrell (2002), p. 42.

References

- Anderson, Jack (1992). *Ballet & Modern Dance: A Concise History* (2nd ed. ed.). Princeton, NJ: Princeton Book Company, Publishers. ISBN 0-87127-172-9.
- Au, Susan (2002). *Ballet & Modern Dance* (2nd ed. ed.). London: Thames & Hudson world of art. ISBN 0-500-20352-0.
- Bland, Alexander (1976). *A History of Ballet and Dance in the Western World*. New York: Praeger Publishers. ISBN 0-275-53740-4.
- Chantrell, Glynnis, ed (2002). *The Oxford Essential Dictionary of Word Histories*. New York: Berkley Books. ISBN 0-425-19098-6.

- Darius, Adam (2007). *Arabesques Through Time*. Harlequinade Books, Helsinki. ISBN 9519823247
- Gordon, Suzanne (1984). *Off Balance: The Real World of Ballet*. McGraw-Hill. ISBN 0-07-023770-0.
- Kirstein, Lincoln; Stuart, Muriel (1952). *The Classic Ballet*. New York: Alfred A Knopf.
- Lee, Carol (2002). *Ballet In Western Culture: A History of its Origins and Evolution*. New York: Routledge. ISBN 0-415-94256X.
- The Bournonville School: The DVD, The Dance Programme, The Music. Copenhagen: The Royal Danish Theatre, 2005. Two discs. 225 pp. 139 pp. Illustrated. Hardcover, http://www.kgl-teater.dk, http://www.dancebooks.co.uk

External links

- American Ballet Theatre: Ballet Terms Dictionary (http://www.abt.org/education/dictionary/index.html)
- "Ballet". *Encyclopædia Britannica* (11th ed.). 1911.

20th century concert dance

20th century → concert dance is the name given to a category of → dance forms that include:

- Free dance
- → Modern dance
- Expressionist dance
- Postmodern dance
- Dance improvisation
- Contemporary dance
- Dance theatre
- Dance for camera

Although *technically* 20th century concert dance, the following dance forms are considered under the separate category of → Ballet or 20th century ballet:

- Contemporary ballet
- Neoclassical ballet
- Deconstructivist ballet / Post-structuralist ballet

lineage of dance forms

Relationship to art movements

Although sharing the name of art movements the dance forms may not relate to them directly. From an ideological and conceptual point of view the connections are shown below:

- **Expressionism**
  - Free dance
  - → Modern dance
  - Expressionist dance
    - Ausdruckstanz
      - Tanztheater (dance theatre)
      - physical theatre
- **Modernism**
  - Postmodern dance
    - Dance improvisation
      - contact improvisation
- **Postmodernism**
  - Postmodern dance
    - Contemporary dance
    - Dance for camera

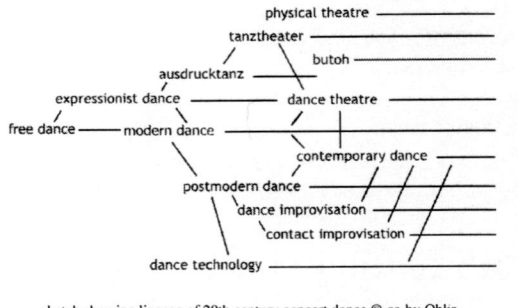

sketch showing lineage of 20th century concert dance ©-cc-by Ohka-

notes:

1. This list is given as an illustrative example and should not be used for re classification
2. Postmodern dance falls under two catergories due to its complex nature (see Postmodernism).
3. Choreographers using a postmodernist process may produce works that are classical, romantic, expressionist, modernist or postmodernist (etc) in appearance (see Postmodernism).

See also

- → Concert dance
- List of dance style categories
- List of dance companies
- → Dance
- Physical theatre

Further reading

- Adshead-Lansdale, J. (Ed) (1994) *Dance History: An Introduction*. Routledge. ISBN 0-415-09030-X
- Anderson, J. (1992) *Ballet & Modern Dance: A Concise History*. Independent Publishers Group. ISBN 0-87127-172-9
- Au, S. (2002) *Ballet and Modern Dance (World of Art)*. Thames & Hudson. ISBN 0-500-20352-0
- Banes, S (1987) *Terpsichore in Sneakers: Post-Modern Dance*. Wesleyan University Press. ISBN 0-8195-6160-6
- Banes, S (Ed) (1993) *Greenwich Village 1963: Avant-Garde Performance and the Effervescent Body*. Duke University Press. ISBN 0-8223-1391-X
- Banes, S (Ed) (2003) *Reinventing Dance in the 1960s: Everything Was Possible*. University of Wisconsin Press. ISBN 0-299-18014-X
- Bremser, M. (Ed) (1999) *Fifty Contemporary Choreographers*. Routledge. ISBN 0-415-10364-9
- Carter, A. (1998) *The Routledge Dance Studies Reader*. Routledge. ISBN 0-415-16447-8
- Cohen, S, J. (1992) *Dance As a Theatre Art: Source Readings in Dance History from 1581 to the Present*. Princeton Book Co. ISBN 0-87127-173-7
- Copeland, R. (2004) *Merce Cunningham: The Modernizing of Modern Dance*. Routledge. ISBN 0-415-96575-6
- Daly, A. (2002) *Critical Gestures: Writings on Dance and Culture*. Wesleyan University Press. ISBN 0-8195-6566-0
- Desmond, J, C. (Ed) (1997) *Meaning in Motion: New Cultural Studies of Dance (Post-Contemporary Interventions)*. Duke University Press. ISBN 0-8223-1942-X
- Dils, A. (2001) *Moving History/Dancing Cultures: A Dance History Reader*. Wesleyan University Press. ISBN 0-8195-6413-3
- Ihde, DD. (2003) *Bodies in Technology*. University of Minnesota Press. ISBN 0-8166-3846-2
- Jowitt, D. (1989) *Time and the Dancing Image*. University of California Press. ISBN 0-520-06627-8
- Novack, C, J. (1990) *Sharing the Dance: Contact Improvisation and American Culture*. University of Wisconsin Press. ISBN 0-299-12444-4
- Reynolds, N. and McCormick, M. (2003) *No Fixed Points: Dance in the Twentieth Century*. Yale University Press. ISBN 0-300-09366-7
- Thomas, H. (2003) *The Body, Dance and Cultural Theory*. Palgrave Macmillan. ISBN 0-333-72432-1

African-American dance

African-American topics

African-American history
Atlantic slave trade · Maafa
Slavery in the United States
African-American military history
Jim Crow laws · Redlining
Civil Rights Movements 1896–1954 and
1955–1968
Afrocentrism · Reparations

African-American culture
African American studies
Neighborhoods · Juneteenth
Kwanzaa · Art · Museums
→ Dance · Literature · Music · Schools · Historic colleges and universities

Religion
Black church · Black theology
Black liberation theology
Doctrine of Father Divine
Black Hebrew Israelites
American Society of Muslims
Nation of Islam · Rastafari

Political movements
Pan-Africanism · Black Power
Nationalism · Capitalism
Conservatism · Populism
Leftism · Black Panther Party
Garveyism

Civic and economic groups
NAACP · SCLC · CORE · SNCC · NUL
Rights groups · ASALH · UNCF
NBCC · NPHC · The Links · NCNW

Sports
Negro league baseball
CIAA · SIAC · MEAC · SWAC

Ethnic sub-divisions
Black Indians · Gullah · Igbo

Languages
English · Gullah · Creole
African American Vernacular

Diaspora
Liberia · Nova Scotia · France Sierra Leone · United Kingdom
Lists
African Americans National firsts · State firsts Landmark legislation Black diaspora Index
Category · Portal

"African-American dance" in the vernacular tradition (academically known as "African American vernacular dance") are those dances which have developed within African American communities in everyday spaces, rather than in dance studios, schools or companies. African American vernacular dances are usually centered on social dance practice, though performance dance and → concert dance often supply complementary aspects to social dancing.

Placing great value on improvisation, African American vernacular dances are characterized by ongoing change and development.

The term 'vernacular dance' is often critiqued by dancers within a tradition as being unnecessarily 'technical'. Despite these issues, the term is commonly used in dance studies literature internationally.

There are a number of notable African American → modern dance companies using African American vernacular dance as an inspiration, amongst these are the Alvin Ailey American Dance Theater and Dance Theatre of Harlem.

History

The Greater Chesapeake area embracing Virginia, Maryland, and much of North Carolina was the earliest and perhaps most influential location of the black-while cultural interchange that produced "African American" dance.[1] Captive Africans from numerous societies in several African regions began pouring into the area as slaves from the late seventeenth to the late eighteenth centuries. Given their cultural heterogeneity, including music and dance, they mostly likely learned to dance together by drawing on the "grammar of culture" shared across much of Western and Central Africa.[2] Something like a regional Chesapeake tradition, a thing entirely novel in European eyes, arose perhaps not long before the eighteenth century had become the nineteenth.[3] Within one or two generations of establishing these creolized African forms, or perhaps simultaneously, elements of European dances were added.[4] "Competitive individuality and [probably] improvisation" were also Choreographic Elements of Seventeenth and Eighteenth Century West African Dance" that were continued in this region.[5]

Based on the limited pictorial record, the typical African practice of bending emphatically at the waist and hips gave way to a more upright, European like style. This may have reflected the African practice of carrying heavy loads on the head, which requires a strong, balancing spine.[4] Black dancing continued strong preferences of other African characteristics such as angularity and asymmetry of body positions, multiple body rhythms or polyrhythms, and a low center of gravity.[6]

Jig, Clog, and Break Down Dancing have been attributed to African Americans.[7] It should be noted, though, that Irish Jig and clogging were both in existence when, in the 1840s in the Five Points area of New York, occupied in part by many Irish, William Henry Lane, aka Masta Juba, combined the shuffle with the Irish jig, a style called a break-down, attracting attention from Charles Dickens who visited Charles Almackk, later called Pete Williams' place, a black American dance hall.

The phrase African American vernacular dance is commonly used to refer to those dances which have developed within the African American communities of the United States from the 1600s. African slaves brought to America from the 1600s were representative of a wide range of ethnic groups, and their dance and cultural lives were similarly diverse. To speak of an 'African American vernacular dance' without qualification is to ignore the vast range of dance practices and traditions which developed from these African roots in communities across the United States. Afro-American dance in the earliest days was a response to the conditions of slavery.

New and different cultural traditions developed not only in different cities across America, but on the properties of different slave owners. There were distinct regional variations in dance in African American communities even in the 1600s, developing as a combination of traditions from different African ethnic groups, the culture of slave owners and other groups within the immediate society, as responses to the musical and social lives of individuals in that community, and in response to different experiences under slavery.

New York and the Harlem Renaissance

Just as the Harlem Renaissance saw the development of art, poetry, literature and theatre in Harlem during the early 20th century, it also saw the development of a rich musical and dance life. Clubs (Cotton Club), Ballrooms (Savoy Ballroom), rent party and other black spaces as the birthplaces of new vernacular dances.

Theatres and the shift from vaudeville to local 'shows' written and choreographed by African American artists. Theatres as public forums for popularising African American vernacular dances.

Genres by period

19th century

Dance genres:

- Tap dancing
- Cakewalk

1930s and 1940s

Dance genres:

- Swing
- Lindy hop
- Charleston
- Texas Tommy

1960s

Music Genres:

- Northern Soul
- Motown

Dance moves and genres:

- Hustle
- Monkey

1970s

Music Genres:

- Funk
- Disco

1980s

Dance genres and moves:

- Break dancing
- Popping
- Locking
- Voguing
- Cabbage patch
- The Worm
- The Robot
- Moonwalk

1990s and 2000s

Dance moves and genres:

→ Krumping, Hyphy, Snap dance, Cha Cha Slide, Lean wit It, Rock wit It, Walk It Out, Breakdance Footwork, Chicken Noodle Soup, Crip Walk, Gangsta Walking, Tootsee Roll, The Roosevelt, Poole Palace, Butterfly Dance, Joc-in, Crank Dat Soulja Boy, A-Town Stomp, Harlem Shake, Aunt Jackie, Heel Toe, D-Town Boogie, Jerkin', Stanky Legg, Botty Dew, Bird Walk.[8]

Performance, competition and social dance

In a vernacular dance culture there is often no distinction between 'dance' spaces and 'non-dances spaces'. Dance and rhythmic movement are as much a part of everyday life as language. In many cases dance has played a more central role than literacy (especially during slavery), particularly in the communication of history, tradition and culture between generations, much as has oral culture. Competition has long played an important role in social dance in African and African American social dance, from the 'battles' of hip hop and lindy hop to the cake walk. Performances have also been integrated into everyday dance life, from the relationship between performance and social dancing in tap dancing to the 'shows' held at Harlem ball rooms in the 1930s.

Social dance spaces

- Juke joint, street parties, rent party and the importance of the front porch
- Ballrooms, cabaret clubs and church halls

Competitive dance

- Cake walks, the Harvest Moon Ball, Breakdance

Learning to dance in an African American vernacular dance tradition

In most African American vernacular dance cultures, learning to dance does not happen in formal classrooms or dance studios. Children often learn to dance as they grow up, developing not only a body awareness but also aesthetics of dance which are particular to their community. Learning to dance - learning about rhythmic movement - happens in much the same way as developing a local language 'accent' or a particular set of social values. Children learn specific dance steps or 'how to dance' from their families - most often from older brothers and sisters, cousins or other older children. Because vernacular dance happens in everyday spaces, children often dance with older members of the community around their homes and neighbourhoods, at parties and dances, on special occasions, or whenever groups of people gather to 'have a good time'. Vernacular dance traditions are therefore often cross-generational traditions, with younger dancers often 'reviving' dances from previous generations, albeit with new 'cool' variations and 'styling'. This is not to suggest that there are no social limitations on who may dance with whom and when. Dance partners (or people to dance with) are chosen by a range of social factors, including age, sex, kinship, interest and so on. The most common dance groups are often comprised by people of a similar age, background and often sex (though this is a varying factor).

African American vernacular dance in the mainstream

Film, Theatre and Video Clips

- Hollywood musicals and stage (theatre)s: the Nicholas Brothers and Gene Kelly; Frankie Manning and Dean Collins
- Music videos: Madonna and Missy Higgins: black dancers in people of non African descent clips, black dances in people of non African descent bodies, black music and dance in black bodies

Black dances in white communities

- Contemporary swing dance communities
- Contemporary tap dance
- Hip hop classes and white b-boys

African American vernacular dance and a continuum of creative cultural expression

Lee Ellen Friedland and other authors argue that to talk about dancing in a vernacular tradition without talking about music or art or drama is like talking about fish without talking about water. Music and dance are intimately related in African American vernacular dance, not only as accompaniments, but as intertwined creative processes.

Jacqui Malone describes the relationships between tap dancers who travelled with bands in the early 20th century, describing the way tap dancers worked with the musicians to create new rhythms. Much has been written about the relationship between improvisation in jazz and improvisation in jazz dance - the two are linked by their emphasis on improvisation and creative additions to compositions while they are in process - → choreography and composition on the spot, in a social context - rather than a strict division between 'creation' and 'performance', as in the European middle class → ballet and operatic tradition.

It is equally important to talk about the relationship between DJs MCs, b-boys and b-girls and graffiti artists in hip hop culture, and John F. Szwed and Morton Marks have discussed the development of jazz and jazz dance in America from European set dances and dance suites in relation to the development of musical artisanship.

African American modern dance

African American modern dance drew on modern dance and African American vernacular dance along with African dance and Caribbean dance influences. Katherine Dunham founded *Ballet Negre* in 1936 and later the **Katherine Dunham Dance Company** based in Chicago, Illinois. She also opened a school in New York (1945). Pearl Primus drew on African and Caribbean dances to create strong dramatic works characterized by large leaps in the air. Primus often based her dances on the work of black writers and on racial and African-American issues, such as Langston Hughes *The Negro Speaks of Rivers* (1944), and Lewis Allan's *Strange Fruit* (1945). Alvin Ailey, a student of Lester Horton and Martha Graham, with a troupe of young African American dancers performed as the Alvin Ailey

American Dance Theater in New York in 1930. Ailey drew on his *blood memories* of Texas, the blues, spirituals and gospel.

See also

- African American History
- Dance in the United States
  - Modern dance in the United States
- Get down
- Jazz dance
- Hip-Hop dance
- Street dance

Further reading

- deFrantz, Thomas. Dancing Many Drums: Excavations in African-American Dance. Wisconsin: University of Wisconsin Press, 2002.
- Emery, Lynne Fauley. Black Dance in the United States from 1619 to 1970. California: National Press Books, 1972.
- Friedland, LeeEllen. "Social Commentary in African-American Movement Performance." Human Action Signs in Cultural Context: The Visible and the Invisible in Movement and Dance. Ed. Brenda Farnell. London: Scarecrow Press, 1995. 136 - 57.
- Gottschild, Brenda Dixon. Digging the Africanist Presence in American Performance. Connecticut and London: Greenwood Press, 1996.
- Hazzard-Gordon, Katrina. "African-American Vernacular Dance: Core Culture and Meaning Operatives." Journal of Black Studies 15.4 (1985): 427-45.
- Hazzard-Gordon, Katrina. Jookin': The Rise of Social Dance Formations in African-American Culture. Philadelphia: Temple University Press, 1990.
- Jackson, Jonathan David. "Improvisation in African-American Vernacular Dancing." *Dance Research Journal* 33.2 (2001/2002): 40 - 53.
- Malone, Jacqui. Steppin' on the Blues: The Visible Rhythms of African American Dance. Urbana and Chicago: University of Illinois Press, 1996.
- Stearns, Marshall, and Jean Stearns. Jazz Dance: The Story of American Vernacular Dance. 3rd ed. New York: Da Capo Press, 1994.
- Szwed, John F., and Morton Marks. "The Afro-American Transformation of European Set Dances and Dance Suites." Dance Research Journal 20.1 (1988): 29 - 36.
- Welsh-Asante Kariamu. "African-American dance in curricula: modes of inclusion." (Pathways to Aesthetic Literacy: Revealing Culture in the Dance Curriculum) American Alliance for Health, Physical Education, Recreation and Dance (AAHPERD) (July 28, 2005)
- Welsh-Asante Kariamu. The African Aesthetic: Keeper of the Traditions (Contributions in Afro-American & African Studies) Greenwood Press, 1993.
- Welsh-Asante Kariamu. African Culture the Rhythms of Unity: The Rhythms of Unity Africa World Press, 1989.

References

[1] Ballroom, Boogie, Shimmy Sham, Shake: A Social and Popular Dance Reader.Julie Malnig. Edition: illustrated. University of Illinois Press. 2009. page 19. ISBN 025207565X, 9780252075650
[2] Ballroom, Boogie, Shimmy Sham, Shake: A Social and Popular Dance Reader.Julie Malnig. Edition: illustrated. University of Illinois Press. 2009. page 21. ISBN 025207565X, 987-0-25207565-0
[3] Ballroom, Boogie, Shimmy Sham, Shake: A Social and Popular Dance Reader.Julie Malnig. Edition: illustrated. University of Illinois Press. 2008. page 21. ISBN 025207565X, 9780252075650
[4] Ballroom, Boogie, Shimmy Sham, Shake: A Social and Popular Dance Reader.Julie Malnig. Edition: illustrated. University of Illinois Press. 2008. page 22. ISBN 025207565X, 9780252075650
[5] All the Mazes of the Dance. Jurretta Jordan Heckscher. PhD dissertation. 2000.
[6] Ballroom, Boogie, Shimmy Sham, Shake: A Social and Popular Dance Reader.Julie Malnig. Edition: illustrated. University of Illinois Press. 2008. page 23. ISBN 025207565X, 9780252075650
[7] Jig, Clog, and Break Down Dancing. Ed James. 1873. (http://memory.loc.gov/cgi-bin/ampage?collId=musdi&fileName=117/musdi117. db&recNum=2&itemLink=r?ammem/musdi:@field(DOCID+@lit(M1171))#1170001&linkText=1)
[8] See also Dancejam.com this list (http://dancejam.com/dances/hip-hop)

Ballroom dance

Ballroom dance refers to a set of partner dances, which are enjoyed both socially and competitively around the globe. Its performance and entertainment aspects are also widely enjoyed on stage, in film, and on television.

While historically *ballroom dance* may refer to any form of formal social dancing as recreation, with the emergence of → dancesport in modern times the term has become much narrower in scope, usually referring specifically to the International Standard and International Latin style dances (see dance categories below). In the United States, two additional variations—"American Smooth" and "American Rhythm"—have also been popularized and are commonly recognized as styles of "ballroom dance".

Vernon and Irene Castle, early ballroom dance pioneers, c. 1910-1918.

Definitions and history

The term "ballroom dancing" is derived from the word *ball*, which in turn originates from the Latin word *ballare* which means "to dance". In times past, ballroom dancing was "social dancing" for the privileged, leaving "folk dancing" for the lower classes. These boundaries have since become blurred, and it should be noted even in times long gone, many ballroom dances were really elevated folk dances. The definition of ballroom dance also depends on the era: Balls have featured Minuet, Quadrille, Polonaise, Pas de Gras, Mazurka, and other popular dances of the day, which are now considered to be historical dances.

The Gaskell Ball

Renaissance Period

Galliard in Siena, Italy, 15th century

The first authoritative knowledge of the earliest ballroom dances were recorded toward the end of the sixteenth century, when Jehan Tabourot, under the pen name "Thoinot-Arbeau", published in 1588 his *'Orchésographie'*, a study of late sixteenth-century French Renaissance social dance. Among the dances described were the solemn basse danse, the livelier branle, pavane, and the galliarde which Shakespeare called the "cinq pace" as it was made of five steps. [1]

In 1650 the Minuet, originally a peasant dance of Poitou, was introduced into Paris and set to music by Jean-Baptiste Lully and danced by the king Louis XIV in public, and would continue to dominate ballroom from that time until the close of the eighteenth century.

Toward the latter half of the seventeenth century, Louis XIV had founded his 'Académie Royale de Musique et de Danse', where specific rules for the execution of every dance and the 'five positions' of the feet were formulated for the first time by members of the Académie. Eventually, the first definite cleavage between → ballet and ballroom came when professional dancers appeared in the ballets, and the ballets left the Court and went to the stage. Ballet technique such as the *turned out* five positions of the stage, however, lingered for over two centuries and past the end of the Victoria era. [1]

Victorian Era

The waltz with its modern hold took root in England about 1812, when Carl Maria von Weber wrote *Invitation à la valse* which *'[marked] the adoption of the Waltz form into the sphere of absolute music'*. The dance was initially met with tremendous opposition due to the semblance of impropriety associated with the closed hold, though the stance gradually softened.[2] In the 1840s several new dances made their apperance in the ballroom, including the Polka, Mazurka, and the Schottische, in the meantime a strong tendeny emerged to drop all 'decorative' steps such as *entrechats* and *ronds de jambes* that had found a place in the Quadrilles and other dances.

An RKO publicity still of Astaire and Rogers dancing to "Smoke Gets in Your Eyes" in *Roberta* (1935)

Early 20th century

In the early 20th century, the on-screen dance pairing of Fred Astaire and Ginger Rogers greatly influenced ballroom dancing in the USA. Although both actors had separate projects and careers, they are associated for their filmed dance sequences together, which included portrayals of early 20th century dancers Vernon and Irene Castle and have reached iconic status.[3] Much of Astaire and Rogers' work portrayed social dancing, although the performances were highly choreographed (often by Astaire or Hermes Pan), and meticulously staged and rehearsed.[4]

Competitive dancing

An International Rumba scene from the 2005 US Nationals

In spite of its historical image as a pastime for the privileged; formal competitions, sometimes referred to as DanceSport, often allow participation by less advanced dancers at various proficiency levels. Ballroom dance competitions take place worldwide at different levels.

The International Olympic Committee now recognizes competitive ballroom dance [5]. It now appears doubtful that it will be included in the Olympic Games especially in light of efforts to reduce the number of offerings, but the application has not been permanently rejected.

In the United States, amateur dance proficiency levels are defined by USA Dance (formerly United States Amateur Ballroom Dance Association, USABDA) as Bronze->Silver->Gold for syllabus dancers, and Novice->Prechampionship->Championship for open competitors.[6] These levels roughly correspond to the "E" to "S" levels in Europe and Australia. Among professionals, levels classify into Rising Star and Open Professional.

Eligibility and "leveling up" requirements will vary greatly between countries and sometimes within. For instance, in addition to USA Dance competitions, amateur dancers in the United States often participate in competitions sanctioned by NDCA or YCN (Youth Collegiate Network), each with its own distinct culture in addition to differing definitions of level and eligibility requirements.

Ballroom dancing competitions in the former USSR also included the Soviet Ballroom dances, or *Soviet Programme*. Australian New Vogue is danced both competitively and socially. In competition there are 15 recognised New Vogue dances, which are performed by the competitors in sequence.

2005 U.S. National Professional Standard Championships, hosted by BYU

Internationally, the Blackpool Dance Festival, hosted annually at Blackpool, England, is considered the most prestigious event a dancesport competitor can attend.

Formation Dance is another style of competitive dance recognised by the IDSF.

Elements of competition

In competition ballroom dancers are judged by diverse criteria such as poise, the hold or frame, posture, musicality and expression, timing, body alignment and shape, floor craft, foot and leg action, and presentation.[7] Judging in a performance-oriented sport is inevitably subjective in nature, and controversy and complaints by competitors over judging placements are not uncommon. The scorekeepers—called scrutineers—will tally the total number recalls accumulated by each couple through each round until the finals, when the Skating system is used to place each couple by ordinals, typically 1-6, though the number of couples in the final may vary.

Intermediate level international style Latin dancing at the 2006 MIT ballroom dance competition. A judge stands in the foreground.

Medal examinations enable dancers' abilities to be recognized according to conventional standards. In medal exams, each dancer performs two or more dances in a certain genre (e.g., International Standard) in front of a judge. In some North American examinations, levels include Newcomer, Bronze, Silver, Gold and Championship; each level may be further subdivided into either two or four separate sections.

Dances

In one common usage "ballroom dance" refers to the ten dances of **International Standard** and **International Latin**, though the term is also often used interchangeably with the five International Standard dances [8] In the United States and Canada, the **American Style** (**American Smooth** and **American Rhythm**) also exists. The dance technique used for both International and American styles is similar, but International Standard allows only closed dance positions, whereas American Smooth allows closed, open and separated dance movements. In addition, different sets of dance patterns are usually taught for the two styles. International Latin and American Rhythm have different styling, and have different dance patterns in their respective syllabi.

Others dances sometimes placed under the umbrella "ballroom dance" include Nightclub Dances such as Lindy Hop, West Coast Swing, Nightclub Two Step, Hustle, Salsa, and Merengue. The categorization of dances as "ballroom dances" has always been fluid, with new dances or folk dances being added to/removed from to the ballroom repertoire from time to time, so no list of subcategories or dances is any more than a description of current practices. There are other dances historically accepted as ballroom dances, and are revived via the Vintage dance movement.

In Europe, Latin Swing dances include Argentine Tango, Mambo, Lindy Hop, Swing Boogie (sometimes also known as Nostalgic Boogie), and Disco Fox. One example of this is the subcategory of Cajun dances that originated in New Orleans, with branches reaching both coasts of the United States.

Standard/Smooth dances are normally danced to Western music (often from the mid-twentieth century), and couples dance counter-clockwise around a rectangular floor following the line of dance. In competitions, competitors are costumed as would be appropriate for a white tie affair, with full gowns for the ladies and bow tie and tail coats for the men; though in American Smooth it is now conventional for the men to abandon the tailsuit in favor of shorter tuxedos, vests, and other creative outfits.

Latin/Rhythm dances are commonly danced to contemporary Latin American music, and with the exception of a few traveling dances (e.g. Samba and Paso Doble) couples do not follow the line of dance and perform their routines more or less in one spot. In competitions, the women are often dressed in short-skirted latin outfits while the men outfitted in tight-fitting shirts and pants; the goal being to bring emphasis to the dancers' leg action and body movements.

See also

- List of DanceSport dances
- List of dance organizations
- Ice dancing, a branch of figure skating that derives from ballroom dance.

External links

- International DanceSport Federation [9]
- USA Dance (formerly U.S. Amateur Ballroom Dance Association) [10]
- Canadian Amateur DanceSport Association [11]
- Ballroom dance photography samples [12]
- Ballroom dance video samples: waltz [13], tango [14], foxtrot [15], quickstep [16], cha-cha [17], samba [18], rumba [19], jive [20]

References

[1] Silvester, V., *Modern Ballroom Dancing* p. 11, Tralfalgar Square Publishing 1993
[2] Silvester, V., *Modern Ballroom Dancing* p.12-13, Tralfalgar Square Publishing 1993
[3] " History of Musical Film, by John Kenrick (http://www.musicals101.com/1930film3.htm)". Musicals101.com. . Retrieved 2008-05-29.
[4] " Review of "Swing Time" (1936) (http://rogerebert.suntimes.com/apps/pbcs.dll/article?AID=/19980215/REVIEWS08/401010363/1023)". rogerebert.com. 1998-02-15. . Retrieved 2008-05-29.
[5] Certificate of Olympic recognition of IDSF (http://www.idsf.net/index.tpl?id=30)
[6] " USABDA 2007-08 Rulebook (http://documents.usabda.org/1341/3114/2007_2008_Rulebook_v12.pdf)". . Retrieved 2007-02-20.
[7] " What Judges Look For (http://www.dancesportireland.org/idsf_news/judging.html)". . Retrieved 2006-12-22.
[8] " History of Modern Ballroom Dancing (http://linus.socs.uts.edu.au/~don/pubs/modern.html)". . Retrieved 2007-02-20..
[9] http://www.idsf.net
[10] http://www.usabda.org
[11] http://www.dancesport.ca
[12] http://www.ballroommedia.com
[13] http://www.youtube.com/results?search_query=waltz&search_type=&aq=f
[14] http://www.youtube.com/results?search_query=ballroom+tango&search_type=&aq=f
[15] http://www.youtube.com/results?search_query=slow+foxtrot&search_type=&aq=f
[16] http://www.youtube.com/results?search_query=quickstep&search_type=&aq=f
[17] http://www.youtube.com/results?search_query=cha+cha&search_type=&aq=f
[18] http://www.youtube.com/results?search_query=ballroom+samba&search_type=&aq=f
[19] http://www.youtube.com/results?search_query=rumba&search_type=&aq=f
[20] http://www.youtube.com/results?search_query=jive&search_type=&aq=f

B-boying

B-boying or **breaking**, commonly referred to as **breakdancing**, is a style of dance that evolved as part of hip-hop culture among Black and Latino American youths in the South Bronx of New York City during the 1970s.[1]:125, 141, 153 It is danced to both hip-hop and other genres of music that are often remixed to prolong the musical breaks. One who practices this style of dance is called a **b-boy**, **b-girl**, or **breaker**. Although "breakdance" is a common term, "b-boying" and "breaking" are preferred by the majority of the art form's pioneers and most notable practitioners.[2][3]

Breaking's intense popularity started to fade in the late 1980s,[4]:137 but in the following decades it became an accepted dance style portrayed in commercials, movies, and print media. Parties, disco clubs, talent shows, and other public events became typical locations for breakers. Instruction in breaking techniques is now available at dance studios where hip-hop dance is taught. Today, breakers maintain a discipline somewhere between that of dancers and athletes.

A b-boy performing in the UK.

Terminology

Though widespread, the term "breakdancing" is looked down upon by those immersed in hip-hop culture. "Breakdancer" may even be used disparagingly to refer to those who learned the dance for personal gain rather than commitment to hip-hop culture.[1]:61 The terms 'b-boys', 'b-girls', and 'breakers' are the preferred terms to use to describe the dancers. B-Boy London of New York City Breakers and Michael Holman refer to these dancers as "breakers".[2] Frosty Freeze of Rock Steady Crew says, "we were known as b-boys", and Afrika Bambaataa says, "b-boys, [are] what you call break boys... or b-girls, what you call break girls."[2] In addition, Jo Jo and Mr. Freeze of Rock Steady Crew and Fab 5 Freddy use the term "b-boy".[2] The dance itself is properly called "breaking" according to figures such as KRS-One, Talib Kweli, Mos Def, and Darryl McDaniels of Run-DMC in the breaking documentary *The Freshest Kids*. Afrika Bambaataa, Fab 5 Freddy, Michael Holman, Frosty Freeze, and Santiago "Jo Jo" Torres (cofounder of Rock Steady Crew) use the original term "b-boying".[2] Purists consider "breakdancing" an ignorant term invented by the media[1]:58[2] that connotes exploitation of the art.[1]:60[2]

- Crazy Legs; Rock Steady Crew: "When I first learned about the dance in '77 it was called b-boying... by the time the media got a hold of it in like '81, '82, it became 'break-dancing' and I even got caught up calling it break-dancing too."[2]
- Action; New York City Breakers: "You know what, that's our fault kind of... we started dancing and going on tours and all that and people would say, oh you guys are breakdancers - we never corrected them."[2]
- Jo Jo; Rock Steady Crew: "B-boy... that's what it is, that's why when the public changed it to 'break-dancing' they were just giving a professional name to it, but b-boy was the original name for it and whoever wants to keep it real would keep calling it b-boy."[2]
- Boston Globe: "Lesson one: Don't call it breakdancing. Hip-hop's dance tradition, the kinetic counterpart to the sound scape of rap music and the visuals of graffiti art, is properly known as b-boying."[3]
- Jorge "Popmaster Fabel" Pabon: "Break dancing is a term created by the media! Once hip hop dancers gained the media's attention, some journalists and reporters produced inaccurate terminology in an effort to present these

urban dance forms to the masses. The term break dancing is a prime example of this misnomer. Most pioneers and architects of dance forms associated with hip hop reject this term and hold fast to the original vernacular created in their places of origin. In the case of break dancing, it was initially called b-boying or b-girling."[5]

The term "breakdancing" is also problematic because it has become a diluted umbrella term that incorrectly includes popping, locking, and electric boogaloo.[1]:60 Popping, locking, and electric boogaloo are not styles of "breakdance". They are *funk styles* that were developed separate from breaking in California.[6]

Dance techniques

There are four basic elements that form the foundation of breaking. These are toprock, downrock, power moves, and freezes/suicides.

Toprock refers to any string of steps performed from a standing position. It is usually the first and foremost opening display of style, and it serves as a warm-up for transitions into more acrobatic maneuvers. Toprock is very eclectic and can draw upon many other dance styles. Though commonly associated with popping and locking (two elements of the funk styles that evolved independently in California during the 1970s) breaking is distinct from both, as its moves require a greater sense of athleticism—as opposed to the contortion of limbs seen in the funk styles. Breakers who wish to widen their expressive range, however, may dabble in all types of hip hop dance.

A b-boy practicing downrock at a studio in Moscow.

Downrock (or "floorwork") includes all footwork performed on the floor, such as the foundational 6-step. It typically involves complicated contortions of the lower body, and may be as highly variable and personalized as toprock. Downrock transitions into more athletic moves known as power moves.

Power Moves are actions that require momentum and physical power to execute. The breaker is generally supported by his upper body, while the rest of his body creates circular momentum. Notable examples are the windmill, headmill, swipe, head spin, and flare. Some moves are borrowed from gymnastics (such as the flare) and martial arts (such as the butterfly kick).

Freezes/Suicides signal the end of a b-boy set. Freezes are stylish poses, and the more difficult require the breaker to suspend himself or herself off the ground using upper body strength in poses such as the pike. Alternatively, suicides can also signal the end to a routine. Breakers will make it appear that they have lost control and fall onto their backs, stomachs, etc. The more painful the suicide appears, the more impressive it is, but breakers execute them in a way to minimize pain. In contrast to freezes, suicides draw attention to the motion of falling or losing control, while freezes draw attention to a controlled final position.

Uprock as a dance style of its own never gained the same widespread popularity as breaking, except for some very specific moves adopted by breakers who use it as a variation for their toprock.[4]:138 When used in a b-boy battle, opponents often respond by performing similar uprock moves, supposedly creating a short uprock battle. Some dancers argue that because uprock was originally a separate dance style it should never be mixed with breaking and that the uprock moves performed by breakers today are not the original moves but poor imitations that only shows a small part of the original uprock style.

Power vs style

Multiple stereotypes have emerged in the breaking community over the give-and-take relationship between technical footwork and physical prowess. Those who focus on dance steps and fundamental sharpness (but lack upper-body brawn, form, discipline, etc) are labeled as "style-heads". Specialists of more gymnastics oriented technique and form—at the cost of charisma and coordinated footwork—are known as "power-heads." Such terms are used colloquially often to classify one's skill, however, the subject has been known to disrupt competitive events where judges tend to favor a certain technique over the other.

History

Elements of breaking may be seen in other antecedent cultures prior to the 1970s,[7] but it wasn't until the '70s that breaking evolved as a street dance style. Street corner DJs would take the rhythmic breakdown sections (or "breaks") of dance records and loop them one after the other. This provided a rhythmic base for improvising and mixing, and it allowed dancers to display their skills during the break. In a turn-based showcase of dance routines, the winning side was determined by the dancer(s) who could outperform the other by displaying a set of more complicated and innovative moves.

A crew is a group of b-boys/b-girls who dance together. A few of the most well known crews are the Jinjo Crew, New York City Breakers, Rock Steady Crew, Recognize Crew, Style Elements Crew, LA Breakers, Last For One, Super Cr3w, Gamblerz, Mortal Combat, Flying Steps, and Massive Monkeys.

B-boy crews such as the Rock Steady Crew and the New York City Breakers changed breaking into a pop-culture phenomenon when they received a large amount of media attention by battling each other in public at the Lincoln Center in 1981.[8] Shortly after the Rock Steady Crew came to Japan, breaking within Japan began to flourish. Each Sunday b-boys would perform breaking in Tokyo's Yoyogi Park.[9] One of the first and most influential Japanese breakers was Crazy-A, who is now the leader of the Tokyo chapter of Rock Steady Crew.[9] He also organizes the yearly B-Boy Park which draws upwards of 10,000 fans a year and attempts to expose a wider audience to the culture.[10]

A related dance form which influenced breaking is Uprock also called rocking or Brooklyn rock. Like toprock, uprock is also performed while standing. The difference is that uprock is a war dance that involves two dancers who mimic ways of fighting each other using mimed weaponry in rhythm with the music.[5] This style involves moves called Yerkes (pron-enl "jerks") which are a set of motions executed to the break of a track and are where most of the battling occurs; outside of the break of a track is where the freestyle element of the dance is executed.

Battles

It has been stated that breaking replaced fighting between street gangs.[11] On the contrary, some believe it a misconception that b-boying ever played a part in mediating gang rivalry. Both viewpoints have some truth. Uprock has its roots in gangs.[4]:116, 138 Whenever there was an issue over turf the two warlords of the feuding gangs would uprock. Whoever won this preliminary battle would decide where the real fight would be.[12] This is where the battle mentality in breaking and hip-hop dance in general comes from.[13] "Sometimes a dance was enough to settle the beef, sometimes the dance set off more beef."[4]:116[5]

Crew vs crew battles are common in breaking. Battles are dance competitions between two individuals or two groups of dancers who try to out-dance each other. They can be either formal or informal but both types of battles are head to head confrontations. They can take the form of a cypher battle and an organized battle.

Informally b-boying began with the cypher, the name given to a circle of breakers (and casual onlookers) who take turns dancing in the center. There are no judges, concrete rules, or restrictions in the cypher, only unspoken traditions. Although participants usually freestyle (improvise) within a cypher, battling does take place. This was the origin of b-boy battles and it is often more confrontational and personal. Cypher dancing is more prevalent in communities with an emphasis on what is regarded as authentic and traditional hip-hop culture. Battling "in the cypher" is also a method of settling differences between individual dancers or crews.

B-boy battle at Hip Hop Festival Serious Side II in Salamanca, Spain.

Organized battles set a format for competition such as a time limit or a cap on the number of participants. Organized battles also have judges, who are usually chosen based on their years of experience, level of cultural knowledge, contribution to the scene, and ability to judge in an unbiased manner. On occasion, organizers invite judges from outside the breaking community, and these events (jams) sometimes meet with disapproval from b-boys/b-girls. Organized battles are publicized to a much greater extent than informal events. They include famous international level championships such as Battle of the Year, UK B-Boy Championships, Red Bull BC One, Freestyle Session, and R-16 Korea. However, the trend in recent years to place excessive emphasis on organized battles, may detract from the spontaneous aspect of the culture that is emphasized in cypher dancing.[14]

Music

The musical selection for breaking is not restricted to hip-hop music as long as the tempo and beat pattern conditions are met. Breaking can be readily adapted to different music genres with the aid of remixing. The original songs that popularized the dance form borrow significantly from progressive genres of jazz, soul, funk, electro, and disco. The most common feature of b-boy music exists in musical breaks, or compilations formed from samples taken from different songs which are then looped and chained together by the DJ. The tempo generally ranges between 110 and 135 beats per minute with shuffled sixteenth and quarter beats in the percussive pattern. History credits Kool Dj Herc for the invention of this concept,[4]:79 later termed the break beat.

Gender inequality

Like the other aspects of hip hop, graffiti writing, MCing, and DJing, males are generally seen as the predominant gender within breaking. However, this belief is being challenged by the rapidly increasing number of b-girls. Critics argue that it is unfair to make a sweeping generalization about these inequalities because women have begun to play a larger role in the breaking scene.[15][16]

Despite the increasing number of female breakers, another possible barrier is lack of promotion. As Firefly, a full-time b-girl says, "It's getting more popular. There are a lot more girls involved. The problem is that promoters are not putting on enough female-only battles."[17][18] More people are seeking to change the traditional image of females in hip-hop culture (and by extension, b-boy culture) to a more positive, empowered role in the modern hip hop scene.[19][20][21] The lower exposure of female dancers is probably caused not by any conscious discrimination, but simply by there being fewer female breakers. Since there are no female divisions in breaking as there are in "official" sports, they have to compete with men on equal terms. In any "b-boy" battle, if it is a one-on-one competition or crew vs crew, b-girls attend the event as equals to the b-boys. They compete solo against other b-boys and as members of a crew alongside b-boys. All female b-girl crews battle against other breaking crews with no negative discrimination. When referencing women, the term "b-girling" is as acceptable as the term b-boying although not as widely used. Aside from the terminology, both males and females practice this art together.

Media Exposure

Film and television

In the early 1980s, several films depicted b-boying, including *Wild Style*, *Flashdance*, *Breakin'*, *Breakin' 2: Electric Boogaloo*, *Delivery Boys*, *Krush Groove* and *Beat Street*. The 1983 PBS documentary *Style Wars* chronicled New York graffiti artists, but also includes elements of breaking. "BreakBoy" (1985) is a view of the determination of one individual to become one of the best. The documentary film *The Freshest Kids: A History of the B-Boy* (2002) provides a comprehensive history of b-boying, its evolution and its place within hip-hop culture. The 2001 comedy film *Zoolander* depicts Zoolander (Ben Stiller) and Hansel (Owen Wilson) performing b-boy moves on a catwalk. *Planet B-Boy* (2007) follows crews from around the world in their quest for a world championship at Battle of the Year 2005.

Break is a 2006 mini series from Korea about a breaking competition. *Over the Rainbow* (Drama series 2006) centers on different characters who are brought together by b-boying. The award-winning (SXSW Film Festival audience award) documentary "Inside the Circle" (2007) goes into the personal stories of three b-boys (Omar Davila, Josh "Milky" Ayers and Romeo Navarro) and their struggle to keep dance at the center of their lives. The character Mugen on the anime TV series *Samurai Champloo* uses a fighting style based on breaking.

Pop culture

- Breakdance was an 8-bit computer game by Epyx released in 1984, at the height of breaking's popularity.
- B-boy (videogame) is a 2006 console game which aims at an unadulterated depiction of breaking.[22]
- Bust A Groove is a video game franchise whose character "Heat" specializes in breaking.
- Pump It Up is a Korean game that requires physical movement of the feet. The game involves breaking and many people have accomplished this feat by memorizing the steps and creating dance moves to hit the arrows on time.
- In 1997, Kim Soo Yong began serialization of the first breaking themed comic,*Hip Hop*. The comic sold over 1.5 million books and it helped to introduce breaking and hip-hop culture to Korean youth.
- The first breaking themed novel, *Kid B*, was published by Houghton Mifflin in 2006. The author, Linden Dalecki, was an amateur b-boy in high school and directed a short documentary film about Texas b-boy culture before writing the novel. The novel evolved from Dalecki's b-boy-themed short story The B-Boys of Beaumont, which won the 2004 *Austin Chronicle* short story contest.
- In 2005, a Volkswagen Golf GTi commercial featured a partly CGI version of Gene Kelly breaking to a new version of "Singin' in the Rain", remixed by Mint Royale. The tagline was, "The original, updated."

External Links
- History of B-boying [23]

References
[1] Schloss, Joseph (2009). *Foundation: B-boys, B-girls, And Hip-Hop Culture In New York*. Oxford University Press.
[2] Isreal (director). (2002). *The Freshest Kids: A History of the B-Boy*. [DVD]. USA: QD3 Entertainment.
[3] Adam Mansbach (24 May 2009). " The ascent of hip-hop: A historical, cultural, and aesthetic study of b-boying (book review of Joseph Schloss' "Foundation") (http://www.boston.com/ae/books/articles/2009/05/24/the_ascent_of_hip_hop/)". *The Boston Globe*. .
[4] Chang, Jeff (2005). *Can't Stop Won't Stop: A History of the Hip-Hop Generation*. New York: St. Martin's Press. ISBN 0-312-30143-X.
[5] Jorge "Popmaster Fabel" Pabon (September 10, 2009). " 25 Things You Should Know About Hip Hop (http://danceruniverse.com/stories/issues/200909/25_things_you_should_know_about_hip_hop/)". Dancer Universe. . Retrieved 2009-09-28.
[6] Freeman, Santiago (July 1, 2009). " Planet Funk (http://www.dancespirit.com/articles/2177)". Dance Spirit Magazine. . Retrieved 2009-09-09.
[7] *1800s Arab street dancer performing head spins and back flips*.
[8] " Hip-Hop Dance History (http://www.dancehere.com/hip-hop-dance-history/)". *DanceHere.com*. Broadway Dreams. July 7, 2008. . Retrieved 2009-07-30.
[9] Condry, Ian. " Japanese Hip-Hop (http://web.mit.edu/condry/www/jhh/)". *mit.edu*. MIT. . Retrieved 2009-09-09.
[10] " Tokyo Rock Steady Crew (http://www.msu.edu/~okumurak/dancers/tokyorsc.html)". *msu.edu*. . Retrieved 2009-09-09.
[11] " Break-dancing, Present at the Creation (http://www.npr.org/programs/morning/features/patc/break-dancing/)". *National Public Radio*. 14 October 2002. . Retrieved 2009-09-09.
[12] Edwards, Bob (April 25, 2003). "Profile: Rerelease of the classic hip-hop documentary "Style Wars"". Morning Edition (NPR).
[13] Crane, Debra (January 23, 2006). "What dance needs: a hip-hop operation". The Times (UK). p. 17.
[14] " When You're In a BATTLE (http://koreanroc.com/zboard/zboard.php?id=document&page=1&sn1=&divpage=1&sn=off&ss=on&sc=on&select_arrange=headnum&desc=asc&no=94)". *BEBE (Ground Zero)*. Korean Roc. . Retrieved 2009-09-09.
[15] La Rocco, Claudia (6 Aug 2006). " A Breaking Battle Women Hope to Win (http://www.nytimes.com/2006/08/06/arts/dance/06laro.html)". *New York Times*. . Retrieved 2009-09-09.
[16] " Girl Power Dances to It's Own Groove (http://politicalpalace.yuku.com/forum/viewtopic/id/10152)". *Yuku.com*. . Retrieved 2009-09-09.
[17] " Firefly aka female breaker (http://www.bbc.co.uk/leeds/features/living/breakdance/firefly.shtml)". *BBC Living section*. . Retrieved 2009-09-09.
[18] " Women Get the Breaks (http://license.icopyright.net/user/viewFreeUse.act?fuid=MjEyOTQ2Mw==)". *The Independent: Independent News and Media*. 18 March 2005. . Retrieved 2009-09-09.
[19] " The Exploitation of Women in Hip-Hop Culture (http://www.mysistahs.org/features/hiphop.htm)". *MySistahs.org*. . Retrieved 2009-09-09.
[20] Arce, Rose (4 March 2005). " Hip-Hop Portrayal of Women Protested (http://www.cnn.com/2005/SHOWBIZ/Music/03/03/hip.hop/index.html)". *CNN*. . Retrieved 2009-09-09.
[21] Shepherd, Julianne (1 June 2005). " Hip Hop's Lone Ladies Call for Backup: The B-Girl Be Summit preaches strength in numbers (http://www.citypages.com/content/printVersion/15970)". . Retrieved 2009-09-09.
[22] " B-boy article (http://www.psp411.com/show/product/1163/0/BBoy.html)". *psp411.com*. . Retrieved 2009-09-09.
[23] http://www.globaldarkness.com/articles/history%20of%20breaking.htm

Dancesport

Dancesport denotes competitive → ballroom dancing[1] at events that are sanctioned and regulated by dancesport organizations.

Internationally, dancesport is governed by the World Dance Council (WDC).[2] This operates through a General Council and two Standing World Committees:

An amateur dancesport competition at MIT.

- The World Dance Sport Committee, which deals with all matters of professional Dance Sport.
- The World Social Dance Committee, which deals with all matters of the dance profession that relate to the activities of Dance Schools and Dance Teachers.
- The WDC Amateur League is charged with developing this area.

The WDC amateur league is the largest free amateur governing body for ballroom dancing in the world. Dance is popular in many countries[3], and competitive ballroom dance is featured in television programs such as *Strictly Come Dancing*, → *Dancing with the Stars* and *Eurovision Dance Contest*.

The status of the International Dancesport Federation (IDSF) in this structure is now somewhat ambiguous. The International Olympic Committee granted full IOC Recognition of DanceSport and of IDSF as sole representative body on September 5th, 1997.[4] At that point, many dance organisations changed their titles to incorporate the words Dance Sport or Dancesport. However, it has become clear that so far no nation organising the Olympic Games will tolerate, let alone promote, Dancesport as an Olympic event. That applies even to London 2012, and England was for decades the centre of ballroom dancing. Thus the hoped-for flow of sport money from governments is unlikely to be realised. Consequently, the IDSF has receded in importance and influence.

The basic membership for both the EDC and the IDSF are the controlling bodies for ballroom dance in each individual country. It is quite consistent for countries to join as many international organisations as they see fit. For all practical purposes, the WDC is the world's senior organisation, and the IDSF is also significant.

History

The first world championship took place in 1909 and the first formation team competed in 1932[11]. Dancesport was first broadcast on TV in 1960[5][6].

Styles

The term *dancesport* applys only to the International Style of competitive ballroom (often referred to as Standard or Modern) dancing and Latin dancing.[7] Today, it includes the following style categories:

- Standard
- Latin American
- Ten Dance
- Rock 'n' Roll

These categories apply to both individual couples and formation dance.

Competitions

There are a wide variety of dance competitions, ranging from the well known Blackpool Dance Festival which is an event open to all competitors. Competitions conducted exclusively for university students, such as those hosted by the Inter Varsity Dance Association in the UK.

Amateur competitions commonly include events that group dancers by age, experience, or both. For example, events might group young dancers by age, such as: juvenile (<12yrs), junior (12-16yrs), and youth (16-19yrs). Events may sometimes cover a wide range of ages, with groupings such as: under 21yrs, adult, Senior I (Over 35yrs), Senior II (Over 45yrs), and Senior III (Over 50yrs). Adult competitions are often further divided into categories such as beginner, novice, intermediate, pre-amateur, and amateur.

Rules

The music for competitions is kept confidential until the event. The music always follows a strict tempo and, for a couples competition, it will usually have a duration of no more than 90 seconds. Some competitions are restricted to "basic" steps and others to "open" steps, but the style of dance and tempo is strictly governed. Lifts are not allowed under the rules Couples are marked under the skating system and judged by timing, footwork, rise and fall, alignment, direction and floor craft. Competitors must meet World Anti-Doping Agency rules.

Dancesport and the Olympics

The IDSF, which has campaigned for dancesport's inclusion at the Olympic games, is recognized by the International Olympic Committee as the governing body for dancesport. To date, dancesport has not been included in the Olympic games.[8]

The physical demands of Dancesport has been the subject of scientific research.[9] [10] [11] [12]

See also

- List of DanceSport dances
- World Ballroom Dance Champions
- World Latin Dance Champions
- World 10 Dance Champions
- List of dance organizations
- Dance basic topics
- Dancesport at the 2005 Southeast Asian Games
- Formation dance
- English amateur dancesport association ltd

External links

- International DanceSport Federation [9]
- World Dance Council [13]
- International Professional DanceSport Council [14]
- World Rock'n'Roll Confederation [15]
- Dancesport Info [16] Comprehensive list of dance competition results and photos
- Information about Dancesport at University Level [17]

References

[1] " History of Dancesport by Dancesport Ireland (http://www.dancesportireland.org/about_dancesport.html)". . Retrieved 2009-03-29.
[2] http://www.dancewdc.org/
[3] "Strictly ballroom steps up to rival the Boat Race". *The Daily Telegraph*. 2005-09-26.
[4] http://www.idsf.net/
[5] http://www.idsf.net/documents/history_of_idsf.pdf IDSF History
[6] http://www.idsf.net/index.tpl?style=news&action=newsItem&id=19 IDSF Media Guide
[7] Lomax, Sondra (2000-09-22). "Sweeping a dance floor near you". *Austin American-Statesman*: p. F1.
[8] " International DanceSport Federation (http://www.olympic.org/uk/organisation/if/fi_uk.asp?id_federation=43)". *Olympic.org - Official website of the Olympic Movement*. .
[9] Biomechanics of dance sport: a kinematic approach ISSN 0025-7826
[10] (Blanksby & Reidy, 1988)
[11] Dancing as a Sport Article (http://dance104.valuehost.co.uk/e107/page.php?12)
[12] IDSF Research Paper (http://www.idsf.net/documents/dancesport_a_sport.pdf)
[13] http://www.wddsc.com/
[14] http://www.ipdsc.org/home.html
[15] http://www.wrrc.org
[16] http://www.dancesportinfo.net
[17] http://www.universitydancesport.com

Krumping

Krumping is an urban street dance form characterized by free, expressive, and highly energetic moves involving the arms, head, legs, chest, and feet.[1] The root word, Krump, is an acronym for **K**ingdom **R**adically **U**plifted **M**ighty **P**raise.[2] The youth who started krumping saw the dance as a way for them to escape gang life and other negative influences in their neighborhood.[3] [4] Krumping has become a major part of hip-hop dance. CBS news has compared the intensity within krumping to what rockers experience in a mosh pit.[5]

A krumper dancing in Australia.

History

Krumping appeared in Los Angeles, CA during the 1990's.[1] Unlike other hip-hop dances krumping is entirely freestyle (improvisational); it is rarely, if ever, choreographed and is danced frequently in battles or sessions.

"Krumping doesn't start moves or your character. It starts with your heart. It starts with what you feel. You gotta' tap into this... It's more that just throwing arms out there on a certain beat, stomping on a certain beat. It has to come from somewhere."

—Ceasare "Tight Eyez" Willis [6]

Krumping includes four primary moves: wobbles, arm swings, chest pops, and stomps.[6] *Clowning* is the less aggressive predecessor to krumping and was created in 1992 by Thomas "Tommy the Clown" Johnson in Compton, CA. In the 90's Tommy and his dancers, the Hip Hop Clowns, would paint their faces and perform *clowning* for children at birthday parties or for the general public at other functions as a form of entertainment.[7] In contrast, krumping focuses on highly energetic battles and movements which Tommy describes as intense, fast-paced, and sharp. "If movement were words, krumping would be a poetry slam."[1] Krumping was not directly created by Tommy the Clown; however, it did grow out of clown dancing.[8] [9]

> "You would never imagine black hip-hop clowns really doing nothing until I brought it to this world. God allowed me to bring it to this world."
>
> —Thomas "Tommy the Clown" Johnson [7]

Tommy eventually opened a clown dancing academy and started the Battle Zone competition where krump crews could come together and battle each other in front of an audience of their peers.[5] Choreographer Lil C, and the leaders of the Krump Kings crew Ceasare (pronounced CHEZ-a-ray) "Tight Eyez" Willis and Jo'Artis "Big Mijo" Ratti are credited with developing krumping.[9] [6] [3] Krumping has appeared in several music videos including Madonna's "Hung Up", Missy Elliott's "I'm Really Hot", Black Eyed Peas' "Hey Mama", and Chemical Brothers "Galvanize".[7] It also appeared in the movie "Bring It On: All or Nothing".

David LaChapelle's *Rize* is a documentary about the clowning and krumping subculture in Los Angeles. He says of the movement:

> "What Nirvana was to rock-and-roll in early '90s is what these kids are to hip-hop. It's the alternative to the bling-bling, tie-in-with-a-designer corporate hip-hop thing."[10]

LaChapelle was first introduced to krumping when he was directing Christina Aguilera's music video "Dirrty". After deciding to make a documentary about the dance, he started by making a short film titled *Krumped*. He screened this short at the 2004 Aspen Shortsfest and used the positive reaction from the film to gain more funding for a longer version.[3] This longer version became *Rize* which was screened at the 2005 Sundance Film Festival.

Vocabulary

- **Battle**: when competitors face-off in a direct dance competition where the use of arm swings and chest movements known as *flares* and *bucks* are extremely common.
- **Session**: when a group of krump dancers form a circle, or *cipher* in hip-hop context, and one-by-one go into the middle and freestyle.
- **Buck**: an expression used by krumpers to describe dancing that is both difficult to execute and impressive/striking.

External links

- Krump Kings [11]
- *Rize* at LondonDance.com [12]

References

[1] Paggett, Taisha (July 2004). " Getting krumped: the changing race of hip hop (http://findarticles.com/p/articles/mi_m1083/is_7_78/ai_n6145252/)". *Dance Magazine*. BNET. . Retrieved 2009-07-30.
[2] Infantry, Ashante (May 21, 2009). "Dancing off the Streets". *The Toronto Star*. ISSN 0319-0781 (http://worldcat.org/issn/0319-0781).
[3] Jones, Jen (September 1, 2005). " Behind the Scenes of David LaChapelle's Documentary "Rize" (http://www.dancespirit.com/articles/1452)". *Dance Spirit magazine*. . Retrieved 2009-09-24.
[4] LaCombe, Jessice (August 29, 2008). " From Ballerina to the Queen of Krump: The Party's Just Begun for Marquisa Gardner (http://danceruniverse.com/stories/issues/200809/from_ballerina_to_the_queen-S9/)". Dancer Universe. . Retrieved 2009-09-28.
[5] Menzie, Nicola (June 30, 2005). " 'Krump' Dances Into Mainstream (http://www.cbsnews.com/stories/2005/06/28/entertainment/main704843.shtml)". CBS News. . Retrieved 2009-08-06.
[6] Shiri Nassim (producer). (2005). *The Heart of Krump*. [DVD]. Los Angeles: Ardustry Home Entertainment, Krump Kings Inc.
[7] Reid; Bella, Mark (April 23 2004). " Krumping: If You Look Like Bozo Having Spasms, You're Doing It Right (http://www.mtv.com/news/articles/1486576/20040423/index.jhtml)". MTV. . Retrieved 2009-07-30.

[8] Thompson, Luke (June 22, 2005). " Dance, Dance, Revolution (http://www.eastbayexpress.com/movies/dance_dance_revolution/Content?oid=289416)". East Bay Express. . Retrieved 2009-08-25.
[9] Voynar, Kim (July 12, 2005). " News Releases: Rize (http://www.cinematical.com/2005/07/12/new-releases-rize/)". *Cinematical.com* (Weblogs Network). . Retrieved 2009-08-27.
[10] Swart, Sharon (2004-01-13). " David LaChapelle: Sundance short take (http://www.variety.com/index.asp?layout=upsell_article&articleID=VR1117898396&cs=1)". Variety. . Retrieved 2007-10-07.
[11] http://www.krumpkings.com
[12] http://www.londondance.com/content.asp?CategoryID=1921

Kandyan dance

Kandyan Dance is a dance form that originated in the area called Kandy of the Central hills region in Sri Lanka. But today it has been widespread to other parts of the country.

A Kandyan Dancer

History

According to the legend, the origins of the dance lie in an exorcism ritual known as the Kohomba Kankariya, which was originally performed by Indian shamans who came to the island.

According to legend, the Indian shamans came to the island upon the request of a king who was suffering from a mysterious illness. The king was said to be suffering from recurring dream in which a leopard directing its longue towards the king. Which is believed as a black magic of "Kuweni" the first wife of the king "Vijaya". After the performance of the Kohomba Kankariya the illness vanished, and many natives adopted the dance.

It was originally performed by dancers who were identified as a separate caste under the Kandyan Fudel system. They were aligned to the Temple of the Tooth and had a significant role to play in the Dalada Perahera (procession) held each year by the temple.

Kandyan Dancers illustrated. A larger version is at[http://www.artwanted.com/imageview.cfm?id=468737

The dance waned in popularity as the support for the dancers from the Kandyan kings ended during the British period. It has now been revived and adapted for the stage, and is Sri Lanka's primary cultural export.

Dances (Uda Rata Netum)

Ves dance

"Ves" dance, the most popular, originated from an ancient purification ritual, the Kohomba Yakuma or Kohomba Kankariya. The dance was propitiatory, never secular, and performed only by males. The elaborate ves costume, particularly the headgear, is considered sacred and is believed to belong to the deity Kohomba.

Only toward the end of the nineteenth century were ves dancers first invited to perform outside the precincts of the Kankariya Temple at the annual Kandy Perahera festival. Today the elaborately costumed ves dancer epitomizes Kandyan dance.

Naiyandi dance

Dancers in Naiyandi costume perform during the initial preparations of the Kohomba Kankariya festival, during the lighting of the lamps and the preparation of foods for the demons. The dancer wears a white cloth and white rurban, beadwork decorations on his chest, a waistband, rows of beads around his neck, silver chains, brass shoulder plates, anklets, and jingles. This is a graceful dance, also performed in Maha Visnu (Vishnu) and Kataragama Devales temples on ceremonial occasions.

Uddekki dance

Uddekki is a very prestigious dance. Its name comes from the Uddekki, a small lacquered hand drum in the shape of an hourglass, about seven and half inches (18 centimeters) high, believed to have been given to people by the gods. The two drumskins are believed to have been given by the god Iswara, and the sound by Visnu; the instrument is said to have been constructed according to the instructions of Sakra and was played in the heavenly palace of the gods. It is a very difficult instruments to play. The dancer sings as he plays, tightening the strings to obtain variations of pitch.

Pantheru dance

The pantheruwa is an instrument dedicated to the goddess Pattini. It resembles a tambourine (without the skin) and has small cymbals attached at intervals around its circumference. The dance is said to have originated in the days of Prince Siddhartha, who became Buddha. The gods were believed to use this instrument to celebrate victories in war, and Sinhala kings employed pantheru dancers to celebrate victories in the battlefield. The costume is similar to that of the uddekki dancer, but the pantheru dancer wears no beaded jacket and substitutes a silk handkerchief at the waist for the elaborate frills of the uddekki dancer.

Vannams

Originally Vannams were kind of recitations. In most Vannams it describes about the behaviours of animals like Elephants, monkeys, rabbits, peacock, cocks, serpents etc. Later dancers have used Vannam as background songs for their performances. There are 18 Vannams in the Kandyan Dance form. Traditionally a dancer would have to learn to perform all these Vannams before they would be gifted the Ves costume. The most well known among these are the Hanuma Vannama (Monkey), The Ukusa Vannama (Eagle) and the Gajaga Vannama (Elephant).

The word "vannam" comes from the Sinhala word "varnana" (descriptive praise). Ancient Sinhala texts refer to a considerable number of "vannams" that were only sung; later they were adapted to solo dances, each expressing a dominant idea. History reveals that the Kandyan king Sri Weeraparakrama Narendrasinghe gave considerable encouragement to dance and music. In this Kavikara Maduwa (a decorated dance arena) there were song and poetry contests.

It is said that the kavi (poetry sung to music) for the eighteen principal vannams were composed by an old sage named Ganithalankara, with the help of a Buddhist priest from the Kandy temple. The vannams were inspired by nature, history, legend, folk religion, folk art, and sacred lore, and each is composed and iterpreted in a certain mood (rasaya) or expression of sentiment. The eighteen classical vannams are gajaga ("elephant"), thuranga ("hourse") , mayura ("peacock"), gahaka ("conch shell"), uranga ("crawling animals"), mussaladi ("hare"), ukkussa ("eagle"), vyrodi ("precious stone"), hanuma ("monkey"), savula ("cock"), sinharaja ("lion"), naaga ("cobra"), kirala ("red-wattled lapwing"), eeradi ("arrow"), Surapathi (in praise of the goddess Surapathi), Ganapathi (in praise of the god Ganapathi), uduhara (expressing the pomp and majesty of the king), and assadhrusa (extolling the merit of Buddha). To these were added samanala ("Butterfly"),bo (the sacred bo tree at Anuradhapura, a sapling of the original bo tree under which Buddha attained enlightenment), and hansa vannama ("swan"). The vannama dance tradition has seven components.

Costume

The dancers wear an elaborate costume including a headdress. The dancer's chest is only covered by a decorative beaded net. This costume is known as the Ves costume. The headdress incorporates a metallic front which makes the dancer look taller than he is. The complete costume also includes anklets that produce a metallic rattle each

The head gear in the ves costume can only be worn by the males & can only be worn after a special ceremony called ves mangalaya in which the male dancerf irst wears the ves vostume

```
& dances.Legend also says that if a female wears the head gear she
will have a lot of bad luck or get very sick even the males if they
have not performed at  the ves mangalaya the same will happen to
them(only males perform at the ves mangalaya & the females have a
separate ceremony called Kalaveny mangalya)
```

Music

The Kandyan Dance is traditionally performed to percussion only. The most common drum is the *Geta Beraya*, which is only used in Kandyan Dance. To assist the dancer to keep rhythm a small pair of cymbals knows as the *Thalampota* is also used. The Vannam's however have lyrics that are sung in tune with the movements of the dancer. These lyrics sing about the virtues of the animal that the Vanna is depicting.

Another form of twin Drums called **Tammettama**[2] used with cane drum sticks.

Thammettam drummer([1])

Kandyan dance today

Even though originally only males were allowed train as dancers, there are now several schools which also train women in the Kandyan dance form. However there is no definite Ves costume for women, and many female dancers have adapted the male costume in different ways.

There are only a few performances of the Kohomba Kankariya now due to many social, economic and political reasons. The dance in its traditional form is still performed each year at the Dalada Perhahera in Kandy.

The Kandyan Dance was adapted for the stage by Chitrasena Dias in the 1970s, in several Ballets he choreographed, he has used kandyan dance movements and features. In some ways his popularity also helped to reduce the caste barriers surrounding the dance, and made it more palatable to an urban, contemporary audience. To date one of the largest school for Kandyan dance is Chitrasena Dance School.

A Nilame on Elephant back in the pageant.([3])

Many contemporary dancers in Sri Lanka have borrowed from the Kandyan form for their work.

References

- video of Ves dance [4]
- An article on Ves dance [5]
- video [6]
- creative kandyan dance [7]

]

- Kandyan [8]
- Kandy Asela Perahara [2]
- Some photos of Kandyan Dancers [9]

A fraction of the Kandy Asela Perahara-the 10-day pageant.. - View a larger version[http://www.comicartfans.com/GalleryPiece.asp?Page=1&Order=Date&Piece=254550&GSub=37663&GCat=0&UCat=0

References

[1] http://www.artwanted.com/imageview.cfm?id=470578
[2] http://www.britishcouncil.lk/kidsintouch/kandy/perahara.htm
[3] http://www.comicartfans.com/GalleryPiece.asp?Page=1&Order=Date&Piece=253813&GSub=37663&GCat=0&UCat=0
[4] http://youtube.com/watch?v=QdLnIN3_Pt0|
[5] http://www.atypon-link.com/INT/doi/abs/10.1386/stap.29.2.187_3?journalCode=stap|
[6] http://youtube.com/watch?v=28y0hMvnpS8|
[7] http://youtube.com/watch?v=TzzDeNSTRFw|
[8] http://kandyan.net
[9] http://www.library.upenn.edu/collections/sasia/mbw/sri_lanka/Sri%20Lanka%20Lecture%20Pages/kandyandance.htm

Irish dance

Irish dance is a group of traditional dance forms originating in Ireland which can broadly be divided into social dance and performance dances. Irish social dances can be divided further into *céilí* and **set** dancing. Irish set dances are quadrilles, danced by 4 couples arranged in a square, while céilí dances are danced by varied formations (ceili) of couples of 2 to 16 people. In addition to their formation, there are significant stylistic differences between these two forms of social dance. Irish social dance is a living tradition, and variations in particular dances are found across the Irish dance community; in some places, dances are deliberately modified and new dances are choreographed.

Irish dancers at St. Patrick's Day parade in Fort Collins, Colorado

Irish performance dancing is traditionally referred to as stepdance. Irish stepdance, popularized in 1994 by the world-famous show "Riverdance," is notable for its rapid leg movements, body and arms being kept largely stationary. Most competitive stepdances are solo dances, though many stepdancers also perform and compete using céilí dances. The solo stepdance is generally characterized by a controlled but not rigid upper body, straight arms, and quick, precise movements of the feet. The solo dances can either be in "soft shoe" or hard shoe".

The dancing traditions of Ireland probably grew in close association with Irish traditional music. Originating in Pre-Christian Ireland, Irish dance was later influenced by dance forms from the Continent, especially the Quadrille. Travelling dancing masters taught all over Ireland, as late as the early 1900s.

Sean-nós dancing in the Irish Diaspora

As Irish people emigrate all over the world, they take their cultural traditions with them. Many people theorize that Sean-nós dancing has influenced various other forms of traditional solo dance, especially those found in areas with strong Irish communities. Historically, it is likely that sean-nós dance influenced the development of many American and Canadian traditional percussive dance forms, such as buck dancing, flatfooting, clogging, and tap dancing. Sean-nós dancing in America and Canada is most commonly seen at folk festivals, although dance workshops are beginning to introduce the style more widely.

Old-Style Step Dancing

(Also termed Munster-style sean-nós dancing.)

Old-style step dancing (a tradition related to, yet distinct from, sean-nós dancing) evolved in the late 18th and early 19th century from the dancing of traveling Irish dance masters. The dance masters slowly formalized and transformed both solo and social dances. Modern masters of old-style step dancing style can trace the lineage of their steps directly back to 18th century dancers.

The Irish dance masters refined and codified indigenous Irish dance traditions. Rules emerged about proper upper body, arm, and foot placement. Also, dancers were instructed to dance a step twice -- first with the right foot then with the left. Old-style step dancers dance with arms loosely (but not rigidly) at their sides. They dance in a limited space. There is an emphasis on making percussive sound with the toes.

The Irish dance masters of this period also choreographed particular steps to particular tunes in traditional music creating the solo set dances such as the Blackbird, St. Patrick's Day, and the Job of Journey Work, which also persist in Modern Irish Step Dancing. In this context, "set dance" signifies a separate tradition from the social dance tradition also called set dance.

Irish Céilí Dances

Irish social, or **céilí** (pronounced /ˈkeɪli/ in English) dances very widely throughout Ireland and the rest of the world. A céilí dance may be performed with as few as two people and as many as sixteen. Céilí dances may also be danced with an unlimited number of couples in a long line or proceeding around in a circle (such as in "The Walls of Limerick", "The Waves of Tory", or "Bonfire Dance"). Céilí dances are often fast and complex. In a social setting, a céilí dance may be "called" -- that is, the upcoming steps are announced during the dance for the benefit of newcomers. The ceili dances are typically danced to Irish instruments such as the Irish hand drum or harp.

Shramore Set, danced by "Cumann Céilí Vín", Vienna, Austria

The term *céilí dance* was invented in the late 19th century by the Gaelic League Céilí as a noun differs from the adjective céilí. A céilí is a social gathering featuring Irish music and dance. Céilí dancing is a specific type of Irish dance. Some céilithe (plural of céilí) will only have céilí dancing, some will only have set dancing, and some will have a mixture.

In various parts of Ireland on St. Stephen's Day, December 26th, **Wrenboys** (**mummers**) celebrate Wren Day (also pronounced as the **Wran**) by dressing up in straw masks and colorful clothing and parading through towns and villages accompanied by traditional céilí music bands. This tradition also exists (or existed) in various parts of Britain, especially Wales.

Irish Stepdance

Roots of Irish Stepdance

Stepdancing as a modern form is descended directly from old-style step dancing. There are several different forms of stepdancing in Ireland (including sean-nós dancing and old style stepdancing), but the style most familiar to the public at large is the Munster, or southern, form, which has been formalised by An Coimisiún le Rincí Gaelacha—the Irish Dancing Commission.

Irish stepdancing is primarily done in competitions, public performances or other formal settings.

Dances

Irish step dancers from Scoil Rince na Connemara in Wilkes-Barre PA dance at the HUB, Penn State University

Irish solo stepdances fall into two broad categories based on the shoes worn: **hard shoe** and **soft shoe** dances.

Soft shoe dances include the **reel, slip jig, light jig and single jig** . Reels have a 4/4 (or sometimes 2/4 or 2/2) time signature. Slip jigs are in 9/8 time. Light and single jigs are in 6/8 time, with different emphasis within the measure distinguishing the music. Hard shoe dances include the **hornpipe** in 2/4 time, the **hard jig (also called the treble jig)** in a slow 6/8, the **treble reel** and **traditional sets**, which are a group of 36 dances with set music and steps. Many traditional sets have irregular musical phrasing. There are also more advanced "non-traditional sets" done by advanced dancers. These have set music, but not steps.

The céilí dances used in competitions are more precise versions of those danced in less formal settings. There is a list of 32 céilí dances which have been standardised and published in An Coimisiún's *Ar Rinncidhe Foirne* as examples of typical Irish folk dances; these are called the "book" dances by competitive stepdancers. Most Irish dance competitions only ask for a short piece of any given dance, in the interests of time.

Shoes and Costume

Two types of shoes are worn in step dancing: hard shoes and soft shoes. The hard shoe is similar to tap shoes, except that the tips and heels are made of fiberglass, instead of metal, and are significantly bulkier. The hard shoes were originally made of wood in the 19th century and early 20th century. The first hard shoes had wooden or leather taps with metal nails. Later the taps and heels were changed into resin or fiberglass to reduce the weight and to increase the footwork sounds. The soft shoes, which are called *ghillies*, resembles a ballet shoe minus the hard toe, the ribbons for laces, and the pink color for black. Gillies are only worn by girls, while boys wear a black leather shoe called a reel shoe, which resembles a black jazz shoe with a hard heel. Boy's soft-shoe dancing features audible heel clicks.

Several generations ago, the appropriate dress for a competition was simply your "Sunday Best". In the 1970s and 1980's ornately embroidered dresses became popular. Today even more ornamentation is used on girls' dresses, including lace, sequins, silk, extensive embroidery, feathers, faux fur and more. Irish Dancing schools have school dresses, which are worn by "Beginner" through "Novice" dancers. When dancers reach a level decided by their school, may get a solo dress of their own design and colors. Today most women and girls curl their hair or wear a wig for a competition or feis (feis pronounced fesh). Today in competition, most men wear a shirt, vest, and tie assigned by their school paired with black pants or a kilt. But when they get into the higher levels, as the girls do, they get to pick their own vest, shirt and tie.

The skirts of the dresses used to be floppy, then they became stiff with a special cardboard and now the skirts are puffy, puffballs, double puffballs, frilly and feathers. The cardboard in the skirts can create paneled skirts. Paneled skirts vary from three panel, four panel, five panel, six+ panel, double panel, panel with frill, side sweep or centre sweep.

Competition Structure

An organized step dance competition is referred to as a *feis* (pronounced fesh, plural *feiseanna*). The word *feis* means "festival" in Irish, and strictly speaking would also have competitions in music and crafts. Féile (/ˈfeɪlə/) is a more correct term for the dance competition, but the terms may be used interchangeably. Dance competitions are divided by age and level of expertise. The names of the levels vary between countries and regions.

An annual regional Championship competition is known as an oireachtas (/oʊˈrɒktəs/). Dancers from each age group may qualify for the World Championships. Qualifying for the World Championships, Oireachtas Rince na Cruinne (roughly translated as Irish Dance Championship of the World), varies slightly by region. Dancers may either qualify at their regional Oireachts or a secondary qualifying event.

The World Championships first took place in Dublin, Ireland in 1970 at Coláiste Mhuire, a school in Parnell Square. In the past, the World Championships have only been held in Ireland, Northern Ireland, or Scotland. However, in 2009, for the first time, the World Championships were held in the United States in Philadelphia. In 2010, the competition will return to Glasgow.

See also

- Ghillies
- Irish stepdance
- Sean-nós dance
- Sean-nós dance in America
- Set dance
- Irish Jig
- World Irish Dance Association

External links

General information

- Irish Dancing & Culture Magazine [1]
- Everything You Need To Know About Irish Dance [2]
- Diddlyi.com: Irish Dance and Music Social Network [3]
- O'Keeffe & O'Brien - A Handbook of Irish Dance (1902) [4]
- Diochra.com: Discover Irish dance! [5]
- Beginners Guide to Irish Dancing [6]
- Information for new dancers [7]
- The History of Irish Dance [8]
- Irish Step Dancing [9]
- Set Dance [10]
- Newcastle Irish Set Dancers (Australia) [11]
- Ealaín Céime Irish Dance School (USA) [12]
- Irish Dance Feisanna Registrations [13]

- Irish dance schools, irish dance dresses, feis dates and more. [14]

Irish Dance Organizations

- An Coimisiún le Rincí Gaelacha / The Irish Dancing Commission [15]
- An Comhdháil Múinteora Rinnce Gaelacha/ Congress of Irish Dance Teachers [16]
- Cumann Rince Náisiúnta [17]
- Cumann Rince Dea Mheasa / Organisation of Goodwill and Excellence in Irish Dancing [18]
- World Irish Dance Association (WIDA) [19]
- American Association of Irish Dancers and Teachers (AADIT) [20]
- Irish Dancing Net [21]
- Comhaltas Ceoltóirí Eireann [22]
- Nordic Society of Irish Dancers [23]
- Danish Society of Irish Dancers [24]
- Japan Irish Dancing Association [25]
- TIDANZ (Traditional Irish Dance Association of New Zealand) [26]
- North American Irish Dance Federation (NAIDF) [27]

References

- Caoimhe Mullen: "Best Irish Dancer Ever" and from Skerries.
- Helen Brennan: *The Story of Irish Dancing*, Mount Eagle Publications Ltd., 1999 ISBN 0 86322 244 7
- John Cullinane: *Aspects of the History of Irish Céilí Dancing*, The Central Remedial Clinic, Clontarf, Dublin 3,(1998), ISBN 0-952-79522-1
- An Coimisiún le Rincí Gaelacha: *Ár Rincí Fóirne-Thirty Popular Céilí Dances*, Westside Press (2003)
- J. G. O' Keeffe, Art O' Brien: *A Handbook of Irish Dances, 1. Edition*, O'Donoghue & Co., (1902)[28]
- Pat Murphy: *Toss the Feathers - Irish Set Dancing*, Mercier Press, 1995 ISBN 1-85635-115-7
- Pat Murphy: *The Flowing Tide - More Irish Set Dancing*, Mercier Press, 2000 ISBN 1-85635-308-7
- An Conhdhail: 'irishdancingorg.com' for the an comhdhail stepdance branch
- An Coimisiún le Rincí Gaelacha [29]

References

[1] http://www.irishdancing.com
[2] http://amazinirishdancer.blogspot.com
[3] http://www.diddlyi.com/
[4] http://ia310911.us.archive.org/3/items/handbookofirishd00okeeiala/handbookofirishd00okeeiala.pdf
[5] http://www.diochra.com/
[6] http://www.irishdancinginsydney.com
[7] http://www.boydirishdance.com/InformationMenu.htm
[8] http://www.irelandseye.com/dance.html
[9] http://histclo.com/act/dance/danceir.html
[10] http://www.setdanceteacher.co.uk
[11] http://users.tpg.com.au/juliasm/Irish_Dance/
[12] http://www.ealainceime.com/
[13] http://www.efeis.com/
[14] http://www.rinceweb.com/
[15] http://www.clrg.ie/
[16] http://www.irishdancingorg.com/
[17] http://www.crn.ie/
[18] http://www.crdm.ie/
[19] http://www.worldirishdance.com/
[20] http://www.aaidt.org/

[21] http://www.irish-dancing.net/
[22] http://www.comhaltas.com/
[23] http://www.nsid.org/
[24] http://www.dsid.dk/
[25] http://www.roisindubh.jp/rincejapan/top/topef.htm
[26] http://www.irishdancenz.co.nz
[27] http://www.naidf.com/
[28] http://www.archive.org/details/handbookofirishd00okeeiala
[29] http://www.clrg.ie/english/content.php?page=1

Indian classical dance

Indian classical dance is a relatively new umbrella term for various codified art forms rooted in Natya, the sacred Hindu musical theatre styles, whose theory can be traced back to the Natya Shastra of Bharata Muni (400 BC). These are:

- Dances performed inside the sanctum of the temple according to the rituals were called Agama Nartanam. Natya Shastra classifies this type of dance form as margi, or the soul-liberating dance, unlike the desi (purely entertaining) forms.
- Dances performed in royal courts to the accompaniment of classical music were called Carnatakam. This was an intellectual art form.
- Darbari Aattam form of dance appealed more to the commoners and it educated them about their religion, culture and social life. These dances were performed outside the temple precincts in the courtyards. Both Carnatakam and Darbari Aattam in particular were predominantly desi forms.

Bharatanatyam, one of the classical dances of India

Indian dancer

For lack of any better equivalents in the European culture, the British colonial authorities called any performing art forms found in India as "Indian dance". Even though the art of Natya includes nritta, or → dance proper, Natya has never been limited to dancing and includes singing, abhinaya (mime acting). These features are common to all the Indian classical styles. In the margi form Nritta is composed of karanas, while the desi nritta consists mainly of adavus.

The term "classical" (Sanscr. "Shastriya") was introduced by Sangeet Natak Akademi to denote the Natya Shastra-based performing art styles. A very important feature of Indian classical dances is the use of the mudra or hand gestures by the artists as a short-hand sign language to narrate a story and to demonstrate certain concepts such as objects, weather, nature and emotion.

Sangeet Natak Akademi currently confers classical status on eight Indian dance styles:

1. Bharatanatyam - Tamil Classical Dance
2. Odissi - Orissa Classical dance
3. Kuchipudi - Telugu Classical dance
4. Manipuri - Manipur Classical Dance
5. Mohiniaattam - Kerala Classical Dance
6. Sattriya - Asamese Classical Dance
7. Kathakali - Malayalam Classical Dance
8. Kathak - North Indian Classical Dance

Out of the 8 styles, the only 2 temple dance styles that have their origin in Natya Shastra and are prescribed by the Agamas are Bharatanatyam and Odissi. These two most faithfully adhere to the Natya Shastra but currently do not include Vaachikaabhinaya (dialog acts), although some styles of Bharatanatyam, such as Melattur style, prescribe the lip movements indicating Vaachikaabhinaya.

Kuchipudi, which also prescribes the lip movements indicating Vaachikaabhinaya, and Mohiniaattam are relatively recent Darbari Aatam forms, just as Kathakali, and two eastern Indian styles, Manipuri and Sattriya, that are quite similar.

Kathak was created in the Mughal period under the influence of Persian dance and various other folk dance forms. As it does not adhere to any shastra and cannot be called Shastriya (classical).

Currently, Sangeet Natak Akademi does not consider the recently reconstructed dance styles of Andhra Pradesh such as Andhra Natyam and Vilasini Natyam as "classical". Bharatanrithyam, despite being the one most closely following Natya Shastra's precepts, is considered as a variety of Bharatanatyam.

Classical Indian dance in the British Raj and since 1947

The British Raj in India was a time of cultural hardship where these traditional dances were viewed by the British rulers as debauched and of doubtful morality. Furthermore, they were all labelled broadly as 'Indian dance' with no regard to the specifics of style. Later, linking dance with tawaifs and devadasis (both groups whom the government considered to be prostitutes), British rule prohibited public performance of dance. In 1947, India achieved independence. The classical forms and regional distinctions of dance were re-discovered, ethnic specialities were honoured.

References

- Ambrose, Kay (1984). *Classical Dances and Costumes of India*. Palgrave Macmillan.
- *Andhra Natyam* [1]. Andhra Pradesh Government. Retrieved 2008-01-29.

See also

- → Dance in India
- Manipuri dance

External links

- Classical Indian dance [1] at the Open Directory Project -- over 250 links to Classical Indian Dance resources

References

[1] http://www.ap.gov.in/aptourism/themes/heritage/heritage_folkarts_bottom5.html

Modern dance

Modern dance is a dance form developed in the early 20th century. Although the term *Modern dance* has also been applied to a category of 20th Century → ballroom dances, *Modern dance* as a term usually refers to → 20th century concert dance.

Modern dance is usually performed in bare feet, often with non-traditional costuming.

Origins

In the early 1900s two American female dancers, Isadora Duncan and Ruth St. Denis, as well as one German female dancer, Mary Wigman, started to rebel against the rigid constraints of Classical → Ballet. Shedding the authoritarian controls surrounding classical ballet technique, costume, and shoes, these early modern dance pioneers focused on creative self-expression rather than on technical virtuosity. Modern dance is a more relaxed, free style of dance in which choreographers use emotions and moods to design their own steps, in contrast to ballet's structured code of steps. It has a deliberate use of gravity, whereas ballet strives to be light and airy.

In the United States

In United States Loie Fuller, Isadora Duncan, Ruth St. Denis, Doris Humphrey and Martha Graham developed their own styles of → dance and laid the foundations of American modern dance with their choreography and teaching.

In Europe

In Europe, Mary Wigman, Francois Delsarte, Émile Jaques-Dalcroze, and Rudolf von Laban developed theories of human movement and expression, and methods of instruction that led to the development of European modern and Expressionist dance. Their theories and techniques spread well beyond Europe to influence the development of modern dance and theater via their students and disciples, and subsequent generations of teachers and performers carried these theories and methods to Russia, the United States and Canada, the UK, Australia and New Zealand.

History

Free dance

- 1891 - Loie Fuller (a burlesque skirt dancer) began experimenting with the effect that gas lighting had on her silk costumes. Fuller developed a form of natural movement and improvisation techniques that were used in conjunction with her revolutionary lighting equipment and translucent silk costumes. She patented her apparatus and methods of stage lighting that included the use of coloured gels and burning chemicals for luminescence, and also patented her voluminous silk stage costumes.
- 1903 - Isadora Duncan developed a dance technique influenced by the philosophy of Friedrich Nietzsche and a belief that dance of the ancient Greeks (natural and free) was *the dance of the future*. Duncan developed a *philosophy of dance* based on natural and spiritual concepts and advocated for that acceptance of *pure dance* as a *high art*.
- 1905 - Ruth St. Denis, influenced by the actor Sarah Bernhardt and Japanese dancer Sada Yacco, developed her *translations* of Indian culture and mythology. Her performances quickly became popular and she toured extensively whilst researching Oriental culture and arts.

Fuller, Duncan and St. Denis all toured Europe seeking a wider and more accepting audience for their work. Ruth St. Denis returned to the United States to continue her work. Isadora Duncan returned to the United States at various points in her life but her work was not very well received there. She returned to Europe and died in Paris in 1927. Fuller's work also received little support outside Europe.

Early modern dance

In 1915, Ruth Dorthy St. Denis founded the Denishawn school and dance company with her husband Ted Shawn. Whilst St. Denis was responsible for most of the creative work, Shawn was responsible for teaching technique and composition. Martha Graham, Doris Humphrey, and Charles Weidman were all pupils at the school and members of the dance company.

- 1923 Graham leaves Denishawn to work as a solo artist in the Greenwich Village Follies.
- 1928 Humphrey and Weidman leave Denishawn to set up their own school and company (Humphrey-Weidman).
- 1933 Shawn founds his all male dance group *Ted Shawn and His Men Dancers* based at his *Jacob's Pillow* farm in Lee, Massachusetts.

After shedding the techniques and compositional methods of their teachers the early modern dancers developed their own methods and ideologies and dance techniques that became the foundation for modern dance practice.

- Martha Graham (and Louis Horst)
- Doris Humphrey and Charles Weidman and Martha Graham
- Helen Tamiris - originally trained in free movement (Irene Lewisohn) and → ballet (Michel Fokine) Tamiris studied briefly with Isadora Duncan but disliked her emphasis on personal expression and lyrical movement. Tamiris believed that each dance must create its own expressive means and as such did not develop an individual style or technique. As a choreographer Tamiris made works based on American themes working in both → concert dance and musical theatre.

- Lester Horton - choosing to work in California (three thousand miles away from the center of modern dance - New York), Horton developed his own approach that incorporated diverse elements including Native American dances and modern Jazz. Horton's dance technique (*Lester Horton Technique*) emphasises a whole body approach including; flexibility, strength, coordination, and body awareness to allow freedom of expression.
- Ted Shawn

European modern and expressionist dance
- Émile Jaques-Dalcroze (Eurhythmics)
- Rudolf Laban
- Kurt Jooss
- Mary Wigman
- Harald Kreutzberg

Popularization of American Modern Dance

In 1927 newspapers regularly began assigning dance critics, such as Walter Terry, and Edwin Denby, who approached performances from the viewpoint of a movement specialist rather than as a reviewer of music or drama. Educators accepted modern dance into college and university curricula, first as a part of physical education, then as performing art. Many college teachers were trained at the Bennington Summer School of the Dance, which was established at Bennington College in 1934.

Of the Bennington program, Agnes de Mille wrote, "...there was a fine commingling of all kinds of artists, musicians, and designers, and secondly, because all those responsible for booking the college concert series across the continent were assembled there. ... free from the limiting strictures of the three big monopolistic managements, who pressed for preference of their European clients. As a consequence, for the first time American dancers were hired to tour America nationwide, and this marked the beginning of their solvency." (de Mille, 1991, p. 205)

Development of modern dance

Whilst the founders of modern dance continued to make works based on ancient myths and legends following a narrative structure, their students, the *radical dancers*, saw dance as a potential agent of change. Disturbed by the Great Depression and the rising threat of fascism in Europe, they tried to raise consciousness by dramatizing the economic, social, ethnic and political crises of their time.

Batsheva Dance Company of Tel Aviv, Israel, was co-founded by Martha Graham and Baroness Batsheva De Rothschild in 1964.

- Hanya Holm - A student of Mary Wigman and instructor at the Wigman School in Dresden, Holm founded the New York Wigman School of Dance in 1931 (which became the Hanya Holm Studio in 1936) introducing Wigman technique, Laban's theories of spatial dynamics, and later her own dance techniques to American modern dance. An accomplished choreographer, she was a founding artist of the first American Dance Festival in Bennington (1934). Holm's dance work *Metropolitan Daily* was the first modern dance composition to be televised on NBC and her labanotation score for *Kiss Me, Kate* (1948) was the first → choreography to be copyrighted in the United States. Holm choreographed extensively in the fields of → concert dance and musical theater.
- Anna Sokolow - A student of Martha Graham and Louis Horst, Sokolow created her own dance company (circa 1930). Presenting dramatic contemporary imagery, Sokolow's compositions were generally abstract, often revealing the full spectrum of human experience reflecting the tension and alienation of the time and the *truth* of

human movement.
- José Limón - In 1946, after studying and performing with Doris Humphrey and Charles Weidman, Limón established his own company with Humphrey as Artistic Director. It was under her mentorship that Limón created his signature dance *The Moor's Pavane* (1949). Limón's choreographic works and technique remain a strong influence on contemporary dance practice.
- Merce Cunningham - A former ballet student and performer with Martha Graham, he presented his first New York solo concert with John Cage in 1944. Influenced by Cage and embracing modernist ideology using postmodern processes, Cunningham introduced *chance procedures* and *pure movement* to choreography and *Cunningham technique* to the cannon of 20th century dance techniques. Cunningham set the seeds for postmodern dance with his non-linear, non-climactic, non-psychological abstract work. In these works each element is in and of itself expressive, and the observer (in large part) determines what it communicates.
- Erick Hawkins - A student of George Balanchine, Hawkins became a soloist and the first male dancer in Martha Graham's dance company. In 1951, Hawkins, interested in the new field of kinesiology, opened his own school and developed his own technique (Hawkins technique) a forerunner of most somatic dance techniques.
- Paul Taylor - A student of the Juilliard School of Music and the Connecticut College School of Dance. In 1952 his performance at the American Dance Festival attracted the attention of several major choreographers. Performing in the companies of Merce Cunningham, Martha Graham, and George Balanchine (in that order), he founded the Paul Taylor Dance Company in 1954. The use of everyday gestures and modernist ideology is characteristic of his choreography. Former members of the Paul Taylor Dance Company included Twyla Tharp, Laura Dean, Dan Wagoner, and Senta Driver.
- Alwin Nikolais - A student of Hanya Holm. Nikolais's use of multimedia in works such as *Masks, Props, and Mobiles* (1953), *Totem* (1960), and *Count Down* (1979) was unmatched by other choreographers. Often presenting his dancers in constrictive spaces and costumes with complicated sound and sets, he focused their attention on the physical tasks of overcoming obstacles he placed in their way. Nikolais viewed the dancer not as an artist of self-expression, but as a talent who could investigate the properties of physical space and movement.

African American modern dance

The development of Modern dance embraced the contributions of African American dance artists regardless of whether they made *pure* modern dance works or blended modern dance with African and Caribbean influences.
- Katherine Dunham - An African American dancer, and anthropologist. Originally a ballet dancer, she founded her first company *Ballet Negre* in 1936 and later the *Katherine Dunham Dance Company* based in Chicago, Illinois. Dunham opened a school in New York (1945) where she taught *Katherine Dunham Technique*, a blend of African and Caribbean movement (flexible torso and spine, articulated pelvis and isolation of the limbs and polyrhythmic movement) integrated with techniques of → ballet and modern dance.
- Pearl Primus - A dancer, choreographer, and anthropologist, Primus drew on African and Caribbean dances to create strong dramatic works characterized by large leaps in the air. Primus often based her dances on the work of black writers and on racial and African-American issues. Primus created works based on Langston Hughes *The Negro Speaks of Rivers* (1944), and Lewis Allan's *Strange Fruit* (1945). Her dance company developed into the *Pearl Primus Dance Language Institute* which teaches her method of blending African-American, Caribbean, and African influences with modern dance and ballet techniques.
- Alvin Ailey- A student of Lester Horton,Bella Lewitzky, and later Martha Graham, Ailey spent several years working in both concert and theater dance. In 1930, Ailey and a group of young African-American dancers performed as Alvin Ailey American Dance Theater in New York. Ailey drew upon his *blood memories* of Texas, the blues, spirituals and gospel as inspiration. His most popular and critically acclaimed work is *Revelations* (1960).

Legacy of modern dance

The legacy of Modern dance can be seen in lineage of → 20th century concert dance forms. Although often producing divergent dance forms, many seminal dance artists share a common heritage that can be traced back to free dance.

Postmodern and Contemporary dance

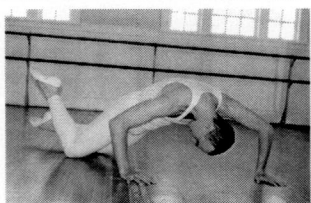

Modern dance often utilizes floor work.

Both Postmodern dance and Contemporary dance are built upon the foundations laid by Modern dance and form part of the greater category of 20th century concert dance. Where as Postmodern dance was a direct and opposite response to Modern dance, Contemporary dance draws on both modern and postmodern dance as a source of inspiration. The social and artistic upheavals of the late 1960s and 70s provoked even more radical forms of modern dance. Modern dance today is much more sophisticated in technique and technology than when modern dance was founded. The founders composed their dances entirely of spirit, sould, heart and mind as opposed to today's modern which has more of a technical aspect as well. The concern with social problems and the condition of human spirit is still expressed, but the issues that are presented would have appalled many of the early modern dancers. The essence of modern dance is to look forward, not back. Ballet and modern sometimes fuse together and enrich both forms, but neither is likely to lose its identity in the process. It is impossible to predict what directions moder dance will take in the future. Each style could go in so many different directions and are usually very radical. If this trend keeps up, future audiences can look forward to an interesting dance forum.

Teachers and their students

This list illustrates the basic teacher / student links in modern dance. For more detailed information see the individual artists entries.

- Loie Fuller
- Isadora Duncan - *Duncan technique*
- Ruth St. Denis
  - Ted Shawn - *Shawn Fundamentals*
  - Denishawn (school and company)
    - Doris Humphrey and Charles Weidman - *The Art of Making Dances* (Humphrey)
      - Humphrey-Weidman school - *Humphrey-Weidman technique (fall and recovery)*
        - José Limón - *Limón technique*
    - Martha Graham - *Graham technique* (and Louis Horst)
      - Erick Hawkins (via George Balanchine) - Hawkins technique
      - Anna Sokolow
      - May O'Donnell
      - Merce Cunningham - *Cunningham technique* (also see Postmodern dance)
        - Yvonne Rainer
        - Steve Paxton
        - Richard Alston
      - Paul Taylor
        - Twyla Tharp
      - Trisha Brown
- Lester Horton

- Bella Lewitzky
- Alvin Ailey
- Rudolf Laban
  - Kurt Jooss (see Ausdruckstanz)
    - Pina Bausch (see Tanztheater)
  - Mary Wigman (see Expressionist dance)
    - Hanya Holm
      - Valerie Bettis
      - Alwin Nikolais - *decentralization*
        - Murray Louis
- Émile Jaques-Dalcroze
  - Mary Wigman
  - Marie Rambert
- Katherine Dunham *Katherine Dunham Technique*
- Pearl Primus
  - Garth Fagan
- Helen Tamiris
  - Daniel Nagrin

See also

- → 20th century concert dance
  - free dance
  - Expressionist dance
  - Ausdruckstanz
  - Postmodern dance
  - Contemporary dance
- List of dance style categories
- Choreographers
- → Dance

References

- Dunning, Jennifer (1991-03-02). "Eleanor King, a modern dancer and choreographer, dies at 85 [1]". *New York Times*.
- Dunning, Jennifer (1989-03-11). "Review/Dance; Recalling the Spirit of Doris Humphrey [2]". *The New York Times*.

Further reading

- Adshead-Lansdale, J. (Ed) (1994) *Dance History: An Introduction*. Routledge. ISBN 0-415-09030-X
- Anderson, J. (1992) *Ballet & Modern Dance: A Concise History*. Independent Publishers Group. ISBN 0-87127-172-9
- Au, S. (2002) *Ballet and Modern Dance (World of Art)*. Thames & Hudson. ISBN 0-500-20352-0
- Brown, J. Woodford, C, H. and Mindlin, N. (Eds) (1998) (*The Vision of Modern Dance: In the Words of Its Creators*). Independent Publishers Group. ISBN 0-87127-205-9

- Cheney, G. (1989) *Basic Concepts in Modern Dance: A Creative Approach*. Independent Publishers Group. ISBN 0-916622-76-2
- Daly, A. (2002) *Done into Dance: Isadora Duncan in America*. Wesleyan Univ Press. ISBN 0-8195-6560-1
- de Mille, A. (1991) *Martha : The Life and Work of Martha Graham*. Random House. ISBN 0-394-55643-7
- Duncan, I. (1937) *The technique of Isadora Duncan*. Dance Horizons. ISBN 0-87127-028-5
- Foulkes, J, L. (2002) *Modern Bodies: Dance and American Modernism from Martha Graham to Alvin Ailey*. The University of North Carolina Press. ISBN 0-8078-5367-4
- Graham, M. (1973) *The Notebooks of Martha Graham*. Harcourt. ISBN 0-15-167265-2
- Graham, M. (1992) *Martha Graham: Blood Memory: An Autobiography*. Pan Macmillan. ISBN 0-333-57441-9
- Hawkins, E. and Celichowska, R. (2000) *The Erick Hawkins Modern Dance Technique*. Independent Publishers Group. ISBN 0-87127-213-X
- Hodgson, M. (1976) *Quintet: Five American Dance Companies*. William Morrow and Company. ISBN 0688080952
- Horosko, M (Ed) (2002) *Martha Graham: The Evolution of Her Dance Theory and Training*. University Press of Florida. ISBN 0-8130-2473-0
- Humphrey, D. and Pollack, B. (Ed) (1991) *The Art of Making Dances* Princeton Book Co. ISBN 0-87127-158-3
- Hutchinson Guest, A. (1998) *Shawn's Fundamentals of Dance (Language of Dance)*. Routledge. ISBN 2-88124-219-7
- Kriegsman, S, A.(1981) *Modern Dance in America: the Bennington Years*. G K Hall. ISBN 0-8161-8528-X
- Lewis, D, D. (1999) *The Illustrated Dance Technique of Jose Limon*. Princeton Book Co. ISBN 0-87127-209-1
- Long, R. A. (1995) *The Black Tradition in Modern Dance*. Smithmark Publishers. ISBN 0831707631
- Love, P. (1997) *Modern Dance Terminology: The ABC's of Modern Dance as Defined by its Originators*. Independent Publishers Group. ISBN 0-87127-206-7
- McDonagh, D. (1976) *The Complete Guide to Modern Dance* Doubleday. ISBN 978-0385050555
- McDonagh, D. (1990) *The Rise and Fall of Modern Dance*. Chicago Review Press. ISBN 1-55652-089-1
- Mazo, J, H. (2000) *Prime Movers: The Makers of Modern Dance in America*. Independent Publishers Group. ISBN 0-87127-211-3
- Minton, S. (1984) *Modern Dance: Body & Mind*. Morton Publishing Company. ISBN 978-0895821027
- Roseman, J, L. (2004) *Dance Was Her Religion: The Spiritual Choreography of Isadora Duncan, Ruth St. Denis and Martha Graham*. Hohm Press. ISBN 1-890772-38-0
- Sherman, J. (1983) *Denishawn: The Enduring Influence*. Twayne. ISBN 0-8057-9602-9
- Terry, W. (1976) *Ted Shawn, father of American dance : a biography*. Dial Press. ISBN 0-8037-8557-7
- A great series of articles on *Analyzing trends in the modern dance movement* can be found here. [3]

References

[1] http://query.nytimes.com/gst/fullpage.html?res=9D0CEEDE1F38F931A35750C0A967958260&scp=2&sq=%22eleanor%20king%22&st=cse

[2] http://query.nytimes.com/gst/fullpage.html?res=950DE4D71330F932A25750C0A96F948260&scp=9&sq=%22eleanor%20king%22&st=cse

[3] http://www.helium.com/tm/264678/impact-advanced-interactive-technologies

Rock and Roll (dance)

Acrobatic Rock'n'Roll refers to a very sporty, competitive form of → dance that originated from lindy hop. Unlike lindy hop, however, it is a choreographed dance designed for performance. It is danced by both couples and groups, either all-female or 4-8 couples together. This is normaly a very fast dance.......

Rock 'n' Roll	
Types:	Pairs, Formation; competition, show
Music:	pop music, rock and roll
Rhythm:	4/4 measure
Speed:	176–208 bpm
Origin:	USA
Creation time:	~1955

History

During the development of the musical genre rock and roll, → dances to go with the music were also created. From swing, which came into being around 1920, Lindy Hop emerged, the first partner dance ever to feature acrobatic elements. Lindy Hop was modified around 1940 to suit faster music, creating the style known as boogie woogie. With rock and roll music coming into fashion around 1955, its adherents converted boogie woogie to the even more athletic rock and roll dance.

A 1959 dance book describes "ROCK-AND-ROLL" as "performed without undue tension, the body and legs being flexible, so that there may be a physical rhythmic expression of co-ordination with the beats of music." "...a dance which leaves much scope for personal expression and interpretation in style, movement, rhythm, and even in the manner in which the figures are constructed." The basic rhythm is Slow, Slow, Quick, Quick. The Slow steps "will be taken first on to the ball of the foot, the heel then lowering".[1]

The double somersault, one of the most demanding acrobatic moves (Daniela Bechtold and Bernd Diel, World Games 2005 in Oberhausen, Germany)

Technique and basics

The most obvious feature of rock and roll dance are its **kicks** (into thin air) and its acrobatic elements like *lifts*, *jumps*, *throws* and *flips*. Today's rock and roll is focused on show and competition dance and - with the exception of its name - has nearly nothing in common with the former rock and roll movement. It is danced in pairs or in formation. Over the years rock and roll dancing has experienced several important changes: the former 6-basic step was converted into the modern tournament's 9-basic step with its typical kick ball change. Other characteristics are techniques such as the man's body wave movement, that he uses to fling his partner from a sitting position upwards, and the throwing basic movement, where she steps onto his hands and is catapulted upwards into neck breaking jumps. Because of its demanding technique, high speed, and acrobatics, rock and roll is a straining high-performance dance and is most often performed by young dancers.

The name of the basic comes from the number of separate actions. With the 6-basic one counts *(1)step (2)step (3)kick (4)settle (5)kick (6)settle* or *(1)kick (2)settle (3)kick (4)settle (5)kick (6)settle*, with the 9-basic it is *(1)kick (2)ball (3)change (4)kick (5)settle (6)settle (7)kick (8)settle (9)settle*. This means that a correct rock and roll kick will have the supporting foot settling on the floor a tiny moment before the kicking foot settles.

Dance categories

Dance categories Youth: No acrobatics allowed. Couples are 12 years old or younger. Juniors: A maximum of three acrobat moves are allowed under the category's safety regulations. Couples are between 12 and 17 years of age. B-Class: Two competitions per couple. One is a dance program with no acrobatics allowed. The acrobatic program requires six acrobatic moves. The male may throw the female into the air, but no flips are allowed. Main Class: Two dances as well, with the dance program allowing no acrobatics. The acrobatic program requires six acrobatics as well, though lifts, jumps, throws and flips are allowed.

Rhythm and music

Rock and roll dance works on the 4/4 measure. One basic comprises six beats and therefore one and a half measures. Differently than the offbeat of rock and roll music, the dance puts stress on the first and third beats of each measure. The music is very fast, between 176 to 208 bpm. Due to non-offbeat stressing and speed traditional rock and roll music has been replaced by modern disco and pop music.

The "swan", a popular acrobatic move in the Junior class.

Clothes

Currently advanced tournament rock and roll dancers don't wear petticoats and jeans - as the original rock and roll dancers did - but rather multi-colored costumes that are made of elastic artificial fibre and can only be purchased as individual pieces by special tailors. One reason for that is that acrobatic elements have grown more and more dangerous, requiring both freedom of movement and enough durability to avoid tearing.

The shoes worn is one of the most important elements in Rock & Roll dancing. Their soles need to possess both "slip" & "grip" characteristics. The most common footwear are light jazz shoes for the dance programs, while the acrobatic programs require more support for the female so sneakers made for aerobics dancers are usually chosen.

Organization

The *World Rock'n'Roll Confederation* is the organization that takes care of national and international rules and guidelines for tournaments. They organize the World Cups, European championships and World championships that occur every year for couples and formations. All international competitors are ranked according to points acquired during competitions.

Famous dancers

- Roman Kolb: The most successful Rock'n'Roll dancer in the history of WRRC, from the Czech Republic. He holds five World Champion titles (1994-1996; 2001-2002) together with former partners Michaela Vecerova and Katerina Fialova. He has retired from his career as an active dancer and now works as a trainer. During his time as a dancer Kolb combined excellent dancing with groundbreaking acrobatic routines.
- Miguel Angueira: One of the best Rock'n'Roll dancers of all time from France. Angueira holds three World Champion titles (1990-1992) together with his former partner Dorothée Blanpain. He has set the standard for aesthetics of Rock'n'Roll for over a decade and still excels due to his elegant dancing and impeccable acrobatic routines. His current partner is Natasha Quoy.

External links

- http://www.wrrc.org/ – World Rock'n'Roll Confederation
- http://www.VRRDA.org.au/ – Victorian Rock'n'Roll Dance Association (Australia). Rock'n'Roll competition dancing in Australia is more "traditional" and more closely related to social Rock'n'Roll dancing.

References

[1] The Girl's Book of Ballroom Dancing. Vera Wilson. Roy Publishers. 1959. pages 117. 118. LoC# 59-12926

Dance squad

A **dance squad** or **dance team**, sometimes called a **pom squad** or drill team, is a sport team that participates in competitive dance. In a routine, a squad will incorparate a specific dance style (i.e. hip-hop, jazz or lyrical), technical work (tumbling, leaps, turns, kicks, splits, jumps) and, depending on the routine, pompon and/or cheers. A pom squad slightly differs from a regular dance squad in that it uses pom-poms in all its dance routines, whilst a regular dance squad may or may not do pom work in a dance routine. Dance teams are also popular in performance dance, especially at sporting events, most commonly performing during the pre-game and halftime periods (and, in a number of cases, on the sidelines) of football and basketball games.

Dance is a highly competitve sport. Youth/association, middle school, high school, collegiate, all-star, and professional teams compete on local, regional, state, national, and international levels. Teams are judged on a number of criteria including form, team unison, showmanship, precision of motions, jumps, leaps, turns, choreography, enthusiasm, and, in the case of pom squads, visual use of poms-poms.

Overview

Dance squads emphasize precise, synchronized motions along with technical dance skills (such as jumps, turns, and leaps). Their routines encompass various styles of dance including the more usually incoprorated hip hop, jazz, lyrical, and kickline styles, to the more unusually used styles like disco, rock and roll, and gospel. A key feature of the dance is the ability to change formations very smoothly.

Types of dance squads

High School and Collegiate

Traditional high school dance/pom squads include competition, performance dance, and promoting school spirit with dance. Dance/pom is usually a year-round sport, performing in competitions and at sporting events, most commonly football and basketball games. Some schools also have their dance team perform short sideline dances. Traditionally, dance teams also perform at school pep rallies [1].

College dance squads are like traditional high school squads in that both include competition and performance dance, but there are many different aspects of being a dancer on a college dance team compared to being on a high school dance squad. For example, a college squad will most likely dance on the sidelines at games or have a specific spot in the stands whilst high schools usually reserve that for cheerleaders. [2]

All-Star

The U.S. All Star Federation governs all-star dance/pom squads.

Tryouts for all-star dance squads may be executed in several different ways. Some all-star teams choose to have just one large tryout in the spring, while other teams may choose to have a large tryout in the spring and another in the fall. A large number of all-star dance squads choose to have year-round open tryouts where anyone can tryout at any time during the season. The opportunity to compete in many large competitions attracts dancers to all star programs. All star dance teams can compete regionally, nationally, and even internationally. [3]

Professional

NFL, NBA, and CFL professional cheerleading are all more Dance Teams than cheerleading squads. "Really, we're a dance team," said Samantha Longo of the New York Jets Cheerleaders. She also said while many people associate cheerleading with back flips and human pyramids, cheering in the NFL is "nothing like that". [4]

Competitions

The prestigious National Dance/Drill Team competitions, from Champion Tours & Events, Inc., are for secondary school and all-star dance teams, with national competitions held in New York City, Los Angeles, and, most famously, in Orlando, Florida. The Flordia team competition is held at the University of Central Florida with the NYC competition held at the College of Staten Island and the L.A. team competition held at the Mater Dei High School arena. [5]

The Universal Dance Association, founded in 1980, holds a national championship for high school and all-star dance teams and is the only national dance team championship endorsed by the National Federation of State High School Associations. The national championship is held at Walt Disney World Resort in Orlando, Florida. Approximately 300 high school and all-star teams compete at the competition annually. [6]

See also

- Competitive dance
- → Dance
- Majorette (dancer)
- *Gotta Kick It Up!*
- Cheerleading
- Ōendan

References

[1] http://www.varsity.com/event/1167/high_school_dance.aspx
[2] http://www.varsity.com/event/1164/college_dance.aspx
[3] http://varsity.com/event/1163/allstar_dance.aspx
[4] http://www.stamfordadvocate.com/ci_13226937?source=rss_viewed
[5] http://www.championtoursandevents.com/regional.html
[6] http://uda.varsity.com/IALC.aspx

Dancing with the Stars

Dancing with the Stars is the name of a group of international television series based on the format of the British TV series *Strictly Come Dancing*, which is distributed by BBC Worldwide - the commercial arm of the BBC. Presently the format has been licensed to more than 30 countries, Australia was the first country to adapt the BBC show, and versions have also been produced in the United States with "Dancing with the Stars", Argentina, Austria, Belgium, Bosnia and Herzegovina, Brazil, Bulgaria, Chile, China, Croatia, The Czech Republic, Denmark, Estonia, Finland, Germany, India, Israel, Italy, Japan, Latvia, The Netherlands, New Zealand, Norway, Poland, Romania, Russia, Slovakia, Slovenia, South Africa, Sweden, and Ukraine. As a result, this contest became the world's most popular television program among all genres in 2006 and 2007, according to the magazine Television Business International,[1] reaching the Top 10 in 17 countries. The show pairs a number of celebrities with professional ballroom dancers, who each week compete by performing dances. These are then given scores by a panel of judges. Viewers are given a certain amount of time to place votes on their favorite dancers, either by telephone or (in some countries) by the Internet. The couple with the lowest combined score (judges plus viewers) is eliminated, and continue in the next week. This process continues until there are only two or three couples left, at which point one couple is declared the champion.

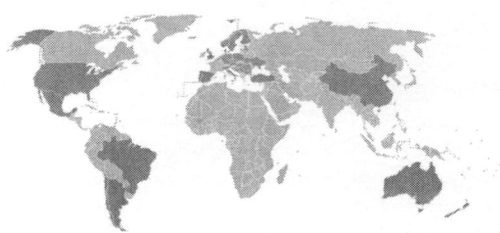

International versions of *Dancing with the Stars*

Franchise records

Cheryl Burke, Julianne Hough, Raimondo Todaro, and Stefano Oliveri made international *Dancing With The Stars* franchise history by becoming the only professional dancers to win two back-to-back championships. Ms. Burke won her first *Dancing With The Stars USA Championship* with the 98 Degrees boy band member Drew Lachey in the second season, and she won her second championship with American National Football League star Emmitt Smith in the third season. Julianne Hough won her first championship with the Olympic Speed Skating Gold Medalist Apolo Anton Ohno in the fourth season, and her second championship with the Indianapolis 500 champion Helio Castroneves in the fifth season. Raimodo Todaro won his first championship in the Italian version of *Dancing with the Stars* called "Ballando con le stelle" with the former Miss Italy and television hostess Cristina Chiabotto during the show's second season. He won again with the Olympic long jump silver medalist Fiona May during the show's third season. Stefano Oliveri won his first championship on *Dancing with the Stars New Zealand* with his dance partner Suzanne Paul, an infomercial hostess in New Zealand during Season three, and he won his second title during Season four with the New Zealander netball champion Temepara George. Brendan Cole is a judge in the New Zealand TV series, and he is a professional dancer in the British version of the show, *Strictly Come Dancing*. There, he won the first series with the British TV news announcer, Natasha Kaplinsky.

Mark Ballas is the only professional dancer to win two seasons that were not back-to-back. He won in Season six of the American version with his partnet Kristi Yamaguchi, and he won in Season eight with his partner Shawn Johnson. Mark also has had the distinction of being the only male professional dancer to win in any two seasons.

In New Zealand, Carol-Ann Hickamore is the only female professional dancer to win. She won in the Season two with the former rugby player Norm Hewitt. Ms. Hickamore later became a dancing judge for Seasons three and four after the Season one judge Donna Dawson had to leave the program.

Julianne Hough became the youngest professional dancer in *Dancing with the Stars* in the United States when she danced with the speed skater Apolo Anton Ohno during Season four at the age of 18.

Shawn Johnson became the youngest contestant on *Dancing with the Stars* in the United States in Season eight at the age of 17. She went on to become the youngest-ever winner of the dance contest.

Kym Johnson, Tobias Karlsson, Ingrid Thompson, Stefano Olivieri, Hayley Holt, Brian Fortuna, Kimberley Smith, and Csaba Szirmai have appeared on two different versions of *Dancing with the Stars*. Ms. Johnson has danced on the American and the Australian versions of the show, while Tobias Karlsson has appeared in bothe the Danish and the Swedish versions. Ingrid Beate Thompson appeared in the Norwegian and the Swedish versions of the show. Csaba Szirmai and Stefano Olivieri appeared in both the Australian and the New Zealander versions. Hayley Holt appeared in the New Zealander version of *Dancing with the Stars* and also in "Strictly Come Dancing" in Great Britain. Kimberley Smith appeared in both the Belgian and the Dutch versionss. Brian Fortuna danced one season in the United States, and he has next signed up to compete in *Strictly Come Dancing*.

Edyta Sliwinska is the only professional dancer in *Dancing with the Stars* to appear in every one of the American seasons. In the original British version of the TV program, *Strictly Come Dancing*, Anton du Beke, Erin Boag, and Brendan Cole have danced in each season.

In the New Zealander version, Rebecca Nicholson is the only professional dancer to have appeared in every season.

Jill Halfpenny and Darren Bennett were the first couple ever to receive a "perfect forty" score in the contest in *Strictly Come Dancing* in the Season two finale.

Two competitors have also hosted a season of the TV show. The winner of Season one of *Strictly Come Dancing*, Natasha Kaplinsky, stood in for the hostess Tess Daly, who was on maternity leave during Season two. Also the winner of Season two of *Dancing with the Stars*, Drew Lachey, filled in for the hostess Samantha Harris, who was also on maternity leave for Season five.

The lowest score that has ever given by a judge in the *Dancing with the Stars* franchise history was a one, which was giving to Rodney Hide, and to Nikki Webster of Australia in 2005. It is an open question of whether a zero score is allowed.

Argentina

Bailando por un Sueño

Based on the format of the program Mira quién baila! Spain or Dancing with the Stars in the U.S., the format was first held in Mexico, where he was commercially successful, so it was decided to adapt it to the Argentine market. Mexican format in Argentina was also adapted to other genres, such as singing (Singing for a Dream), figure skating (Skating for a Dream), musicals (Musical Comedy for a Dream), which also were issued in Showmatch. Until the year 2009 have been performed 5 complete editions and will be sixth in 2009.

In competition, a "dreamer" anonymous (male or female) should also be an amateur dancer, is accompanied by a celebrity in a dance contest, where, week after week, the couple must prove their dancing skills at different rates musical, which in Argentina until today are: Disco, Cha Cha Cha, Hip Hop, Salsa, Milonga, Rock And Roll, Chamamé, Jazz, Waltz, Ax, Merengue, Swing, Charleston, Lambada, Mambo, Reggaeton, Pole dance, Striptease, Cumbia, Cuarteto, Jive, Beat, Arabic, Video, Pop Latino, Rumba Flamenca, Dancing In The Rain, Samba, Ballroom, Country, Adagio, Adagio Latino, Flamenco, Chacarera, Aero Dance, Music Telenovelas, Paso Doble Kids, Aquadance, Cabaret, Dancing under the Snow, Pop, Rock Nacional, Double Cano. The three couples who obtained the fewest points by the jury and be sentenced to either the public who their SMS text messages), or telephone calls, vote which couple should be followed in the program, thanks to this program gives significant gains for each message sent.

Jurors in the various editions are celebrities from the art scene in Argentina. They have been Carmen Barbieri, Zulma Faiad, Jorge Lafauci, Moria Casan, Reina Reech, Graciela Alfano, Gerardo Sofovich, Laura Fidalgo, Florencia de la V, Antonio Gasalla, Samuel Gelblung.

Editions of Bailando por un sueño

- 1ª Editión, 2006: Carmen Barbieri and Cristian Ponce
- 2ª Editión, 2006: Florencia De La V and Manuel Rodríguez
- 3ª Editión, 2006: Carla Conte and Guillermo Conforte
- 4ª Editión, 2007: Celina Rucci and Matías Sayago
- 5ª Editión, 2008: Carolina Ardohain and Nicolas Armenghol

Cantando por un Sueño

Singing for a dream is a television singing contest program of Showmatch Argentine. There have been two editions: one in 2006 and one more in 2007. It is hosted by Marcelo Tinelli and broadcast by Channel 13 of Buenos Aires.

Editions of Cantando por un Sueño

- 1ª Editión, 2006: Iliana Calabró and Ricardo Rubio
- 2ª Editión, 2007: Miguel Fernandez and Micaela Salinas

Patinando por un Sueño

Skating for a Dream is a contest in figure skating, was telecast in 2007 and 2008. The celebrity ice skates with a professional skater to fulfill the dream of a foundation. They are evaluated by a jury of four judges from television and radio. The format is the same as for "Dream Dancing" and "Singing for a Dream".

Editions of Patinando por un Sueño

- 1ª Editión, 2007: Ximena Capristo and Marcelo Porce.
- 2ª Editión, 2008: Leonardo Tusam and Analía Papa.

Bailando por un Sueño Kids

Kids Dancing for a Dream, better known as Dancing Kids, was an Argentine dance contest where couples made up of children involved (ages 7 to 12 years), which are judged by a jury. The driver was Marcelo Tinelli (during the first three weeks) and then was Jose Maria Listorti (during the next four). It premiered on Thursday, 7 May 2009 and has been criticized by some quarters for what they view as handling of child actors, ending on 19 June of that year

Editions of Bailando por un Sueño Kids

- 1ª Editión, 2009: Pedro Maurizi and Candela Rodríguez

El Musical de Tus Sueños

The Music of Your Dreams is a television program where CONTEST 1 famous together with 5 dancers, this group of 6 people is directed by its choreographer and manager. Musicals do every week where they sing and dance and act. The jury is responsible for rating and the 3 couples with the lowest score or more are sentenced, and the day of the elimination dance again, so the jury saves all the best couples danced until there are 2 and the public is who decides who remains in the competition by voting via SMS to 9009. Each week 1 couple is being eliminated until semifinalists are the 4 pairs of partners there are the 2 finalists, perform a series of rhythms and the jury vote for the couple you like most, which has more vote takes 1 point or maybe a tie. The winning couple will fulfill his dream production. Common Something usually happens is that I undertake to abide famous.

Editions of El Musical de Tus Sueños

- 1ª Editión, 2009: *Issuing*

Australia

Dancing with the Stars has aired on the Seven Network since late 2004 and is hosted by Daniel MacPherson and Sonia Kruger. In late 2007, previous host Daryl Somers left the series after seven seasons. For the first seven seasons, there were four judges:

- Paul Mercurio, ballroom dancer and star of the Australian film, *Strictly Ballroom*.
- Todd McKenney, former Latin dance champion and theatre star. He starred as Peter Allen in *The Boy From Oz*.
- Helen Richey, former international Latin champion and one of the world's leading coaches and most sought after adjudicators.
- Mark Wilson, Five time Australian Dancesport champion and adjudicator.

Before the eighth season aired, Paul Mercurio was dropped from the judging panel.

The series has won the prestigious Logie Award, and has been named one of the most successful television programs to air on Australian television. The show averages around 2 million viewers a week nationally across Australia.[2] The program was made by the BBC in conjunction with Granada but since season eight, has been produced by Freehand. The most recent season commenced mid 2009.

Winners

- Season One (Late 2004) - Bec Cartwright
- Season Two (Early 2005) - Tom Williams
- Season Three (Late 2005) - Ada Nicodemou
- Season Four (Early 2006) - Grant Denyer
- Season Five (Late 2006) - Anthony Koutoufides
- Season Six (Early 2007) - Kate Ceberano
- Season Seven (Late 2007) - Bridie Carter
- Season Eight (Late 2008) - Luke Jacobz
- Season Nine (Late 2009) - Adam Brand

Austria

The first season of "Dancing Stars" started airing in Autumn of 2005 on ORF1, the second season started in Spring 2006, the third season in Spring of 2007 and the fourth season in 2008.

Dancing Stars hosts:

In Season 1, 2 and 3 the show was Alfons Haider (Main Host) and Mirjam Weichselbraun (Backstage and Interviews). In Season 4 Mirjam Weichselbraun replaced Alfons Haider and winner of Season 3 Klaus Eberhartinger took her place

Season 1

In the first season, no couple had to leave the first show and only two pairs were left in the final show. In all other seasons, one couple had to leave the first show and three pairs were left in the final show.

- Mat Schuh (Singer and Entertainer) with Kelly Kainz (8th place)
- Arabella Kiesbauer (Host) with Balázs Ekker (7th place)
- Peter Rapp (ORF Host) with Julia Polai (6th place)
- Patricia Kaiser (Miss Austria 2000 and track and field athlete) with Alexander Kreissl (5th place)
- Stefano Bernardin (Actor) with Christina Auer (4th place)
- Barbara Rett (ORF Host) with Manfred Zehender (3rd place)
- Toni Polster (Ex soccer player) with Michaela Heintzinger (2nd place)
- Marika Lichter (Musicalactress) with Andy Kainz (winner)

Season 2

- Gerda Rogers (Astrologer) with Andy Kainz (10th place)
- Ulrike Beimpold (Actress and Comedian) with Manfred Zehender (9th place)
- Edi Finger jun. (Radio-sportscaster) with Nicole Kuntner (8th place)
- Barbara Karlich (Talkshow Host) with Alexander Zaglmeier (7th place)
- Gregor Bloéb (Actor) with Michaela Heintzinger (6th place)
- Simone Stelzer (Singer) with Alexander Kreissl (5th place)
- Hans Georg Heinke (Journalist and Newscaster) with Elke Gehrsitz (4th place)
- Nicole Beutler (Actress) with Balázs Ekker (3rd place)
- Andreas Goldberger (Ex Ski jumper) with Julia Polai (2nd place)
- Manuel Ortega (Singer) with Kelly Kainz (winner)

Scorecard

Couple	EP 1	EP 2	EP 3	EP 4	EP 5	EP 6
Manuel & Kelly	25	29	**34**	**35**	34	**36+34=70**
Andreas & Julia	24	*21*	24	*28*	27	24+*32*=56
Nicole & Balázs	**30**	**32**	32	**35**	33	**36**+33=69
Hans & Elke	24	23	22	32	*24*	*21*+*32*=53
Simone & Alexander	28	27	29	33	27	28+*32*=60
Gregor & Michaela	23	30	32	31	30	
Barbara & Alexander	24	29	29	32		
Edi & Nicole	*16*	*21*	23			
Ulrike & Manfred	29	26				
Gerda & Andy	20					

Season 3

- Timna Brauer (Singer and Artist) with Manfred Zehender (10th place)
- Hera Lind (bestselling author) with Alexander Kreissl (9th place)
- Stephanie Graf (Ex Runner) with Andy Kainz (8th place)
- Michael Konsel (Ex soccer player) with Nicole Kuntner (7th place)
- Harry Prünster (Host) with Michaela Heintzinger (6th place)
- Nina Proll (Actress) with Balázs Ekker (5th place)
- Michael Tschuggnall (Starmania-Winner 2002) with Alice Guschelbauer (4th place)
- Zabine Kapfinger (Singer) with Alexander Zaglmaier (3rd place)
- Peter L. Eppinger (Ö3-Host) with Julia Polai (2nd place)
- Klaus Eberhartinger (Singer, EAV-Frontman) with Kelly Kainz (winner)

Season 4

- Claudia Stöckl (Ö3-Host) with Alexander Kreissl (10th place)
- Peter Tichatschek (Host) with Michaela Heintzinger (9th place)
- Oliver Stamm (Beach volleyball player) with Julia Polai (8th place)
- Christine Reiler (Miss Austria 2007) with Manfred Zehender (7th place)
- Marc Pircher (Singer) with Kelly Kainz (6th place)
- Jeannine Schiller (Charity-lady) with Balázs Ekker (5th place)
- Hans Kreuzmayr (Waterloo & Robinson) with Alice Guschelbauer (4th place)
- Elke Winkens (Schauspielerin) with Andy Kainz (3rd place)
- Elisabeth Engstler (Host) with Alexander Zaglmaier (2nd place)
- Dorian Steidl (Host) with Nicole Kuntner (winner)

Special Episodes

One Week after the final of each Season a "Dancing Stars Best of" was aired and after the "Best of" of Season 3 there was a special episode called " Dancing Stars - Die Traumhochzeit" (Dancing Stars - The Dream Wedding) in which the professional ballroom dancers Balázs Ekker and Alice Guschelbauer got married.

Bulgaria

See: Dancing Stars

The first season of the show started on 22 September 2008, it is called *Dancing Stars* and is aired on bTV. The show is hosted by Radost Draganova and Todor Kolev. The show airs from Monday to Thursday with two live shows - on Monday (main show) and Thursday (results show) and two background episodes on Tuesday and Wednesday. *Dancing Stars* proved to be a huge success reaching an average audience share over 40%, beating Nova Television's *Big Brother 4*.

Judges:

Vladimir Bozhilov

Galena Velikova

Neshka Robeva

Contestants:

Anya Pencheva (born 12 September 1957) - Actress

Niki Kunchev (born 26 December 1960) - TV host

Alisia - Pop-folk singer

Galena - Pop-folk singer

Bojidar Iskrenov (born 1 August 1962) - Former football player

Kalki (born 9 December 1962) - Singer

Violeta Markovska (born 24 April 1987) - Actress

Neti (born 14 September 1975) - Actress and singer

Andrei Batashov (born 10 September 1965) - Actor

Georgi Mamalev (born 5 August 1952) - Actor

Iliana Raeva - Ex gymnast (born 15 March 1963)

Georgi Kostadinov (born 20 September 1979) - Winner of Survivor BG 2

Orlin (born 23 April 1979) - Pop singer

Elena Yoncheva (born 27 May 1964) - Journalist

Official Site [3]

Chile

El Baile en TVN ("The Ball on TVN") is aired in Televisión Nacional de Chile since October 16, 2006. It's hosted by Rafael Araneda and Karen Doggenweiler.

Season 1

Since October 16, 2006. The winners of this season were Juvenal Olmos and Claudia Miranda.

Season 2

Since March 5, 2007. The winners of this season were Cristian Arriagada and Paz Bustos.

Season 3

Since August 22, 2007. The winners of this season were Francisco Reyes and Irene Bustamante.

- Carolina "Pampita" Ardohain (Argentine Top Model, partnered by Diego Heilig)
- Maria Eugenia Larrain "Kenita Larrain" (Chilean Top Model, partnered by Rodrigo Escobar)
- Amaya Forch (Chilean Singer and Actress, partnered by William Orrock)
- Catalina Palacios (Entertainer of Infantile televising programs, partnered by Darwin Ruz)
- Adrea Tessa (Chilean singer, partnered by Alfredo Araya)
- Gianella Marengo (ex-reality show participant, partnered by Emilio Rubilar)
- Leandro Martínez (Chilean singer and member of the televising program "Rojo Fama Contrafama", partnered by Maria Isabel Sobarzo)
- Francisco Reyes (Chilean actor of the national television network TVN, partnered by Irene Bustamante)
- Juan Pablo Matulic (ex-reality show participant, partnered by Francini Amaral)
- Eliseo Salazar (Chilean Automovilistic Runner, partnered by Claudia Miranda)
- Hotuiti Teao (Chilean model from Easter Island, partnered by Monica Valenzuela)
- Carlos von Mühlenbrock (Chilean Chef and entertainer of Chilean televising programs, partnered by Viví Rodriguez

Season 4

The winners of this season were Fernando Godoy and Paz Bustos.

The contestants of this season are :

Sebastian Ferrer (Stylist & panelist of T.V show "Pollo en conserva")

Mario Guerrero (Singer)

Sandra O Ryan (Actress)

Reinaldo González (Military instructor of reality shows "Pelotón")

Cristian Riquelme (Actor)

Denisse Malebrán (Singer)

Fernando Godoy (Actor, comediant & T.V host)

Mariana Derderian (Actress, singer & T.V host)

Sergio Vargas (Ex - football player)

Paola Camaggi (Model & T.V host)

Raquel "KEL" Calderón (Young actrees, singer, model & Panelist of TV shows)

Iván Torres ("The Weather man")

Rosita Parsons (Model)

China (including Hong Kong)

The Chinese version is a co-production between Hong Kong's TVB and the mainland's Hunan TV under licence from the BBC. It is available free-to-air in Hong Kong on TVB Jade. In mainland China it is aired on Hunan Satellite Television, which is free-to-air in Hunan, and available in urban areas throughout the rest of mainland China through widespread cable systems.

The Chinese title (simplified Chinese: 舞动奇迹; traditional Chinese: 舞動奇跡; pinyin: *Wǔdòngqíjì*) is difficult to translate, but could be rendered as *Miracle Dancing* or "Miracles of Dance Moves". The official English title is *Strictly Come Dancing*.

Each broadcaster provides five male and five female dancers, for a total of twenty. Pairs were determined by audience SMS votes.

The programme began airing in late 2007, in order to mark the anniversary of the 1997 handover of Hong Kong from the UK to the People's Republic of China.[4]

Croatia

Hosted by Barbara Kolar and Duško Čurlić.

Judges:

- Elio Bašan
- Milka Babović
- Dinko Bogdanić
- Davor Bilman

Official Site [5]

Season 1

The first season of *Ples sa zvijezdama* (*Dancing with the Stars*) started airing on December 2, 2006 on HRT1. The contestants were:

- Zrinka Cvitešić (actress) with Nicolas Quesnoit (**Winners**)
- Rene Bitorajac (actor) with Mirjana Žutić (runner-up)
- Maja Šuput(singer) with Ištvan Varga (6th eliminated)
- Žarko Radić (actor) with Ivana Antinac (5th eliminated)
- Zoran Vakula (meteorologist) with Ksenija Plušćec (4th eliminated)
- Sandra Bagarić (opera singer) with Leon Ajtlbez (3rd eliminated)
- Dubravko Šimenc (water polo player) with Tamara Despot (2nd eliminated)
- Zdenka Kovačićek (singer) with Hrvoje Kraševac (1st eliminated)

Highest score of the season (40):

- Zrinka & Nicolas (Jive - 3rd episode)
- Zrinka & Nicolas (Slowfox - 4th episode)
- Maja & Ištvan (Paso Doble - 4th episode)
- Maja & Ištvan (English Waltz - 6th episode)
- Zrinka & Nicolas - *total* - *80 points* (English Waltz & Paso Doble - 7th episode)
- Maja & Ištvan (Slowfox - 7th episode)
- Zrinka & Nicolas - *total* - *120 points* (English Waltz, Samba & Freestyle - final episode)
- Rene & Mirjana (Freestyle - final episode)

Lowest score of the season:

- Žarko & Ivana - 16 points (Samba - 5th episode)

Season 2

The second season of *Ples sa zvijezdama* ("Dancing with the Stars") started airing on November 3, 2007 on HRT1. The contestants were:

- Luka Nižetić (singer) with Mirjana Žutić (**Winners**)
- Lana Jurčević (singer) with Hrvoje Kraševac (runner-up)
- Davor Gobac (singer) with Tamara Despot (6th eliminated)
- Nikolina Pišek (TV hostess) with Ištvan Varga (5th eliminated)
- Danijela Martinović (singer) with Nicolas Quesnoit (4th eliminated)
- Iva Majoli (tennis player) with Marko Herceg (3rd eliminated)
- Damir Markovina (actor) with Ana Herceg (2nd eliminated)
- Mirko Fodor (TV host) with Žana Alerić (1st eliminated)

Highest score of the season (40):

- Luka & Mirjana (Paso Doble - 6th episode)
- Lana & Hrvoje - *total* - *80 points* (Quickstep & Paso Doble - 7th episode)
- Luka & Mirjana - *total* - *80 points* (Tango & Cha-cha-cha - 7th episode)
- Luka & Mirjana (Paso Doble & Freestyle - final episode)

Lowest score of the season:

- Davor & Tamara - 20 points (Samba - 5th episode)

Season 3

The third season of *Ples sa zvijezdama* ("Dancing with the Stars") started airing on October 25, 2008 on HRT1. The contestants were:

- Mario Valentić (actor, model and former Mister Croatia) with Ana Herceg (**Winners**)
- Zlata Mück (TV and radio hostess) with Ištvan Varga
- Daniela Trbović (TV hostess) with Nicolas Quesnoit
- Martina Zubčić (bronze olympic medal in taekwondo) with Robert Schubert
- Antonija Šola (singer) with Hrvoje Kraševac
- Goran Grgić (actor) with Sara Stojanović
- Luka Vidović (magician and actor) with Mirjana Žutić
- Nikša Kaleb (handball player) with Tamara Despot

Highest score of the season:

- Zlata & Ištvan- 40 points (Tango - final episode)
- Mario & Ana - 40 points (Freestyle - final episode)

Lowest score of the season:

- Goran & Sara - 17 points (Jive - 3rd episode)

Scorecard

Couple	Average	EP 1	EP 2	EP 3	EP 4	EP 5	QF	SF	F
Mario & Ana	34.8	**33**	**32**	34	36	32	32+31=*63*	35+36=*71*	39 + 38 + 40 = **117**
Zlata & Ištvan	31.9	23	22	29	30	27	31+33=64	39+33=72	40 + 38 + 38 = *116*
Daniela & Nicolas	**35.8**	25	30	**37**	**39**	**37**	**38+38=76**	**39+39=78**	
Martina & Robert	30.7	29	29	31	31	26	33+36=69		
Antonija & Hrvoje	31	20	**32**	35	**39**	29			
Goran & Sara	21	20	22	*17*	25				
Luka & Mirjana	21.3	20	23	*21*					
Nikša & Tamara	*19.0*	*18*	*20*						

Bold numbers indicate the couples with the highest score for each week.

Italic numbers indicate the couples with the lowest score for each week.

indicates the couples eliminated that week.

indicates the returning couple that finished in the bottom two.

Dances are:

Cha-cha-cha

Waltz

Rumba

Quickstep

Jive

Tango

Paso doble

Slowfox

Samba

Freestyle

Czech Republic

Named "StarDance ... When the Stars are Dancing" and aired (so far) 3 seasons by Czech Television. Hosted by Tereza Kostková & Marek Eben.

Judges:

- Vlastimil Harapes (Season 1)
- Michael Kocáb (Season 1)
- Eva Bartuňková (Season 1)
- Richard Hes (Season 2)
- Zdeněk Chlopčík (Season 1, 2, 3)
- Mahulene Bočanová (Season 2)
- Tatiana Drexler (Season 2, 3)
- Jaroslav Kuneš (Season 3)
- Leona Kvasnicová (Season 3)

Season 1 (2006)

The contestants were:

- **Roman Vojtek (musical singer) with Kristýna Coufalová (Winners)**
- Václav Vydra (actor) with Petra Kostovčíková (runner-up)
- Tomáš Dvořák (olympionic) with Kamila Tománková (6th eliminated)
- Mahulena Bočanová (actress) with Jaroslav Kuneš (5th eliminated)
- Jolana Voldánová (TV News host) with Jan Tománek (4th eliminated)
- Jana Švandová (actress) with Zdeněk Fenčák (3rd eliminated)
- Jan Čenský (actor) with Tereza Bufková (2nd eliminated)
- Helena Zeťová (singer) with Eduard Zubák (1st eliminated)

Season 2 (2007)

The contestants were:

- **Aleš Valenta (ski jumper) with Iva Langerová (Winners)**
- Tatiana Vilhelmová (actress) with Petr Čadek (runner-up)
- Jiří Schmitzer (actor, singer) with Simona Švrčková (6th eliminated)
- Michal Dlouhý (actor) with Michaela Gatěková (5th eliminated)
- Robert Záruba (TV SPORT NEWS host) with Vanda Dětinská (4th eliminated)
- Monika Žídková (model) with Jan Halíř (3rd eliminated - because of Jan's car crash)
- Lenka Filipová (singer) with Michal Petr (2nd eliminated)
- Štěpánka Hilgertová (olympionic) with Michal Němeček (1st eliminated)

Season 3 (2008)

The contestants were:

- **Dana Batulková (actress) and Jan Onder (Winners)**
- Zuzana Norisová (actress, singer) and Jan Kliment (runner-up)
- Jaromír Bosák (TV sport host) a Eva Krejčířová (6th eliminated)
- Vladimír Kratina (actor) a Laura Klimentová (5th eliminated)
- Jana Doleželová (model) and Michal Necpál (4th eliminated)
- David Suchařípa (actor) and Albina Zaytseva (3rd eliminated)
- Iva Frühlingová (singer) a Michal Kostovčík (2nd eliminated)
- Bohouš Josef (singer) and Lenka Tvrzová (1st eliminated)

Denmark

The first season of *Vild med dans* ("Mad about Dancing") was aired on the Danish TV-channel TV 2 in 2005 and the contestants were:

Season 1 (Spring 2005)

- **Mia Lyhne (actress) and Thomas Evers Poulsen (winners)**
- Erik Peitersen (TV workman) and Marianne Eihilt
- Klaus Bondam (politician and actor) and Soffie Dalsgaard
- Jesper Skibby (racing cyclist) and Julia Petrovic
- Stine Stengade (actress) and Lars Christensen
- Marianne Florman (handball player) and René Christensen
- Sofie Stougaard (actress) and Tobias Karlsson

Season 2 (Autumn 2005)

- **David Owe (actor) and Vickie Jo Ringgaard (winners)**
- Eskild Ebbesen (Olympic-winning oarsman) and Marianne Eihilt
- Sisse Fisker (TV hostess) and Steen Lund
- Peter Mygind (actor) and Mie Moltke
- Zindy Laursen (singer) and Tobias Karlsson
- Bettina Aller (magazine editor) and René Christensen
- Kim Milton Nielsen (soccer referee) and Ann Wilson
- Allan Olsen (actor) and Soffie Dalsgaard
- Mayianne Dinesen (radio hostess) and Lars Christensen

Birthe Kjær (folk singer) and Bo Loft Jensen, left the show because of health problems

Season 3 (2006)

- **Christina Roslyng (Olympic-winning handballplayer) and Steen Lund (winners)**
- Simon Mathew (singer) and Viktoria Franova
- Nikolaj Christensen (singer) and Soffie Dalsgaard
- Anna David (singer) and René Christensen
- Ole Olsen (speedway racer) and Marianne Eihilt
- Master Fatman (TV DJ) and Mie Moltke
- Annette Heick (singer/TV hostess) and Thomas Evers Poulsen
- Liv Corfixen (actress) and Mads Vad
- Gert Bo Jacobsen (boxer) and Vickie Jo Ringgaard
- Lærke Winther Andersen (actress) and Klaus Kongsdal

Season 4 (2007)

- **Robert Hansen (actor) and Marianne Eihilt (winners)**
- Vicki Berlin (comedian/actress) and Steen Lund/Jesper Dalsgaard
- Rikke Hørlykke (Olympic-winning handball player) and Mads Vad
- Lai Yde (actor) and Mie Moltke
- Lisbeth Østergård (TV-hostess) and Thomas Evers Poulsen
- Anne Louise Hassing (actress) and Michael Olesen
- Said Chayesteh (actor) and Mette Georgio
- Paula Larrain (TV hostess) and René Christensen
- Nicolai Moltke-Leth (military man) and Soffie Dalsgaard
- Benedikte Hansen (actress) and Bo Loft Jensen

Joachim Boldsen (handball player) and Vickie Jo Ringgaard, went out because of health problems

Christmas Gala 2007

- **Simon Mathew and Viktoria Franova (winners)**
- David Owe and Vickie Jo Ringgaard
- Mia Lyhne and Thomas Evers Poulsen
- Christina Roslyng and Steen Lund
- Robert Hansen and Marianne Eihilt
- Master Fatman and Mie Moltke

Season 5 (2008)

- **Joachim B. Olsen (shot put olympic medalist) and Marianne Eihilt (winners)**
- Tina Lund (European show jumping champion) and Tobias Karlsson (2nd)
- Anne-Grethe Bjarup Riis (actress) and Michael Olesen (3rd)
- Anne-Mette Rasmussen (kindergarten teacher and Prime Minister's wife) and Thomas Evers Poulsen
- Hans Pilgaard (TV presenter) and Mie Moltke
- Szhirley Rasmussen (singer) and Silas Holst
- Kenneth Carlsen (tennis player) and Katrine Bonde
- Søren Bregendal (singer/actor) and Ashli Williamson
- Jette Torp (singer) and Mads Vad
- Oliver Bjerrehuus (model) and Viktoria Franova

Season 6 (2009)

- Lisa Lents (model/European taekwondo champion) and Michael Olesen
- Casper Elgaard (racing driver) and Vickie Jo Ringaard
- Malena Belafonte (model) and Silas Holst
- Noam Halby (singer) and Katrine Bonde
- René Dif (singer/actor) and Luise Crone Dons
- Pernille Højmark (actress/singer) and Thomas Evers Poulsen
- Lotte Friis (European swimming champion) and Mads Vad
- Line Baun Danielsen (TV presenter) and Morten Kjeldgaard
- Basim Moujahid (singer) and Claudia Rex
- Sven-Ole Thorsen (retired actor/stuntman) and Mie Moltke

The show features four judges. Anne Laxholm, Britt Bendixen, and Jens Werner have been featured in all seasons. The first season (2004) featured Kim Dahl as the fourth judge. In the second season (2005), he was replaced by Thomas Evers Poulsen. Since the third season (2006-), Allan Tornsberg has been the fourth judge.

Estonia

The show is called *Tantsud tähtedega* (*Dances with the stars*) and is aired on Kanal 2. The 3rd season is hosted by Mart Sander and Gerli Padar.

Season 1

Hosts Mart Sander and Kristiina Heinmets-Aigro. Judges: Ants Tael, Merle Klandorf, Kaie Kõrb, Jüri Nael

Mikk Saar (singer) and Olga Kosmina

1. Gerli Padar (singer) and Martin Parmas
2. Erki Nool (athlete, Olympic gold medalist) and Ave Vardja
3. Aivar Riisalu (businessman, singer) and Kristina Tennokese
4. Vilja Savisaar (politician) and Veiko Ratas
5. Ingrid Tähismaa (journalist) and Aleksandr Makarov
6. Reet Linna (singer, TV-presenter) and Eduard Korotin
7. Indrek Tarand (director of museum) and Kaisa Oja

Season 2

Hosts Mart Sander and Merle Liivak. Judges: Ants Tael, Merle Klandorf, Kaie Kõrb, Jüri Nael

Koit Toome (singer) and Kerttu Tänav

1. Luisa Värk (singer) and Martin Parmas
2. Peep Vain (top-instructor) and Olga Kosmina
3. Andrus Värnik (athlete, World Championship gold medalist) and Kaisa Oja
4. Dag Hartelius (Swedish ambassador to Estonia) and Kristina Tennokese
5. Kristiina Ojuland (politician) and Aleksandr Makarov
6. Katrin Karisma (actress) and Veiko Ratas
7. Beatrice (model) and Eduard Korotin

Season 3

Hosts Mart Sander and Gerli Padar. Judges: Ants Tael, Merle Klandorf, Riina Suhotskaja, Märt Agu

- Maarja-Liis Ilus (singer) and Veiko Ratas - Runner-ups
- Piret Järvis (singer) and Mairold Millert, third eliminated
- Erika Salumäe (politician, athlete, 2 times Olympic gold medalist) and Kristjan Kuusk, second eliminated
- Evelyn Sepp (politician) and Marko Kiigajaan, fifth eliminated
- Lauri Pedaja (actor, hairdresser) and Kristina Tennokese, sixth eliminated
- Henrik Normann (actor) and Kaisa Oja, fourth eliminated
- Arne Niit (designer) and Olga Kosmina, first eliminated
- Argo Ader (bodybuilder) and Helena Liiv - **Winners**

Finland

Season 1

The series (titled *Tanssii tähtien kanssa* (Dances with Stars); a pun on the title of the film Dances with Wolves, *Tanssii susien kanssa*) aired in spring 2006, featuring

- Tomi Metsäketo (tenor) partnered by Sanna Hirvaskari, eventual winners
- Kristiina Elstelä (actress) partnered by Marko Keränen, runners-up
- Jone Nikula (music executive, Idols judge) partnered by Katja Koukkula, sixth eliminated
- Keith "Keke" Armstrong (soccer coach) partnered by Helena Ahti-Hallberg, fifth eliminated
- Markus Pöyhönen (track athlete) partnered by Sanna Hento, fourth eliminated
- Katja Kannonlahti (news anchor) partnered by Jussi Väänänen, third eliminated
- Suvi Miinala (model, Miss Finland 2000) partnered by Juha Pykäläinen, second eliminated
- Leena Harkimo (member of Parliament) partnered by Erik Hento, first eliminated

Season 2

(spring 2007) featured

- Mariko (musician) partnered by Aleksi Seppänen, eventual winners
- Sari Siikander (actress) partnered by Mikko Ahti, runners-up
- Sami Sarjula (actor) partnered by Sanna Hirvaskari, sixth eliminated
- Eppu Salminen (actor) partnered by Anna Sainila, fifth eliminated
- Jani Sievinen (swimmer) partnered by Helena Ahti-Hallberg, fourth eliminated
- Vanessa Kurri (model, Miss Finland 1999) partnered by Marko Keränen, third eliminated
- Roman Schatz (TV personality, writer) partnered by Saara Huovinen, second eliminated
- Pirkko Arstila (journalist, writer) partnered by Vesa Anttila, first eliminated

Singer Kirill Babitzin was to take part in the competition, but he suddenly died on January 31. His place was taken by Schatz.

Season 3

(spring 2008) featured

- Maria Lund (singer, actress) partnered by Mikko Ahti, eventual winners
- Nicke Lignell (actor) partnered by Susa Matson, runners-up
- Tuuli Matinsalo (athlete) partnered by Aleksi Seppänen, eighth eliminated
- Antti Kaikkonen (member of Parliament) partnered by Satu Markkanen, seventh eliminated
- Joonas Hytönen (TV personality) partnered by Kati Koivisto, sixth eliminated
- Vappu Pimiä (TV and radio personality) partnered by Jani Rasimus, fifth eliminated
- Merja Larivaara (actress) partnered by Janne Talasma, fourth eliminated
- Jimi Pääkallo (singer, actor) partnered by Anna Sainila, third eliminated
- Jyrki Anttila (tenor) partnered by Satu Suomi, second eliminated
- Sikke Sumari (TV personality, restaurateur) partnered by Daniel Ylimäki, first eliminated

Season 4

(spring 2009) featured

- Satu Tuomisto (Miss Finland 2008, model) partnered by Janne Talasma eventual winners
- Pirkko Mannola (actress) partnered by Mika Jauhiainen, runners-up
- Rosa Meriläinen (writer, ex-politician) partnered by Sami Helenius, eighth eliminated
- Wilson Kirwa (long distance runner) partnered by Susa Matson, seventh eliminated
- Kim Herold (musician, ex-model) partnered by Sanni Siurua, sixth eliminated
- Miia Nuutila (actress) partnered by Vesa Anttila, fifth eliminated
- Bettina Sågbom (TV reporter) partnered by Jani Rasimus, fourth eliminated
- Mato Valtonen (musician, actor) partnered by Janica Mattsson, third eliminated
- Rolf Nordström (plastic surgeon) partnered by Nitta Kortelainen, second eliminated
- Simo Frangén (comedian) partnered by Satu Markkanen, first eliminated

Germany

The series is called *Let's Dance*. Season 1 aired in April 2006 on RTL. Season 2 aired in May 2007. Both seasons have been hosted by Hape Kerkeling & Nazan Eckes.

Contestants season 1

- Sandy Mölling (singer) With Roberto Albanese
- Wolke Hegenbarth (actress) With Oliver Seefeldt
- Heike Henkel (former athlete) With Dirk Bastert
- Heide Simonis (former politician) With Hendrik Höfken
- Axel Bulthaupt (TV-host) With Anna Karina Mosmann
- Wayne Carpendale (actor) With Isabel Edvardsson - **Winners**
- Jürgen Hingsen (former decathlethe) With Uta Deharde
- Jochen Horst (actor) With Sofia Bogdanova

Contestants season 2

- Ben (singer/TV-host) With Christine Deck
- Katja Ebstein (singer) With Oliver Seefeldt
- Jenny Elvers-Elbertzhagen (actress/TV-host) With Sascha Karabey
- Giovane Élber (former soccer-player) With Isabel Edvardsson
- Guildo Horn (singer) With Motshegetsi Mabuse
- Markus Majowski (actor) With Anastasiya Kravchenko

- Margarethe Schreinemakers (former TV-host) With Jürgen Schlegel
- Susan Sideropoulos (actress) With Christian Polanc - **Winners**
- Jasmin Wagner (singer) With Hendrik Höfken
- Eralp Uzun (actor) With Anna Karina Mosmann

    *Further information (**German**): Let's Dance*

India
Winners:
- Season 1: Mona Singh
- Season 2: Prachi Desai
- Season 3: Bhaichung Bhutia

Israel
Winners:
- Season 1: Eliana Bekier
- Season 2: Guy Arieli
- Season 3: Rodrigo Gonzáles
- Season 4: Galit Giat

Italy
Four season of the show, called *Ballando con le Stelle*, have been aired on Rai Uno. All the series have been hosted by Milly Carlucci. Singer and TV presenter Amanda Lear has been part of the judging panel in series 1,2,4 and 5

The first series (titled *Ballando con le Stelle* [6]) aired in Autumn 2004, featuring:

- Fabrizio Frizzi (partnered by Samanta Togni)
- Francesco Salvi (partnered by Natalia Titova) - Runners-up
- Paola Ferrari (partnered by Andrea Placidi)
- Igor Cassina (partnered by Denise Abrate)
- Gianni Ippoliti (partnered by Valentina Vincenzi)
- Carla Paneca (partnered by Lucio Cocchi)
- Anna Maria Barbera (partnered by Ilario Parise)
- Hoara Borselli (partnered by Simone Di Pasquale) - Winners

The second series (titled *Ballando con le Stelle*) aired in Autumn 2005, featuring:

- Syusy Blady (partnered by Emanuele Ricci)
- Alessandra Canale (partnered by Simone Di Pasquale)
- Loredana Cannata (partnered by Samuel Peron) - Runners-up
- Cristina Chiabotto (partnered by Raimondo Todaro) - Winners
- Mario Cipollini (partnered by Marina Aleksejeva)
- Youma Diakite (partnered by Giuseppe Albanese)
- Fabio Fulco (partnered by Claudia Nicolussi)
- Diego Maradona (partnered by Angela Panico)
- Stefano Masciarelli (partnered by Francesca Vispi)
- Marco Mazzocchi (partnered by Vincenza Farnese)
- Vincenzo Peluso (partnered by Natalia Titova)
- Francesca Reggiani (partnered by Sergio Sampaoli)

The third series (titled *Ballando con le Stelle*) aired Autumn 2006, featuring:

- Massimiliano Rosolino (partnered by Natalia Titova)
- Antonio Cupo (partnered by Giada Giacomoni)
- Rodolfo Laganà (partnered by Hildegard Salvatore)
- Sean Kanan (partnered by Tinna Hoffman)
- Biagio Izzo (partnered by Samanta Togni)
- Rudy Smaila (partnered by Lucia Annese)
- Eva Grimaldi (partnered by Simone Di Pasquale)
- Fiona May (partnered by Raimondo Todaro) - Winners
- Chiara Boni (partnered by Samuel Peron)
- Pamela Camassa (partnered by Angelo Madonia) - Runners-up
- Sofia Bruscoli (partnered by Manuel Favilla)
- Martina Pinto (partnered by Umberto Gaudino)
- Tiberio Timperi (partnered by Elena Coniglio)
- Orietta Berti (partnered by Andrea Placidi)

The fourth series (titled *Ballando con le Stelle*) aired in Autumn 2007, featuring:

- Irene Pivetti (partnered by Mauro Rossi)
- Massimo Lopez (partnered by Serena Lecca)
- Giovanni Muciaccia (partnered by Ola Karieva)
- Catherine Spaak (partnered by Benedetto Capraro)
- Gabriele Cirilli (partnered by Vicky Martin)
- Anna Falchi (partnered by Stefano Di Filippo) - Runners-up
- Riccardo Sardonè (partnered by Annalisa Di Filippo)
- Ivan Zazzaroni (partnered by Natalia Titova)
- Maria Elena Vandone (partnered by Samuel Peron) - Winners
- Elisa Silvestrin (partnered by Sante Mandolini)
- Michael Reale (partnered by Marta Faiola)
- Licia Colò (partnered by Raimondo Todaro)

The fifth series (titled *Ballando con le Stelle*) aired in January 2009, featuring:

- Maurizio Aiello (partnered by Sara Di Vaira)
- Carol Alt (partnered by Raimondo Todaro)
- Emanuela Aureli (partnered by Roberto Imperatori)
- Stefano Bettarini (partnered by Samanta Togni)
- Corinne Clery (partnered by Chuck Danza)
- Alessio Di Clemente (partnered by Alessandra Mason)
- Metis Di Meo (partnered by Simone Di Pasquale)
- Andrea Montovoli (partnered by Ola Karieva) - Runners-up
- Licia Nunez (partnered by Dima Pakhomov)
- Andrea Roncato (partnered by Vicky Martin)
- Emanuele Filiberto, Prince of Venice and Piedmont (partnered by Natalia Titova) - Winners
- Valentina Vezzali (partnered by Samuel Peron)

The Netherlands

Series one was shown in Summer/Autumn 2005. It featured

- Inge de Bruijn (sportswoman) (partnered by Remco Bastiaansen)
- Joris Lutz (presenter) (partnered by Euvgenia Parakhina)
- Koert-Jan de Bruijn (actor) (partnered by Charissa van Dipte)
- Inge Ipenburg (actress) (partnered by Koen Jan Willem Brouwers)
- Ans Markus (artist) (partnered by Peter Bosveld)
- Irene van de Laar (presenter) (partnered by Marcus van Teijlingen)
- Rudolph van Veen (cook) (partnered by Roemjana de Haan)
- Jim Bakkum (singer) (partnered by Julie Fryer)

Jim Bakkum was eventually declared the winner.

Series two is shown in Winter/Spring 2006. It features:

- Lieke van Lexmond (actress) (partnered by Remco Bastiaansen)
- Winston Post (actor) (partnered by Euvgenia Parakhina)
- Maik de Boer (stylist) (partnered by Charissa van Dipte)
- Myrna Goossen (presenter) (partnered by Koen Jan Willem Brouwers)
- Edsilia Rombley (singer) (partnered by Peter Bosveld)
- Barbara de Loor (speed-skater) (partnered by Marcus van Teijlingen)
- John de Wolf (sportsman) (partnered by Roemjana de Haan)
- Frits Sissing (presenter) (partnered by Julie Fryer)

The finale will be aired 13-05-2006. The two contestants who got this far are Barbara de Loor and Winston Post. The winner was declared Barbara de Loor, who got the highest amount of points from the jury, and most votes as well.

On New Year's Eve 2005, a New Year's special was shown. It featured:

- Catherine Keyl (Presenter) (partnered by Marcus van Teijlingen)
- Tatjana Šimić (actress, model) (partnered by Koen Jan Willem Brouwers)
- Marit van Bohemen (sporter) (partnered by Peter Bosveld)
- Lieke van Lexmond (actress) (partnered by Remco Bastiaansen)
- Bas Muijs (actor) (partnered by Roemjana de Haan)
- Christijan Albers (Formula 1-driver for Spyker-MF1) (partnered by Julie Fryer)
- Hans Klok (partnered by Charissa van Dipte)
- Ernst Daniël Smid (Singer) (partnered by Euvgenia Parakhina)

This was won by Tatjana Šimić and Koen Brouwers

Special Christmas and New Year's Eve 2006, with

- Yolanthe Cabau van Kasbergen (actress) and Peter Bosveld
- Wilbert Gieske (actor) and Roemjana de Haan
- Do (singer) and Koen Brouwers
- Arnold Vanderlyde (bronze medal winner Los Angeles 1984,Seoul 1988, Barcelona 1992) and Charissa van Dipte
- Patricia Paay (member of girl-group the star-sisters) and Remco Bastiaansen
- Bastiaan Ragas (singer/musicalstar) and Julie Fryer
- Eric van Tijn (musicproducent) and Euvgenia Parakhina
- Anita Witzier (presenter) and Marcus van Teijlingen

Do and Koen Brouwers won this special.

On March 31 2007 the third season started. This featured:

- Bart Chabot (writer) and Kimberly Smith

- Christophe Haddad (actor) and Ilse Lans
- Bob de Jong (olympic champion skating) and Euvgenia Parakhina
- Martijn Krabbé (presenter) and Roemjana de Haan
- Lodewijk Hoekstra (TV-gardener) and Charissa van Dipte
- Aukje van Ginneken (actress/singer) and Remco Bastiaansen
- Nikkie Plessen (presenter) and Peter Bosveld
- Fabienne de Vries (former VJ) and Koen Brouwers
- Helga van Leur (meteorologist) and Marcus van Teijlingen

This season was won by Helga van Leur and Marcus van Teijlingen

Scoring charts

week.
  indivates the couple was in the bottom 3.
  indicates the couple in the bottom 2.
  indicates the winning couple.
  indicates the runner-up couple.
  indicates the third place couple.

Team	Place	1	2	1+2	3	4	5	6	7
Jim & Julie	1	29	30	59	**36**	*26*	**36**	28+35=63	*29+36=65*
Irene & Marcus	2	24	31	55	31	**35**	33	33+38=71	**34+37=71**
Inge B & Remco	3	**32**	31	**63**	35	29	31	30+34=64	**38**+*30*=68
Joris & Euvgenia	4	25	*19*	44	24	32	27	*21+25=46*	
Koert-Jan & Charissa	5	*21*	31	52	26	34	28		
Inge I & Koen	6	23	**32**	55	27	*26*			
Rudolph & Roemjana	7	27	25	52	28				
Ans & Peter	8	27	26	**53**					

Team	Place	1	2	1+2	3	4	5	6	7
Barbara & Marcus	1	27	28	55	**35**	30	33	**38+36=74**	*37+32=69*
Winston & Euvgenia	2	30	30	60	29	**38**	35	33+37=70	**38+35=73**
Frits & Julie	3	**32**	27	**59**	33	31	31	32+**40**=72	*29+36=65*
John & Roemjana	4	23	27	50	25	29	22	*31+25=56*	
Lieke & Remco	5	30	**32**	**62**	27	33	31		
Edsilla & Peter	6	30	24	54	32	32			
Myrna & Koen	7	24	*21*	45	*24*				
Mike & Charissa	8	*20*	23	*43*					

Team	Place	1	2	1+2	3	4	5	6	7	8	9
Helga & Marcus	1	27	30	57	31	30	33	33+29=62	31+28=59	*33*+36=*69*	*34+36+38=108*
Christophe & Ilse	2	**32**	**31**	**63**	**35**	**37**	**38**	**40**+34=**74**	**34+36=70**	39+36=75	**38+40+40=118**
Nikkie & Peter	3	29	25	54	30	31	36	34+**39**=73	*28*+33=61	**40**+36=**76**	
Bob & Euvgenia	4	24	23	47	27	27	28	32+27=59	28+27=55		
Martijn & Roemjana	5	29	28	57	30	35	28	36+31=67			
Bart & Kimberly	6	21	21	42	24	25	21				
Aukje & Remco	7	28	29	57	31	34					
Lodewijk & Charissa	8	*16*	20	36	18						
Fabienne & Koen	9	26	30	56							

New Zealand

Winners of Each Series:

- Norm Hewitt and Carol-Ann Hickmore (Season 1)
- Lorraine Downes and Aaron Gilmore (Season 2)
- Suzanne Paul and Stefano Olivieri (Season 3)
- Temepara George and Stefano Olivieri (Season 4)
- Tamati Coffey and Samantha Hitchcock (Season 5)

Norway

The series was named *Skal vi danse? (en: Shall We Dance?)*.

Season 1

The first Season was broadcast in Winter/Spring 2006 on TV 2. It featured:

- Simen Agdestein (chess player/coach) (partnered by Gyda Kathrine Bloch Svela-Thorsen)
- Terje Sporsem (comedian) (partnered by Cecilie Brink Rygel)
- Katrine Moholt (TV hostess) (partnered by Bjørn Wettre Holthe)
- Caroline Dina Kongerud (singer) (partnered by Gustaf Lundin)
- Signy Fardal (publisher and magazine editor) (partnered by Geir Gundersen)
- Finn Schjøll (flower decorator) (partnered by Lena Granaas Lillebø)
- Tom A. Haug (actor) (partnered by Therese Cleve)
- Anita Moen (Former Cross-country skier) (partnered by Thomas Kagnes)
- Otto Robsahm (handyman) (partnered by Michelle Lindøe)
- Guri Schanke (actress and singer) (partnered by Tom Arild Hansen)

The Season Finale took place in March 2006. Winners were TV hostess Katrine Moholt and her partner Bjoern Wettre Holthe.

The professional jury in "Skal Vi Danse"s 1st Season were:

- Trine Dehli Cleve
- Tor Fløysvik
- Anita Langset
- Trond Harr

Season 2

The second Season of *Skal vi danse? (en: Shall We Dance?)* premiered in September 2006. It featured:

- Jeanette Roede, administrative manager. She was partnered by Jan-Eric Fransson
- Trude Mostue, TV-Veterinarian. She was partnered by Tom Arild Hansen
- Christer Torjussen, comedian. He was partnered by Lena Granaas Lillebø
- Elisabeth Andreassen, singer. She was partnered by Mats Brattlie
- Tone Damli Aaberge, singer. She was partnered by Tom-Erik Nilsen
- Susann Goksør Bjerkrheim, former handball-player. She was partnered by Asmund G. S. Grinaker
- Eirik Newth, writer and radio host. He was partnered by Therese Cleve
- Steffen Tangstad, former professional boxer, now a sports manager. He was partnered by Ingrid Beate Thompson
- Kristian Ødegård, TV-producer and comedian/joke host. He was partnered by Alexandra Kakurina
- Ingar Helge Gimle, actor. He was partnered by Gyda Kathrine Bloch Svela-Thorsen

The Season Finale took place on 24 November 2006. Winners were TV-producer/comedian/joke host Kristian Ødegård and his dancing partner Alexandra Kakurina.

The professional jury in "Skal Vi Danse"s 2nd Season were:

- Trine Dehli Cleve
- Tor Fløysvik
- Cecilie Brinck Rygel
- Trond Harr

Isdans

In the spring of 2007, TV 2 will air a programme called *Isdans* (en: Figure Skating)[7], in which six celebrities have been paired with professional skaters. The show is similar to Dancing with the Stars, with the difference being that figure skating rather than ballroom dancing is performed. The participants are:

- Dorthe Skappel, TV show hostess, partnered by Janusz Komendera
- Sandra Lyng Haugen, Artist, partnered by Aleksander Sunde Iversen
- Per Christian Ellefsen, Actor, partnered by Marianne Fjørtoft
- Pål Anders Ullevålsæter, Rally motor cyclist, partnered by Anna Pouchkov
- Anette Bøe, Retired cross-country skier, partnered by Aleksandr Smokvin
- Jim Martinsen, Retired ice hockey player, partnered by Kaja Hanevold

Season 3

The third season was aired in the autumn 2007. It featured:

- Tshawe Baqwa, rapper - Winner
- Esben Esther Pirelli Benestad, transvestite doctor
- Mona Grudt, former Miss Universe
- Pia Haraldsen, TV host
- Trine Hattestad, former athlete
- Finn Christian Jagge, former alpine skier
- Dag Otto Lauritzen, former cyclist
- Mari Maurstad, entertainer
- Jostein Pedersen, TV host
- Liv Marit Wedvik, country singer

Season 4

The fourth season, aired autumn 2008, features

- Hans Petter Buraas, alpine skier - *eliminated 3rd*
- Tor Endresen, singer *eliminated 5th*
- Tore Andre Flo, football player - *runner-up*
- Janne Formoe, actress - *eliminated 1st*
- Mikkel Gaup, actor
- Siri Kalvig, meteorologist
- Hanne Krogh, singer -*eliminated 4th*
- Gaute Ormåsen, singer
- Jenny Skavlan, actress - *eliminated 2nd*
- Sigurd Sollien, TV host - *withdrawn*
- Lene Alexandra Øien, singer and model - *winner*

Poland

The first season of "Taniec z Gwiazdami" ("Dancing with the Stars") aired in Poland on TVN in Spring of 2005, the second in Fall of 2005, the third edition in Spring of 2006, the fourth edition in Fall of 2006, the fifth edition in Spring of 2007, the sixth edition in Fall 2007 and the seventh edition in Spring of 2008. Since September, 7th 2008 the eighth season has been aired.

When on air, every Sunday the average of 5 - 7 million viewers tune in to watch the show. The highest rated episode was the second season finale with over 8 million people watching.

Winners of Each Series:

- Olivier Janiak and Kamila Kajak (Season 1)
- Katarzyna Cichopek and Marcin Hakiel (Season 2)
- Rafał Mroczek and Aneta Piotrowska (Season 3)
- Kinga Rusin and Stefanoo Terazzino (Season 4)
- Krzysztof Tyniec and Kamila Kajak (Season 5)
- Anna Guzik and Łukasz Czarnecki (Season 6)
- Magdalena Walach and Cezary Olszewski (Season 7)
- Agata Kulesza and Stefano Terazzino (Season 8)
- Dorota Gardias-Skóra and Andrej Mosejczuk (Season 9)
- ? (Season 10) TBA

Romania

The show uses the name "Dansez pentru tine" (en: "Dancing for you"). Every pair of dancers is dancing for a cause. The pair is composed of a star and someone affected by the cause (if the cause is helping a person) or a supporter of the cause. The show presents the cause, the training and of course the dancing. The last two pairs in the order given by the jury, will dance next week extra dances and will be eliminated as decided by phone voters (based on the dance or the cause).

According to official Romanian website [8] there have been 8 editions until Summer 2009.

After dancing in the 3rd edition, Andreea Bălan (music star) & Petrişor Ruge participated in Mexico at "Dancing with the Stars World Championship". They danced very well in the local show but didn't win. Instead they took a very good 2nd place in Mexico.

Sweden

The Swedish version is called "Let's Dance" and is produced by MTV Mastiff. The first two seasons were hosted by Agneta Sjödin and David Hellenius, then from season three to current season have Agneta been replaced by Jessica Almenäs. One of the popular judges is the British dance teacher, Tony Irving. The series had a large audience, and with almost 2 million viewers the final gave TV4 the highest rating for that Friday evening. It was the first time since 1997 that TV4 had more viewers than the public service company SVT's perennially popular music game show "Så Ska Det Låta". In September 2006, it won the Swedish equivalent of the Emmy award, Kristallen (The Crystal), in the Entertainment category. The second season started broadcasting in January 2007 and aired every Friday.

Season 1

(January-March 2006) on TV4

- **Måns Zelmerlöw (singer) partnered by Maria Karlsson - WINNERS**
- Anna Book (singer) partnered by David Watson - *runner-up / 2nd place*
- Viktor Åkerblom Nilsson (actor) partnered by Carin da Silva - *eliminated 8th / 3rd place*
- Arja Saijonmaa (singer) partnered by Tobias Karlsson - *eliminated 7th*
- Peppe Eng (sports journalist) partnered by Malin Watson - *eliminated 6th*
- Kishti Tomita (jury member in the Swedish Idol) partnered by Tobias Wallin - *eliminated 5th*
- Tone Bekkestad (Norwegian TV-weather reporter) partnered by Peter Broström - *eliminated 4th*
- Paolo Roberto (former professional boxer) partnered by Helena Fransson - *eliminated 3rd*
- Carolina Gynning (winner of Swedish Big Brother 2004) partnered by Daniel da Silva - *eliminated 2nd*
- Melker Andersson (star chef) partnered by Ingrid Beate Thompson - *eliminated 1st*

Carin da Silva and Daniel da Silva are siblings. Daniel is the older of the two, having been born in 1981; Carin was born in 1984.

Season 2

(January-March 2007) on TV4

- **Martin Lidberg (wrestler) partnered by Cecilia Erling - WINNERS**
- Tobbe Blom[1] (TV-host och magician) partnered by Annika Sjöö - *runner-up / 2nd place*
- Erica Johansson (athlete) partnered by Daniel da Silva – *eliminated 10th / 3rd place*
- Lasse Brandeby (actor) partnered by Ann Lähdet – *eliminated 9th*
- Ebba Hultkvist (actress) partnered by Jonathan Näslund - *eliminated 8th*
- Anna Sahlin (singer) partnered by Tobias Karlsson - *eliminated 7th*
- Yvonne Ryding (Miss Universe 1984) partnered by Tobias Wallin – *eliminated 6th*
- Harald Treutiger (TV-host) partnered by Maria Karlsson - *eliminated 5th*
- Patrick Ekwall (TV-sport reporter) partnered by Carin da Silva - *eliminated 4th*
- Malou von Sivers (TV-hostess) partnered by Björn Törnblom - *eliminated 3rd*
- Mårten Andersson[2] (comedian) partnered by Helena Fransson - *eliminated 2nd*
- Birgitte Söndergaard (actress and artist) partnered by Johan Andersson - *eliminated 1st*

The winners Martin Ledberg and Cecilia Erling became a couple during the running of the show and participated in the Eurovision Dance Contest in 2007 where they ended in a 14th place.

Note 1: Singer and entertainer Markoolio was supposed to compete in the second season, but broke his foot and was replaced by Tobbe Blom.
Note 2: Actor Emil Forselius chose to leave the show before start. Mårten Andersson replaced him.

Season 3

(January-March 2008) on TV4

- **Tina Nordström (TV-chef) partnered by Tobias Karlsson - WINNERS**
- Tony Rickardsson (speedway driver) partnered by Annika Sjöö - *runner-up / 2nd place*
- Karl Petter Bergvall (star of Bonde söker fru (Farmer seeking wife)) partnered by Jeanette Carlsson - *eliminated 10th / 3rd place*
- Danny Saucedo (singer) partnered by Malin Johansson - *eliminated 9th*
- Mats "Matte" Carlsson (TV-carpenter) partnered by Carin da Silva - *eliminated 8th*
- Linda Lampenius (musician) partnered by Daniel da Silva - *eliminated 7th*
- Mi Ridell (actress) partnered by Johan Andersson - *eliminated 6th*
- Richard Herrey (singer) partnered by Cecilia Ehrling - *eliminated 5th*
- Dilba Demirbag (singer) partnered by Tobias Wallin - *eliminated 4th*
- Susanne Lanefelt (TV-exercise instructor) partnered by Björn Törnblom - *eliminated 3rd*
- Tilde Fröling (model) partnered by Alfred Palmgren - *eliminated 2nd*
- Ulf "Uffe" Larsson (actor) partnered by Christina Samuelsson - *eliminated 1st*

Even though Tina Nordström & Tobias Karlsson won Let's Dance, it was Danny Saucedo & Jeanette Carlsson who competed in Eurovision Dance Contest 2008 and finished in 12th place.

Season 4

(Airs Fridays (January 9th - March 27th) 2009) on TV4

- **Magnus Samuelsson (strongman) partnered by Annika Sjöö - WINNERS**
- Laila Bagge (jury member from the Swedish Idol) partnered by Tobias Wallin - *runner-up/ 2nd place*
- Morgan Alling (actor) partnered by Helena Fransson *eliminated 10th / 3rd place*
- Elisabet Höglund (journalist) partnered by Tobias Karlsson *eliminated 9th*
- Niclas Wahlgren[1] (artist & songwriter) partnered by Jeanette Carlsson *eliminated 8th*
- Carl-Jan Granqvist (professor in meal knowledge) partnered by Maria Lindberg *eliminated 7th*
- George Scott (former professional boxer) partnered by Maria Karlsson *eliminated 6th*
- Kitty Jutbring (radiohost) partnered by Anders Jacobson - *eliminated 5th*
- Hasse Aro (journalist & TV-host) partnered by Charlotte Sinclair - *eliminated 4th*
- Magdalena Graaf (author) partnered by Daniel da Silva - *eliminated 3rd (withdrew[2])*
- Isabella Löwengrip (famous blogger) partnered by Jonathan Näslund - *eliminated 2nd*
- Linda Haglund (former Olympic sprinter) partnered by Martin Ragnarsson - *eliminated 1st*

Note 1: Morgan "Mojje" Johansson had to withdraw from the competition due to a heart attack after the first episode. Niclas Wahlgren replaced him.

Note 2: Magdalena Graaf had to withdraw from the competition due to a subdural hematoma.

Judges' scoring summary

The judges in Let's Dance 2009 is Maria Öhrman, Dermot Clemenger, Ann Wilson and Tony Irving.

Green numbers indicate the couples with the highest score for that week.

Red numbers indicate the couples with the lowest score for that week.

indicates the couple eliminated that week.

indicate the couple who was in the bottom two that week.

Team	Place	1	2	1+2	3	4	5	4+5	6	7
Morgan & Helena		22	17	39	25	40	34	74	38	39
Magnus & Annika		15	19	34	29	21	26	47	31	33
Laila & Tobias		18	28	46	25	30	27	57	27	28
Niclas & Jeanette		16	17	33	23	26	16	42	24	28
George & Maria		9	12		8	20	11	31		15
Elisabet & Tobias		13	10	23	16	16	23	39	14	17
Carl-Jan & Maria		4	7	11	6	14	10	24	8	14
Kitty & Anders	8th	5	4	9		16	15		21	
Hasse & Charlotte	9th	8	8	16	16	15	14	29		
Magdalena & Daniel	10th	21	12	33	19	WD				
Isabella & Jonathan	11th	8	13	21	11					
Linda & Martin	12th	14	8	22						

Ukraine

In Ukraine show started at September 2006 on television channel 1+1 under name "Танці з зірками" ("Tantsi z zirkamy") which stands for "Dances With The Stars". The show was hosted by Yuriy Horbunov and Tina Karol. The star contestants were paired with famous Ukrainian dancers, who had won major international competitions. The winners of the show were awarded with the tour to the Rio Carnival, while the runners-up went to the Carnival on Cuba. The show was extremely popular with Ukrainian viewers. The show finale held on the November 26, 2006 had the TV rating of 26.83% with the share of 54.64%, meaning that the quarter of Ukrainian population and more than half of all TV viewers at that moment watched the finale. The show overall was watched by nearly 16 million Ukrainians. The pair of Volodymyr Zelenskyy (leader of a famous Ukrainian comic troupe) and Olena Shoptenko won the main prize.

United Kingdom

In the United Kingdom, where the show originated, it is known as *Strictly Come Dancing*.

United States

The American version of *Dancing with the Stars* premiered in the summer of 2005. Its 9th season began on September 21, 2009.

Winners: (by season)

Season	Celebrity	Professional
1	Kelly Monaco	Alec Mazo
2	Drew Lachey	Cheryl Burke
3	Emmitt Smith	Cheryl Burke
4	Apolo Anton Ohno	Julianne Hough
5	Hélio Castroneves	Julianne Hough
6	Kristi Yamaguchi	Mark Ballas
7	Brooke Burke	Derek Hough
8	Shawn Johnson	Mark Ballas

Other countries

The **Russian** this TV show is called "Танцы со звездами" ("Tantsi so zvezdami", transliterated). The first season, which began in 2005, became extremely popular. Its second season is in progress after a long delay. The format of the show is identical to that of other countries. Each pair is composed of a famous celebrity and a professional dancer.

The **German** show is called *Let's Dance* in English. ("Tanzen wir" in German).

The **Danish** show is called *Vild Med Dans*. Its fourth season ended November 16, 2007.

The **Indian** version is called *Jhalak Dikhhla Jaa*. It was first broadcast in September 2006 on Sony Entertainment Television (SET). A lot of people confuse Dancing With The Stars with *Nach Baliye* [9] which airs on StarPlus [10]. *Nach Baliye* and *Jhalak Dikhhla Jaa* have similar content and presentation but there are minor differences in the concept. The celebrity dancers on *Nach Baliye* are real life couples, and work with an assigned choreographer. The dancers on *Jhalak Dikhhla Jaa* has one celebrity paired with a trained dancer/choreographer. A notice at the end of the show verifies that the *Jhalak Dikhhla Jaa* is indeed a version of *Dancing With The Stars*.

The **Japanese** version is called *Shall We Dance?* It has the same title as the 1996 movie by the same name, but it has no relation to the movie beyond the shared name. Due to the fact that there was already a season-special dancing program, and that and many cast members from it also appeared in the new program, the Japanese version was confused with a regularly-scheduled version of the season-special, rather than its own version of the TV series. This one ran from April 8, 2006, to March 17, 2007.

A **Slovakian** version of the dancing program is called *Let's Dance* (in English), and it was broadcasted by TV Markiza in the autumn of 2006, hosted by Adela Banasova and Martin Rausch (both of them also hosted the program Slovensko hľadá SuperStar on STV in 2005 and 2006). The winners were Zuzana Fialová (a noted Slovakian actress) and Peter Modrovský (a professional dancer).

World Championship

In 2007, the first edition of the Dancing with the Stars World Championship took place. Countries which took part in the event, staged in Mexico, included teams Romania, Argentina, Colombia, Costa Rica, Mexico, Slovakia, Panama, Paraguay and Ecuador. The winner of the event was the host nation, Mexico.

- 1st place - Mexico
- 2nd place - Romania
- 3rd place - Argentina

External links

- http://www.axmo.com/profile_blog.php
- "The Girls of Dancing With the Stars" photo gallery [11] at Maxim.com [12]
- "Reality Dancing" [13] at ContentQuake TV [14]
- Dancing With The Stars Unofficial Blog [15]
- "Dancing with the Stars" [16] at Yahoo! TV [17]
- Australia official website [18]
- (Czech) StarDance ...když hvězdy tančí [19] - Czech Republic official website
- (German) Austria official website [20]
- Belgium official website [21]
- (Spanish) Chile official website [22]
- Finland official website [23]
- Italy official website [24]
- German official website [25]
- India official website [26]
- Israel official website [27]
- Japan official website [28]
- Malaysia official website [29]
- Netherlands official website [30]
- Poland official website [31]
- Official website of first season in Poland [32]
- Official website of second season in Poland [33]
- Official Romanian website [8]
- official website Slovakian version [34]
- Sweden official website [35]
- Turkish version [36]
- Chilean version El Baile en TVN [37]
- Ukrainian official website [38]
- U.S. official website [39]
- Tony Dovolani [40] at Ballroom Dance Channel [41]
- U.K. official website [42]
- Strictly Come Dancing Online and Dancing With the Stars fansite [43]
- *Dancing with the Stars (Australia)* [44] at the Internet Movie Database
- *Dancing with the Stars (US)* [45] at the Internet Movie Database
- Dancing With the Stars at AOL Television [46]
- RealityTV Magazine *Dancing with the Stars* blog [47]
- Top Votes Abc's Dancing with the Stars [48]
- Dancing with the Stars news, photos and videos [49]

- Dancing with the Stars [50] at BuddyTV
- Dancing with the Stars [51] at Biogs
- Dancing with the Stars Recaps and Results [52] at Reality-Tv-Online.com

References

[1] " Strictly 'world's most watched' (http://news.bbc.co.uk/1/hi/entertainment/7719968.stm)". BBC News. 2008-11-08. . Retrieved 2008-11-08.
[2] TV ratings for Australian Dancing with the Stars (http://www.thinktv.com.au/SiteMedia/w3svc371/Uploads/Documents/5e28b79e-2e34-4466-9414-abe544854856.pdf)
[3] http://dancingstars.btv.bg/
[4] Hunan TV press release on the launch of *Strictly Come Dancing* (http://news.hunantv.com/English/FCD/200712/t20071227_24985.html)
[5] http://www.hrt.hr/htv/emisije/plessazvijezdama/
[6] http://it.wikipedia.org/wiki/Ballando_con_le_stelle
[7] Isdans (en: Figure Skating) (http://pub.tv2.no/TV2/magasiner/isdans/article918222.ece) Norwegian
[8] http://dansezpentrutine.protv.ro/
[9] http://starone.indya.com/specials/nachbaliye/index.html
[10] http://starplus.indya.com/
[11] http://www.maximonline.com/Thegirlsofdancingwiththestars/girls_of_maxim/413.aspx?src=GM7070:MD
[12] http://www.maxim.com?src=GM7070:MD
[13] http://realitydancing.contentquake.com
[14] http://contentquake.com
[15] http://dancing-with-the-stars1.blogspot.com
[16] http://tv.yahoo.com/dancing-with-the-stars/show/38456
[17] http://tv.yahoo.com/
[18] http://seven.com.au/seven/dancing
[19] http://www.star-dance.cz/
[20] http://insider.orf.at/dancingstars/
[21] http://www.vtm.be/sterren/
[22] http://programas.tvn.cl/elbaileentvn/2006/
[23] http://www.mtv3.fi/tanssiitahtienkanssa/
[24] http://www.ballandoconlestelle.rai.it/
[25] http://www.rtl.de/tv/letsdance
[26] http://www.setindia.com/shows/shows_inside.php?id=71
[27] http://rokdim.bezeqint.net/
[28] http://www.ntv.co.jp/dance/
[29] http://www.astro.com.my/sehatiberdansa/
[30] http://www.rtl.nl/shows/dancingwiththestars/home/
[31] http://tanieczgwiazdami.onet.pl/
[32] http://tanieczgwiazdami.onet.pl/2edycja/pierwszaedycja.html
[33] http://tanieczgwiazdami.onet.pl/2edycja/
[34] http://www.markiza.sk/letsdance/?77696e=77950
[35] http://www.tv4.se/tvprogram/letsdance/
[36] http://www.showtvnet.com/programlar/bakkimdansediyor/
[37] http://es.wikipedia.org/wiki/El_baile_en_TVN/
[38] http://www.tanci.tv/
[39] http://abc.go.com/primetime/dancing/
[40] http://ballroomdancechannel.com/tony-dovolani
[41] http://ballroomdancechannel.com
[42] http://www.bbc.co.uk/strictlycomedancing/
[43] http://strictlydancing.utopian-totality.co.uk/
[44] http://www.imdb.com/title/tt0434676/
[45] http://www.imdb.com/title/tt0463398/
[46] http://tvshows.aol.com/show/dancing-with-the-stars/SH7473660000/main
[47] http://www.realitytvmagazine.com/blog/dancing_with_the_stars/
[48] http://www.dancingwithstars.info/
[49] http://www.dancingstarfan.com

[50] http://www.buddytv.com/dancing-with-the-stars.aspx
[51] http://www.biogs.com/dancing/
[52] http://www.reality-tv-online.com/dancing-with-the-stars.html

Article Sources and Contributors

Dance *Source*: http://en.wikipedia.org/w/index.php?title=Dance *Contributors*: (jarbarf), --Elle--, 0pulse, 12 Noon, 2004-12-29T22:45Z, 206.63.106.xxx, 37.186, 5678friend, 69me, A. Balet, Abrech, Accurizer, Ace ETP, AdamSpark2007, Adashiel, Adnenlaa, Agel to alive, Agogin, Ahoerstemeier, Aim Here, Ajh16, Akkeresu, Alansohn, Alex LaPointe, Alexofantarctica, Alma Pater, Alphachimp, Altenmann, Amatulic, Amelia The Weird, AmiDaniel, Amog, Amp0207, Ams80, Andreas Kaganov, Andres, Andreworkney, Andy Marchbanks, Andycjp, Angela, Angr, Angus Lepper, Animum, Anitaa, Antandrus, Antonio Lopez, Aphaia, Arpingstone, Artaxiad, Atomiktoaster, Autocratique, Auximines, Axeloide, Balaji, Bardsandwarriors, Bart133, Bartledan, Basz, BeefRendang, Beginning, Bemoeial, BenFrantzDale, BertieBasset, Betacommand, Biggysize, Bill37212, Bitter iris, Bkkbrad, BlastOButter42, Blobglob, Bluezy, Bobo192, Borameer, Borgx, Bovlb, BozoTheScary, Bradeos Graphon, Branbon, BrianY, Brianga, Brion VIBBER, Briséis, BrokenSegue, Brusegadi, Bryan Derksen, Bsdlogical, Bsimmons666, Bsroiaadn, C777, CJLL Wright, COMPFUNK2, Caknuck, Calliopejen, CambridgeBayWeather, Camembert, Camw, Can't sleep, clown will eat me, CanadianLinuxUser, Canadienmonkey, Capricorn42, Captain panda, Causa sui, Cautionsaywhat, Cenarium, Cescsanj, Chasingsol, Chessguydudeman, Chevinki, Chewy lol, Chinesedancer, Christian List, Chuck Smith, Chumki91, Ciaccona, Citicat, Closedmouth, Coffee, Comafibiosa, Cometstyles, CommonsDelinker, Complex (de), Condem, Conversion script, Cosettey, CrookedAsterisk, Crossoveranx, Crystallina, Csari, Cswrye, Ctjf83, Curps, DVD R W, Dafyd, DanMS, Dance City, DanceScape, Danceguide, Danceoff, Dancer english99, Dancerlnh, Dancersrock9211, Dancewat12, Danceweb, DancingPenguin, Danicools, Danny, Danny-w, Danski14, Dark Shikari, DarkAudit, Dave6, David spector, Dawn Bard, Dbachmann, DeadEyeArrow, Deeptrivia, Dekisugi, Den fjättrade ankan, Deor, DerHexer, Dina, Discospinster, Disneycat, Dmcq, DoctorW, Dod1, DoubleBlue, Douglas Whitaker, Dramaticme, Dreadlady, Drsloth, Durova, Dysepsion, E Wing, ERK, ESkog, EVula, EarthPerson, Eclectic hippie, Edancer, Eddie.willers, Edit teh treez, El C, El Krem, Ela112, Elipatwood, Emc2, Enviroboy, Epbr123, Erc, Erebus555, Eric-Wester, Ericorbit, Escape Orbit, Esprit15d, Eternally Devoted To Jesus, Ethongdog, Evercat, Everyking, Ewawer, Explicit, Exploding Boy, Exq bea, Fabiform, Fang Aili, Fastcars00, Feezo, Fieldday-sunday, Fiet Nam, Fjbfour, Flewis, Fluffyaragorn, FlyingToaster, Fplay, Franamax, Frankiefrankie, Freedom skies, FreplySpang, Frogman541, Frosty0814snowman, Funglufn, Futurebird, Galaxiaad, Geneb1955, General Jazza, Giggles95, Gilliam, Gimmetrow, Glacier Wolf, Glamorous-indie-rock-n-roll-95, Glen, Glenn, Gogo Dodo, Gogodancer123, Golbez, GoneAwayNowAndRetired, Goodnightmush, Graceferguson, GraemeL, Greatgavini, Greg Lindahl, GregLindahl, Gregfitzy, Gristow, Gtstricky, Guaka, Gunnar Hendrich, Gurch, Gurchzilla, Guy Peters, Gwernol, H1es-, Hadal, Hamedog, Harriv, Hatch68, Hdt83, Hgilbert, Hongooi, Howcheng, Htaccess, Hu12, Husond, Hut 8.5, Hyacinth, Hydrogen Iodide, IAMTHEEGGMAN, II MusLiM HyBRiD II, IRP, Iain99, Idril, Ignatzmice, Ilovedaddymartinez, Iloveyou0726, Iloveyou4477, Imaninjapirate, Imipolex, Indon, Indosauros, IndulgentReader, Infrogmation, Inge-Lyubov, Inklein, Inter16, Invinciblechampion, Iran2, Irish Souffle, It Is Me Here, Ixfd64, J.delanoy, JDubman, Jacek Kendysz, Jaerok, Jakethelad, Jam1444, Jamesontai, JanessaKK, Jean11221122, Jeffhos, JenkinzTCW, Jennavecia, Jeremyb, Jerzy, Jess b, JesseW, Jesus Saves!, Jfdwolff, Jfracchia, Jianrong95, Jim bob05, Jimmy, Jkelly, Jkiddo24, Jleo181, Jlocalled, John254, Johndburger, Johnhenry312, Jongleur100, Jonyshin, Joshua Issac, Joyous!, Jredmond, Jtalledo, Juliancolton, Justinfr, Jvhertum, JzG, KJS77, Kaihsu, Kajasudhakarababu, Karenjc, Kayla182, Kchishol1970, Kdrinnen, Keilana, Kenny sh, Kerowyn, Kevin Breitenstein, Kimchi.sg, Korg, Kpjas, Kristen Eriksen, Kroevyn, Kubigula, Kulshrax, Kumarrajendran, Kungfuadam, Kungming2, Kurt Shaped Box, Kuru, Kurykh, La Pianista, Lala, Lala696969, Lambtron, Lanma726, Largoplazo, Lars Washington, Laurenlotz, Lavrentii, Leafyplant, Learntodance, LeaveSleaves, Leonariso, Lexor, Lightmouse, Lights, Lindmere, Llort, Logical2u, Lowellian, Lozzykj, Lradrama, Luna Santin, Lunkwill, Lycurgus1920, Lyellin, MBisanz, MER-C, MK8, MZMcBride, MacTire02, Macy, Madangry, Magnus Manske, Mahitgar, Maitch, Man vyi, Mani1, MantisEars, Marianocecowski, Mark K. Jensen, Martin S Taylor, Matt.smart, Mattcornell, Matthew Auger, Mattisse, Mav, McSly, Medgrlsc, Megleesmith, Mel Etitis, MeltBanana, Mendaliv, Mendel, Merchbow, Mexcellent, Mfield, Michael Hardy, Michael Rawdon, Midnightcomm, Mietchen, Mike Rosoft, Miranda, Mischler96, Miskatonic, Misterconginialtastical, Misterx2000, Mitico, Mo0, Monkey123456789, Montrealais, Moomoomoo, Morenooso, Moriori, Morphious142777, Moverton, Mr. moose, MrOllie, Mrholybrain, Mrlopez2681, Mrmuk, Mufka, Mukadderat, Muzoben, Mwanner, Myznt, NHRHS2010, NSR77, Nae'blis, Nagy, Nakon, NastalgicCam, Natalie Erin, Nauticashades, NawlinWiki, Neesha C, NeoChaosX, Neurolysis, Neutrality, Neverquick, Nevilley, Newly, Newsaholic, Nexus Seven, NickBush24, Nivix, Nlu, Nokia288, NotJackhorkheimer, Nunh-huh, Nv8200p, Obli, Ohka-, Olof, Onthedancefloor, Orange-bum-cleavage, Oroso, Orrelly Man, Ottis05, Owen, Oxymoron83, P4k, PMDrive1061, Pamboersma, Parkjunwung, Pathaugen, Patrick, Patrick-br, PatrickJ83, Paul foord, Pax:Vobiscum, Pearle, Pedro, Penniedreadful, Pethan, Pharaoh of the Wizards, PhilipMW, Piano non troppo, Pigman, Pigsonthewing, Pingku, Pink!Teen, Pnkrockr, Pojunis, Pooki, Pooky1234567890, Postdlf, Pretzels, Primate, Proffessor Hugh, Prokopenya Viktor, PrometheusX303, PseudoSudo, Pseudoserpent, Psy guy, PubliusFL, Puli, Pumeleon, Pvmoutside, Qxz, R'n'B, R. S. Shaw, RHaworth, Ramachandran24, Ranveig, Rdeknijf, Rdsmith4, RedWolf, Regibox, Retiono Virginian, Rettetast, RexNL, RichardF, RickK, Rlitwin, Robertgreer, RodC, Roguelibrarian, Roland2, Romanm, Romanskolduns, Roshanak, Rossami, RoyBoy, Royalguard11, RyanCross, Ryulong, S3000, SBKT, SDC, Salsa Shark, Sam 1123, Samay2, Sandstein, Sanya, Saoshyant, SatuSuro, SchuminWeb, Sean D Martin, Sean William, Secretlondon, Seemagoel, Seifabdoun, Seraphim, Serlin, Sfacets, Sfdan, Shakeitdo, Shanes, Shell Kinney, Shirulashem, SiobhanHansa, Sita ram7, Sj, Sjakkalle, Skarebo, Skeetch, Skeleton m, Skier Dude, Slowking Man, Smalljim, Soman, Someone42, Spellcast, Squiddy, StAkAr Karnak, Stainless steel, Steeev, SteinbDJ, Stephen G. Brown, Stephen Gilbert, Stephenb, Steve Pucci, Steven Zhang, Stwalkerster, Subdolous, SuperDude115, SuperSkannie, Susice, Swollib, Symane, THEN WHO WAS PHONE?, Tachyon01, Tagishsimon, TalentRock, Talkie tim, Tarheelz123, Tempodivalse, Terrytheunwantedspider, Texture, Thatoneguyuknow, Thaurisil, The Shadow-Fighter, The Transhumanist, The Transhumanist (AWB), TheMeEvan, TheRanger, ThierryVignaud, Thingfive, Thingg, Thrashmetal4, Throwing, Tiles, Timir2, Tinkeramy4, Tnxman307, Torontodance, Travel2dance, Trevor MacInnis, Tyrenius, Unit, Until It Sleeps, Usedbook, Useight, Utcursch, Vanish2, Vansice, Vectro, Veinor, Verkhovensky, Versageek, Versus22, Vilerage, Virtual Cowboy, Voxpuppet, Walden, Walor, Wapcaplet, Ward3001, Warda45, Wayward, WereSpielChequers, Wesredhawk, Wetman, Whitewolf1679, Wiki alf, WikiBone, Wikiklrsc, Will.i.am, Wimt, Window, Wintran, Wknight94, Wookie planet, Work permit, Wutt, Wålberg, Xevi, Xezbeth, XxDangerDangerxx, Yartamis, YeaaBoii, Yintan, Ykhwong, Ynhockey, Yodalover, YourEyesOnly, Yugarunadhar, Yvwv, Zigger, Zingdoodle, Zoe, Zsinj, Zundark, Александр, 1365 anonymous edits

Motion (physics) *Source*: http://en.wikipedia.org/w/index.php?title=Motion_%28physics%29 *Contributors*: 2384213, Abhishek, Addshore, Alansohn, Algebraist, Anameforwiki, Andres, AndrewHowse, Anthony, Antonio Lopez, Arnesh, Atamyrat, Avono, Babakathy, Bakken, Banus, Black and White, Bobo192, Bomac, Borgx, Boud, BrokenSegue, Bruyninc, Buzybeez, Callipides, CanadianLinuxUser, Canaima, Chowbok, Chuy1530, Cjmnyc, Cometstyles, Conversion script, D6, Da monster under your bed, Danleo, Dead paulie, Deb, Dell12342, Denaje, Dominus, Dougofborg, Doyley, Dr Dec, EPM, ESkog, Earthdirt, East718, Edcolins, Eliyak, Eloc Jcg, Emoloisirc, Epbr123, Esanchez7587, EscapingLife, Evil saltine, Excirial, Exteray, F3meyer, FiddyCent, Flewis, GB fan, GDonato, Georgia guy, Georgiabiker, Giftlite, Glacialvortex, Gogo Dodo, Gram123, Guiltyspark, Gurch, HalfShadow, Hashimi, Headbomb, Heisenbergthechemist, HexaChord, Hirohisat, Husond, IRP, Igorwindsor, J.delanoy, J04n, JBellis, JaGa, Jaranda, Jerzy, JiangL90, Jj137, JoeSmack, Jredmond, KathrynLybarger, Kbh3rd, Keilana, Kingboyk, Kolyma, Kroevyn, L33th4x0rguy, La goutte de pluie, Lambiam, Laogeodritt, Lar, Latka, LeaveSleaves, Leuqarte, MagneticFlux, Mahanga, Matthew Yeager, Mbell, Mentisock, MetsFan76, Michaelas10, Mnbitar, Morqueozwald, Most-wanted124, Mxn, Neutrality, NewEnglandYankee, Newbyguesses, Nk, Oleg Alexandrov, Oscabat, Panoptical, Paolo.dL, Pauli133, Peak, Persian Poet Gal, Peterlin, Philip Trueman, Pkbharti, Psychonaut, Pyfan, Quibik, Qxz, Ravneetgill, Red Bowen, RexNL, Ridethesnow, Rjanag, Robert P. O'Shea, Robert Skyhawk, Ronhjones, SMC, Samw, Sceptre, Scetoaux, Scientizzle, Seans Potato Business, Skwisgaar skwigelf45, Slicedoranges, Steve Pucci, SteveOOMB, TakuyaMurata, Tang Wenlong, The Transhumanist, Thingg, Thinradred9, Tide rolls, Tim Ivorson, Tim Q. Wells, Tom harrison, Troy 07, VASANTH S.N., Voyagerfan5761, WadeSimMiser, Wadems, Waraba, Warofdreams, Wesaq, Whitepaw, WikiNetti3, WojciechSwiderski, XJamRastafire, Xiong Chiamiov, Yurik, Zigger, 321 anonymous edits

Performance *Source*: http://en.wikipedia.org/w/index.php?title=Performance *Contributors*: 16@r, 3Coins, ACupOfCoffee, Alansohn, Andycjp, Angela, AnnaP, Anyep, Argon233, Bahar101, Bardsandwarriors, BarretBonden, Bart133, Branddobbe, CALR, Cfailde, Chris the speller, ChrisCork, Cstubbies, Danfrost, Danyoung, Davin, DeadEyeArrow, Diddi, Dlcstory, Dolphin51, Drbreznjev, Dunse, El C, Elf, Esrever, Fg2, Grafen, Grebaldar, Grotendeels Onschadelijk, Gypsiesoul420, Hah4545, Harry Potter, Hohum, Hyacinth, Ilyasozgur, J04n, JoJan, Jonnyp68, Josh Parris, Katieh5584, Laftronic, Levineps, LiDaobing, MER-C, Macaddct1984, Martpol, Mboverload, Michael Hardy, Miquonranger03, Mr. Lefty, MrMacMan, N2e, Natalya, Papa Lima Whiskey, Patrick, Pearle, Pedant17, Philip Trueman, Quadell, Rich Farmbrough, RyanCross, Sesshomaru, Sfdan, Simon12, Skarebo, Snoyes, Someguy1221, SpK, StaticGull, Struthious Bandersnatch, Tarquin, Thseamon, Until It Sleeps, UtherSRG, Zigger, Zzuuzz, 74 anonymous edits

History of dance *Source*: http://en.wikipedia.org/w/index.php?title=History_of_dance *Contributors*: A. Balet, Adelesse, AgnosticPreachersKid, Altenmann, Alyaly94, Amazins490, Andreas Kaganov, Andrew Parodi, AnonGuy, Antialias, Ascending Star Dance, Aspects, Barticus88, Basketball110, Bibi Saint-Pol, Binksternet, Caerwine, Caltas, Ccacsmss, Chodorkovskiy, Clubmarx, D6, Darkfred, Defrenrokorit, Deltabeignet, Dfrg.msc, Discospinster, DropDeadGorgias, El C, Ela112, Elassint, Falk47, Flockmeal, Flyguy649, Galithia, Geoffr, Gimboid13, GlassFET, Gogo Dodo, Golbez, IRP, Igiffin, Insouciance, J.delanoy, Khoikhoi, Kubigula, Lahiru k, Lexor, Luna Santin, Lydss, Lyellin, Lyricmac, Malerin, MatchDancer, MrFizyx, NawlinWiki, Nehrams2020, Ohka-, Omnipaedista, Onlyt tooth, ParkerHiggins, Paul foord, Pigsonthewing, Pwqn, RexNL, Rise Above the Vile, Rubicon, S3000, Sannse, Seemagoel, Tagishsimon, ThierryVignaud, Thomas Ludwig, Tylarw2006, Ubermuffin, Ultrapowerbeyond, Until It Sleeps, Versus22, WODUP, Waggers, Winerock, ZX81, Zereshk, Zoicon5, 217 anonymous edits

Choreography *Source*: http://en.wikipedia.org/w/index.php?title=Choreography *Contributors*: 100110100, Ahoerstemeier, AlbertSM, Alfred Dengan, Altenmann, Amit A., Andrea.gf, Armeria, Atomiktoaster, Bardsandwarriors, Borgx, Bruce1ee, COMPFUNK2, Can't sleep, clown will eat me, Caper13, Catherine breillat, Ckatz, Dantadd, Dawn Bard, Dbachmann, Dfrg.msc, Discospinster, Disneycat, Drhaggis, Drini, Edcolins, El C, Fosnez, Gbern3, Germaine01, Ginkgo100, Ginsengbomb, GraemeMcRae, Graham87, Gurch, Island, J.delanoy, JForget, Jcrock, Jiddisch, Jimp, Jlin, Kalathalan, Kingpin13, Kukini, Kungfuadam, Lambtron, Littleolive oil, Magioladitis, Mani1, Marek69, Matthewflorence, Matturn, MeltBanana, Mendaliv, Michael Hardy, Morphious142777, Mothmolevna, MsDivagin, Neelix, Nihonjoe, Nopira, Nsaa, Ohka-, Onebyone, Onlyt tooth, Panda, Paul foord, Postdlf, Quentin X, Radagast83, Riceflan, Robertgreer, Robina Fox, Sevela.p, SlimVirgin, Spike Wilbury, StephanieWilkinson, Stephenb, Stevekeiretsu, Subitosera, SynchronizedSkating, Terathe, Thailek, Tientao, Ukexpat, Viriditas, Vonkje, Wars, Wayland, Woohookitty, Ynhockey, 137 anonymous edits

Dance therapy *Source*: http://en.wikipedia.org/w/index.php?title=Dance_therapy *Contributors*: Addshore, Altenmann, AndrewCarey, Ashleyy osaurus, B9 hummingbird hovering, Bonniemeekums, C.Fred, CarrieT, Chx1975, Daniel1177, Deli nk, Devonian Strata, Dmcq, Dspradau, El C, FreeKresge, Gaius Cornelius, Greenrd, Hu12, J04n, Jlittlet, JohnCD, Landon1980, Larmeniox, Laurel719, Leontes, Loydenk2, Lumos3, MER-C, MarcoTolo, Mattisse, Meco, Ohka-, Ohnoitsjamie, Onebravemonkey, Onodevo, Ot, Paul foord, Piano non troppo, Samdance, Shirar18, Tabletop, Template namespace initialisation script, Twinkling, Woohookitty, Xtian59, 52 anonymous edits

Health risks of professional dance *Source*: http://en.wikipedia.org/w/index.php?title=Health_risks_of_professional_dance *Contributors*: Cayte, CerealBabyMilk, Dmcq, Editor at Large, Geniac, Keitei, Kenneth M Burke, Miraclebaby, Myznt, Nateland, Paul foord, Puddhe, Radagast83, Rjwilmsi, Sedonaarizona, Slhogan94, Sumahoy, Tainter, Vary, Werdna, Woohookitty, 14 anonymous edits

Dance in India *Source*: http://en.wikipedia.org/w/index.php?title=Dance_in_India *Contributors*: 11K, A.Ou, Ahoerstemeier, Ashwinijaya, Bharatanatyam scholar, BrokenSegue, Charles Matthews, Chopper Dave, CommonsDelinker, Danceteacher333, DigitallyBorn, Dwaipayanc, Ekabhishek, Emperor Genius, Enigma Blues, Eric-Wester, Gail, Gaius Cornelius, Gnanapiti, Gurch, Guruchandrasekharan, Harianand3, Incidious, JForget, Jagged 85, Jayajaya, Kajasudhakarababu, Katieh5584, Maedin, MarcAurel, Moonriddengirl, Neelix, Padmanabhan1, Paul foord, Pooja Narang, Pranathi, Rasanubhava, Redheylin, Seemagoel, Shruti14, Tariq25, Themfromspace, Tis2k, Tsemii, Venu62, Warofdreams, Wavelength, Wmahan, کشرز, 83 anonymous edits

Dances of Sri Lanka *Source*: http://en.wikipedia.org/w/index.php?title=Dances_of_Sri_Lanka *Contributors*: Aazathm, Aelfthrytha, Barticus88, Beano, CambridgeBayWeather, Chamal N, Edward, Ela112, Elonka, G41rn8, Guroadrunner, Hazel77, Kirrages, Laudak, Mattisse, Mild Bill Hiccup, Netmonger, Oxymóron83, Paul foord, Senero, Shanes, The Rambling Man, Vishvax, 15 anonymous edits

Concert dance *Source*: http://en.wikipedia.org/w/index.php?title=Concert_dance *Contributors*: Altenmann, Ccacsmss, Classicfilms, Crazy-dancing, Cswrye, Dan Pelleg, Danny lost, Enviroboy, Exq bea, Gogo Dodo, Hgilbert, Jan11989, Kcordina, Lambtron, Lkinkade, Mimihitam, Ohka-, Onlyt tooth, Paul foord, Piano non troppo, Roland2, Scraggy1978, Sdream93, Signalhead, Sluzzelin, Tabletop, Tufkaa, Unschool, Wintran, 14 anonymous edits

Ballet *Source*: http://en.wikipedia.org/w/index.php?title=Ballet *Contributors*: *drew, 7, @pple, A Softer Answer, A. B., AKeen, ALargeElk, Abberley2, Adam Carr, Adrian.benko, Aeon1006, Ah Boon King, Ahirzel, Ahoerstemeier, Ahubbard2012, Aksi great, Alansohn, Alasdair, Allstarecho, Altenmann, Amandatim, Amitch, AnKrol, Andrarias, Andre Engels, Andreagritton, Angela, Angusmclellan, Anne226, Annrules, Anomalocaris, Anonymous anonymous, Antandrus, Antique Rose, Antonrojo, Antopi, Appleattic, Appleboy, Arienh4, ArtEnvOrg, Atomiktoaster, Avnjay, Az1568, BETM, Bagatelle, Baiji, Ballerina15, Ballet2m, Balletdancerch, Balletprincess69, Bart133, Beach000, Big Bird, Bigbigbigdog, Biopresto, BitterMan, Blanchardb, Blehfu, Bob Burkhardt, Bobo192, Bonadea, Bongwarrior, Bookermorgan, Bookgrrl, BorgQueen, Brain control, Breno, Briaboru, Brian Kendig, Brianga, BrokenSegue, Btharper1221, Buttsrule132, C.Fred, C45207, CIreland, CJ, CWY2190, Calabraxthis, Calliopejen1, Caltas, Caltrop, Calvin 1998, Camembert, Camw, Can't sleep, clown will eat me, Can't wake, clown will vomit me, CapitalR, Capricorn42, Captain B, Catgut, CatherineMunro, Catherinedemedici, Cayte, Ccacsmss, Celithemis, CerealBabyMilk, Charlieb63, Cherry19, Chillum, Cholmes75, Chrestomanci, Chris421234567890, Christianw7, Chumki91, Ckatz, Clayoquot, Closeapple, Closedmouth, CloudNine, Coffee, CommonsDelinker, Condem, Crazy-dancing, Cryptic, Csari, Curps, Cxz111, Cyan, D. D. Recorder, DMacks, DWarrior, DanceScape, Danceguide, Danceoff, Dancer1234567890, Dancercoaster, Dancerman, Dancinginmagic, DanielCD, Danndylion00, Danzadance, DarkFalls, Darkhallsredfloors, Darth Panda, Dasani, David Sneek, Dawn Bard, DeadEyeArrow, Dekaels, Dell1995, Delldot, Denny, DennyColt, DerHexer, Dethme0w, Dfrg.msc, Diane 85, Dipics, Disavian, Discospinster, DocWatson42, Doctormatt, Donarreiskoffer, Dori, DorisH, DoubleBlue, Dougofborg, DougsTech, Dprestonwiki, Drini, Dsmdgold, Ductape, ESkog, Earthmuscle, Eclecticology, Ecurran, Editor at Large, Ehheh, Ekmtap, El C, ElizBallet@verizon.net, Ellolovelyy, Enviroboy, Epbr123, Epolk, Eras-mus, Ericjlee, EscapingLife, Excirial, Explicit, Exq bea, Ez212, Faithcote, Falcon21893, Faradayplank, Fashionslide, FayssalF, Femto, Fenice, Ferdyg, Finnegar, Fraggle81, Frode Inge Helland, Funandtrvl, Fvasconcellos, GRider, GT5162, GUllman, Gadfium, Gail, Galoubet, Garion96, Gavriliada, Gazimoff, Gene Nygaard, General Wesc, Germaine01, Ghirlandajo, Ghét màu đỏ, Gidonb, Gilliam, Gimmetrow, Gjd001, Gogo Dodo, Golab17, Graham87, Grahamec, Green day obsessed, Greg Lindahl, GrooveDog, Gscshoyru, Gurch, Gutsul, Gzornenplatz, Hannahc999, Harry Wood, Haukurth, Hektor, Hemmingr, Hersfold, Hhielscher, Hyacinth, II MusLiM HyBRiD II, Iammaxus, Iamtheultimatenoob, Ian Pitchford, IceDragon64, Imogenation, Indrian, Inferno, Lord of Penguins, Infrogmation, Instinct, Iokseng, Iridescence, Iridescent, Irock2007, Isocephaly, Ixfd64, J.delanoy, JForget, JFreeman, JLaTondre, JNW, JaGa, Jacek Kendysz, Jake Wartenberg, Janka, Jaranda, Jchthys, Jennifu, Jessirex, Jhfireboy, Jimmy Society, Jimpaz, Jirt, Jklin, Jmaynard, Jnivekk, Joanjoc, Joel7687, Joethepyro, Johannesjones, John254, Johnhenry312, Jojhutton, Jon Awbrey, Jon helgem, Jonojet, JorgeGG, Joyous!, JuJube, Jwissick, JzG, KC0ZHQ, Kaare, KaragouniS, Karol Langner, Katharine Kanter, KathyAnne, Kbh3rd, Kdrinnen, Keilana, Keitei, Keith D, Kenneth M Burke, KeybladeSephi, Khatru2, KinczelA, Kingpin13, Klinkyclaire, Kmg90, Kocio, Kocsonya, Kpjas, Kubigula, Kurykh, Kw93, Kylu, LOL, La Pianista, Labeasley, LachlanA, LadyEarth, Laj168, Lambiam, Lambtron, LarRan, Lardman, Lauracs, Lawilkin, LibLord, Lisalars, Luke dillon, Luna Santin, Lupo, Lyellin, MER-C, MPerel, Mailyn, Malcolm Farmer, Mannelamies, MartinC, Marysays, Masqueunadanza, Matt Deres, Matthew Stannard, Maurreen, Mav, Maxcrean, McSly, MegA, Melaen, Melburnian, Melissaguerramanzo, MeltBanana, Mercury, Michael Hardy, Mintleaf, Miraclebaby, Missmarple, Mkeranat, Moeron, Montrealais, Mordant21, Mordkin, Movetheframe, Mpaluszek, Mrlopez2681, Mrwojo, Mschel, Mvasaly, Myanw, Mygerardromance, Naddy, NaminesPetals, Navy Blue, NawlinWiki, Neverquick, NigelR, Nivelon, Nrswanson, Nubiatech, O1ive, Octahedron80, Oda Mari, Ogg, Ohka-, Olderbeast83, Omicronpersei8, Onathinwhiteline, Onlyt tooth, Ontopic, Opelio, Open2universe, Oxymoron83, PDH, PMDrive1061, Pacaro, Paiskar, Panchitaville, Parishan, Parkwells, Pathaugen, Paul foord, Pcpcpc, Perkmashin, Peteb16, Philip Trueman, Phmerz, Piano non troppo, Picaroon, Poccil, Poeloq, Poshoeda, Possum, Prashanthns, Prolog, Prom3th3us, Puchiko, Puddhe, Puplover4, Puremitch, Pwqn, Qatter, Queenofthewilis, Quentin X, Quintote, R'n'B, RHB, RJN, Rachelle4731, Radagast83, Ramita, Raydarnbead, Rayuwish, Rdikeman, Read-write-services, RedCoat10, RedWolf, ReeceW93!, RegentsPark, RexNL, Rhobite, RickK, Rjeezy, Rlitwin, Rmhermen, Rnrfstar, Robert Merkel, RobertG, Robertgreer, Robogun, RodolfoPiskorski, RogDel, Roland2, Romanm, Rudys, RupertMillard, ST47, Sam Korn, Sandahl, Sanfranman59, Sapita, Sarah w-j, Sasha Callahan, Sceptre, Schoen, SchuminWeb, Sciurinæ, Scjessey, Sclaster1, Scythian99, Sephiroth BCR, Sexy love123, Sfmammamia, Shanel, Shorething000, Simon12, SimonP, Skiracer0093, Slhogan94, SlimVirgin, Smalljim, SmartGuy, Smartybutt1234, Smb1001, Snowolf, Snoyes, Snud Swimp, Someone else, Spike Wilbury, Spiraling, Spitfire, Splash, Springeragh, Squirepants101, Staffwaterboy, Stamboultrain, StephanCom, Stephenb, Steven Zhang, StitchHasGlitch, Stizz, Stoboe, Sud-Pol, Sue Michael Canuck, Sunderland06, SuperSkannie, Sweetiecoco, Sweetness46, Symane, TFriesen, THEN WHO WAS PHONE?, TUF-KAT, Tawker, Techman224, Tempodivalse, The Anome, The Fiddly Leprechaun, TheBallerinaDoll, Thefunkygibson, Thingg, Thumperward, Tide rolls, Tinderface, Tizio, Tmg1107, Tobycat, Tohd8BohaithuGh1, TomPhil, TomTheHand, Totorotroll, Tresiden, Tufkaa, Tylarw2006, Ubermuffin, Ulric1313, Unsy770, Until It Sleeps, Urmumisfat, Versus22, Voyagerfan5761, Vsmith, W1k13rh3nry, Wallie, Waterjuice, Wavelength, Weeliljimmy, Weirdy, Whopkins1, WideArc, Wiki alf, WikiTyper2009, Wikiscient, WillDarlock, WillWikiWontWiki, William Avery, Williamb, Willking1979, Wknight94, Wolfrock, Woohookitty, Wtmitchell, Wwwmute, Xed, Yiyikatie, Yourmama, Yuckfoo, Zadcat, Zaheen, Zaslav, Zeimusu, Zidane tribal, Михајло Анђелковић, 1475 anonymous edits

20th century concert dance *Source*: http://en.wikipedia.org/w/index.php?title=20th_century_concert_dance *Contributors*: Altenmann, Bobblewik, Chris the speller, Classicfilms, Hraefen, Ohka-, Paul foord, Timo Honkasalo, Topbanana, 4 anonymous edits

African-American dance *Source*: http://en.wikipedia.org/w/index.php?title=African-American_dance *Contributors*: Aitias, Altenmann, Anna Lincoln, Backslash Forwardslash, Bluemoose, Bobblehead, Crystallina, D, Dbtfz, Deeceevoice, Discospinster, DoubleBlue, Elonka, Epbr123, Eric-Wester, Ethanlbrooks, Futurebird, Gogo Dodo, Ifasehun, Jakah, Jersey Devil, Jlittlet, Kollision, KrissyJ, Leontes, N00bcannonball, Nikai, Omnipaedista, Paul foord, Peecee1978, Penniedreadful, Pharos, PlainJane, Rees11, Saga City, Sardanaphalus, Srushe, Steve Pastor, The Man in Question, Wintran, Wtmitchell, Yahel Guhan, Ytrottier, Yungeddie1, Zoicon5, ZooFari, 94 anonymous edits

Ballroom dance *Source*: http://en.wikipedia.org/w/index.php?title=Ballroom_dance *Contributors*: 21655, 2D, 65.13.223.xxx, AKeen, Aaron charles, AdjustShift, Alexthe5th, Altenmann, AnakngAraw, Andrewrp, Angela, AnnaFrance, Aranel, Backbaychef, Bajamircea, Balroomdancing, Balthazarduju, Barticus88, Beginning, Ben James Ben, Benwildeboer, Bll6969, Bobblewik, Bobo192, Bonadea, Borisblue, Brian Crawford, Bus stop, Caltas, Camw, CanisRufus, Capricorn42, Caroline.marshall, Celarnor, Celithemis, Chris421234567890, Chumki91, Classic1010, Codey53, Cometstyles, Conversion script, Cool3, Csari, Cswrye, Ctballroom, D-Rock, D6, Dance Business, DanceScape, Danceoff, Dancingmagician, Dantadd, Dekay, Deltabeignet, Deltasquared, DoctorW, Dominick, DoubleBlue, DragonflySixtyseven, Durova, Faeryty, Fenice, Filipe de Moraes Paiva, Flappychappy, Flyguy649, Fremsley, FreplySpang, GabeOdess, Gamgee, Gavri, Gerrit, Gig Guide, Gilliam, Graham87, Grayfair, Griffinofwales, Gurch, Habj, HaltonRattlesnake, Hyacinth, Icono Clast, ImperatorExercitus, Infrogmation, Ixfd64, J.delanoy, JaGa, Jack in the green, JanCK, Java7837, Jordan1000, KRRK, Kalamkaar, Kazubon, Khazzhar, King of Hearts, Koreth, Kosebamse, KyleDantarin, Lambtron, Lang rabbie, Largoplazo, Latka, Ld100, Learntodance, Lilweezy123, Loonymonkey, Lowellian, Lunkwill, Lyellin, Màcdonald-ross, Madangry, Marcika, Mariánocecowski, Martin451, McSly, Mdebets, MegX, Merphant, Mervyn, Michael Hardy, Michael Snow, Miskatonic, Mpalais, Mrh30, MuZemike, Mwanner, NAHID, Neutrality, Nightstallion, Niteowlneils, Nneonneo, Oliana, Onlyt tooth, Orinoco-w, Oxymoron83, ParisianBlade, Patstuart, Pawebster, Pearle, Pepe123456789, Persian Poet Gal, Plau, Porfitron, Pschemp, Qu3a, Quaternionic, Quidam65, Quill, RG2, RTC, RagnarokG, Researchassistant2006, Rich Farmbrough, Riveira2, RobertG, Robina Fox, Rogpyvbc, Roland2, Romanm, Rror, Salli, Sedasa, Sfdan, Sinii, Skyewitt, Smb1001, Spangineer, Staeiou, StaticGull, Stuartyeates, Svenji, TEB728, Tangopaso, Tempodivalse, Tendancer, Tis rin, Tohd8BohaithuGh1, Trevor MacInnis, Tualha, Turnstep, Until It Sleeps, Versageek, Vina, Voyagerfan5761, WISo, Waggers, Wallie, Wj32, WriterHound, Wuzzy, Xevious, Yke, Zigger, Zoicon5, יבצ לאינד, 396 anonymous edits

B-boying *Source*: http://en.wikipedia.org/w/index.php?title=B-boying *Contributors*: B.s.n.R.N., Deli nk, Draeco, Gbern3, Jennnsterrr, Licriss, Mrernesto, Myominane, Tide rolls, Wintran, 25 anonymous edits

Dancesport *Source*: http://en.wikipedia.org/w/index.php?title=Dancesport *Contributors*: Altenmann, Alx skinner, Anclation, Anoko moonlight, Aranel, Bwesseling, Caroline.marshall, Chumki91, Clarityfiend, Clockwork Laser, Csari, D3, DanceScape, DanceSportFriend, Danssport, Davidwr, Docrx, Dravecky, Dycedarg, Esrever, GalaxiaGuy, Ged UK, Gragox, JLaTondre, Just Another Dan, Lambtron, Landon1980, Lyellin, Macdonald-ross, Mickidk, Moogle, Mountforddrive, Mrh30, Mushroom Man, Niteowlneils, Nitsansh, Oda Mari, Orpheus, Paul foord, Perakhantu, Piechjo, Pilou4, Quarl, Quicksilvre, Rcstretch, Rjwilmsi, Skeleton m, Smb1001, Spangineer, Welsh, Yandman, Yoggysot, Zogin, 63 anonymous edits

Krumping *Source*: http://en.wikipedia.org/w/index.php?title=Krumping *Contributors*: Aaron Brenneman, Aazn, Abc4, Academic Challenger, Accurizer, Aderylak, AeroIllini, Agnte, Aiken fever, Aitias, Alansohn, AlexTG, Altenmann, Amcbride, Andreas Toth, AndrewHowse, AnnaAniston, ArielGold, Arru, Asa Winstanley, Atama, Az1568, Backpackadam, Backslash Forwardslash, Barneca, Bartledan, Bboyzheng, Bdve, Beetstra, Belovedfreak, Belthazor696, Bikeable, BillC, Bitchen, Bobo192, Bosox822, Bsadowski1, Bubba hotep, Bucked, CWii, CaNNoNFoDDa, Cacycle, Can't sleep, clown will eat me, CanadianLinuxUser, CanisRufus, Catapult, Catgut, Cenarium, Chairman S., Charles Matthews, Chasingsol, Ched Davis, Chimaera156, Chinasaur, Chopper99, Chozen1, Christopher Parham, Ckatz, Cmdrjameson, Coin945, Compton city g, Corvus cornix, DNewhall, Dafyd, Dakinijones, Dalecki, DancingMan, Dangerousnerd, Dardorosso, Darth Panda, Deathawk, Declare, Deewhite, Delbert Nagle, Deon, Dinkytown, Dodo von den Bergen, Doniago, Doulos Christos, Download, EchoBravo, Eclipse08, EdiTor, Editor2020, Eggymusic, Elassint, Element ag, Eli lilly, Elliotharmon, Epbr123, Esanchez7587, Esperant, Etkh1, Euchiasmus, EvKnight13, Footballfan190, FreplySpang, Fusionall, Fuzzygerdes,

GQsm, Gadfium, Gbern3, Gewat, Gidonb, Gilliam, Giroro60, Gman124, Gobonobo, Gogo Dodo, Graevemoore, Greudin, Groyolo, Grübzück, Gtg204y, Gulley07, Gurch, Gwernol, Gzkn, HSOtrumpet1, Hadal, HaltonRattlesnake, Harland1, Hendrix67, Hipster21, Hjh123, Hokieguy001, Hu12, Husond, Hydrogen Iodide, Hypnochimp, ICAPTCHA, Icestorm815, Icewedge, Icseaturtles, IdLoveOne, Ilija Pavlic, Iloveparis, Iridescent, Irsobuck, J Milburn, J.delanoy, Jaganath, Jamesooders, Javguerre, Jedravent, JesseGarrett, JetLover, Jkyoung, JohnnyCalifornia, Johnnymiller, Jon Rob, Jpgordon, Jr hollywood, Junius49, JustAGal, KConWiki, Kaed9285, Kaiser matias, Karlhendrikse, Kate, Kcordina, Keilana, Keke101092, Kellywatchthestars, Kemalaysel, Kgroover, Kloud916, KnowledgeOfSelf, Kodster, Kotra, Krumper72, Kummi, Kyrun, LAX, Laserszandjon, Lectonar, Leodrome, Leonard^Bloom, LilHelpa, Lilrafe, Lindsey8417, Liveste, Luna Santin, Luva90, Lyriclover911, MBisanz, Marek69, Masamage, Matrx10503, Mazca, Mbryanton, Mike Rosoft, Mikeblas, Mikelieman, Mitchell Stevenson, Mjblink, Molly1234, Mrf, Muntuwandi, NPswimdude500, Nakon, NeilN, Netkinetic, Niteowlneils, Nivix, Nootau, Nuttycoconut, Orasis, Outasync, Oxymoron83, PFHLai, PTSE, Pandacomics, Patriarch, Paul foord, Pearle, Pedant, Persian Poet Gal, Peruvianllama, Petersam, Philip Trueman, Piano non troppo, Pinoygatas, Plasticup, Plusman, Pnkrockr, Pteron, Puckly, Pyrogenix, RainbowOfLight, Razorflame, Rees11, Renice, Reviloliver, RexNL, Rgoodermote, RiRiDazzel, Robomaeyhem, Rockero, RodC, Ronhjones, RoyBoy, Rror, Ruff HoodRat, Runtime, S3000, SMC, Saaga, Schneelocke, Ser Amantio di Nicolao, Skier Dude, Smarties775, Snori, Snowolf, SoWhy, Sorelle, Spartaz, Stezton, Sturm55, Stwalkerster, Super-Magician, Szabolcs, T for Tendetta, Tagishsimon, Ted87, Teemeah, Tennekis, Tevildo, That Guy, From That Show!, The wub, TheDJ, Thedeadlypython, Thehelpfulone, Themightyquill, Thingg, Thomas Hopkins, Throop, Tim Ivorson, Titoxd, Toby Woodwark, TomCerul, Trivialist, Triwbe, Ttiotsw, Underwater, Until It Sleeps, User529, Utcursch, Versus22, Voyagerfan5761, WDavis1911, WETaylor, Wainstead, Waterspyder, Wendiesel, Whirlingdervish, WiFiWalrus, Willking1979, Wimt, Wintran, Woohookitty, Yakksoho, YoungAnarchy, ZS, Zro, 永, 1157 anonymous edits

Kandyan dance *Source*: http://en.wikipedia.org/w/index.php?title=Kandyan_dance *Contributors*: AtulaSiriwardane, Blackknight12, BuddhikaD, Chanakal, Edward, Elagatis, John, JustAGal, Lahiru k, Lanka7, Lucky number 49, Melchoir, Morquendi, Parsecboy, Paul foord, Sudeshm, Svm1 63, Welsh, 27 anonymous edits

Irish dance *Source*: http://en.wikipedia.org/w/index.php?title=Irish_dance *Contributors*: 30.215, 64.218.173.xxx, A bit iffy, ABF, Academic Challenger, Aetheling, Ahoerstemeier, Aitias, Ale jrb, Alexand875, Alison, Altenmann, Antiuser, Antonio Lopez, Ardfern, Argyriou, Awickert, Bagatelle, Banes, Bboy14, Beaumont, Becky Sayles, Bmicomp, Bobo192, Bonadea, Booyabazooka, Bridgetwow13, C2r, CSProfBill, Caltas, Calvin 1998, Canterbury Tail, Captain-tucker, Caspian blue, Ceilt101, Celarnor, CelticSeimi, Chase me ladies, I'm the Cavalry, Chris the speller, ClemMcGann, Closedmouth, Coco Fontana, Cometstyles, Conti, Conversion script, Corcairlus, Craig Stuntz, Cryptoid, Crystallina, Cuchullain10, Daboombest, Dancegal100, Dancerules, DarkAudit, Darkar, Dcdancer859, Decumanus, Deeptrivia, Dellkw, Demiurge, Deor, Derek Ross, Di4gram, Diberri, Donncha77, Dougiehowlett25, Download, Dpm64, Drkshadowmaster, Dycedarg, EamonnPKeane, Ecarn4225, Egil, Epbr123, Eric-Wester, Fanuilos, Folk Life, Fyz-en, Gaff85, Gail, George The Dragon, Georgelikesboys, Ghilliegal, Gilliam, Gogo Dodo, Gold heart, Graham87, Gramscis cousin, Greybeard, Grievous Angel, Guyclone, Huntster, Hydrogen Iodide, Ian Pitchford, Irishdancing, Irishdancingbabe, Irishguy, Isilelentari, Ixfd64, J.delanoy, JForget, John, Joyous!, Jpbowen, Juliancolton, KYSoh, Kateshortforbob, Kcflood, Kerowyn, Kilclaren, Kirrages, Kitchner, Krellis, Kukini, Kwamikagami, Lambtron, Larry_Sanger, Leah Mayotte, Leuko, LittleOldMe, LongZ, Lostinletterkenny, Lovelylisa90, Luk, Lupin, Lyellin, Mais oui!, Maithcailin, Martin Kozák, Mav, Maximillion, McSly, MelForbes, MichaelH99, Microtony, MiddleEarth, Mimijackson, Mlouns, Mopyboy, Moriori, Mulcher, Munci, Mygerardromance, Neelix, Newcastle Irish Set Dancers, Njg, Norm, Nuclare, Numbo3, Ogg, Ohnoitsjamie, Omicronpersei8, P3net, Paul Magnussen, Phaedriel, PhilKnight, Pishogue, Plugwash, Ponder, Prairie dancer, Prodego, Prolog, Pschemp, Raven in Orbit, Rebi13, Red blaze, Reel.dancer, Reelgirl, Rgamble, RickK, Rincemom, Rinceoir, RitaBar, Rjm656s, Rjstott, Scoilrince, Sdgdenise, Seamasmac, SfsuStudent, Shoaler, Smile4pink3, Stifle, Superfopp, Swwarmuth, THEN WHO WAS PHONE?, Tcncv, Teashark, Teddyzapoodle, Thebrooklet, Thingg, Thryduulf, Tim!, TimNelson, Tobias Hoevekamp, TreadLightly, Trinitywriter, TruthbringerToronto, Valerieadeam, Veinor, Vesperholly, Viriditas, Vishahu, Watch As I Wander, Wavelength, Xezbeth, Zhukora, Zora, 646 anonymous edits

Indian classical dance *Source*: http://en.wikipedia.org/w/index.php?title=Indian_classical_dance *Contributors*: A Ramachandran, A. B., AA, AKA MBG, Abhinavagupta, After Midnight, Ahoerstemeier, Altenmann, Anitaa, Annamacharya51, Anthony Appleyard, Ashokaloof, Buddhipriya, Chaipau, Chumki91, CommonsDelinker, DanceExpert, Dobromila, Giraffedata, Gnanapiti, Goethean, Govender U.J, H1es-, Hegades, Icairns, JaGa, Jafer3, Jag Ju, Jayajaya, Kaberi, Kerowyn, King of Hearts, LordGulliverofGalben, Madan Img, Mahayogini, Mwanner, Natyakr, Natyayogini, Ncmvocalist, Paul foord, Raguks, Ramachandran24, Ranireji, Rasmus Faber, Redheylin, Rlandmann, Robert1947, Rupa Srikanth, Salih, Samsoonah, Sangeetapriya, Santap, Sfacets, SiobhanHansa, Soumyamji, SteinbDJ, Tamilselvam, Tariqabjotu, The Sunshine Man, Thunderboltz, Timichal, Tschild, Until It Sleeps, Utcursch, Vajaram, Viriditas, Yogagates, అహ్మద్ నిసార్, 63 anonymous edits

Modern dance *Source*: http://en.wikipedia.org/w/index.php?title=Modern_dance *Contributors*: 206.63.106.xxx, Accounting4Taste, Ahoerstemeier, Allstarecho, Altenmann, Amakuha, Amberrock, Amcbride, Andre Engels, Andrew Parodi, Angela, AnnaP, Aruam.Aruam, Azer Red, BMF81, Bartonpoulson, Bkonrad, Blackbyrus, Bmiller1109, Bobby1011, Bobo192, BrianGV, Caco de vidro, CanisRufus, Chris the speller, Ckatz, Classicfilms, Community88thStreet, Conversion script, Coppertwig, Crazy-dancing, DabMachine, Dancingbeenie, Danndylion00, David Shankbone, DavidLevinson, Dekisugi, Dfrg.msc, Dralwik, Earlypsychosis, Eclecticology, Elmo1, Elonka, Enviroboy, Epbr123, Esanchez7587, FastLizard4, Filll, FordPrefect42, Fredrik, Gladiolii2, Graymornings, Gregfitzy, Grunt, Gurch, HaeB, Halibutt, Harmil, Haskellbronson, Ikeeverett, J. Van Meter, J.delanoy, JRHorse, JamesMLane, Jbailey, Joel7687, Jonojet, Josh Parris, Jpers36, Jpgordon, Jsecret11, Jweinbe0, Keesiewonder, Keitei, Larry_Sanger, LeaveSleaves, Leontes, Lethe, Lexor, Lotrtkdchic, Lyellin, Mackensen, Maximus Rex, Metamagician3000, Mjwaxman, Mmoneypenny, Modernist, Montrealais, Natkeeran, NawlinWiki, Number1spygirl, Ohka-, Oxymoron83, Paul foord, Paullisa, Politepunk, Quercusrobur, Rachelle4731, RedWolf, Riceflan, Roland2, Romanticcynic, Rookkey, SDC, Sam Hocevar, Sanbeg, Secret cracker, Seraphimblade, Serein (renamed because of SUL), Seth Ilys, Shalom Yechiel, Sheynhertz-Unbayg, Shimgray, Spartan, Spreck, Staffwaterboy, Stagehand, StaticGull, Steven Walling, Stirling Newberry, The cattr, Thingg, Ticklemepinkfor, Tide rolls, Timeineurope, Tm8992, Tomchiukc, Ubermuffin, Vina, Wmahan, Woohookitty, Wrp103, Yair-haklai, Z10x, ZoBlitz, יבצ לאינד, 250 anonymous edits

Rock and Roll (dance) *Source*: http://en.wikipedia.org/w/index.php?title=Rock_and_Roll_%28dance%29 *Contributors*: Altenmann, Chris19910, Cswrye, Danssport, Discospinster, EivindJ, FreeKresge, Gaius Cornelius, Gurch, Hoof Hearted, J.delanoy, JLaTondre, Jake Wartenberg, Kallidroni, Kicking222, Lyellin, Mukadderat, Nintendude, Oxymoron83, Paul foord, Pavel Vozenilek, Pengo, Pretzels, Sleske, Steve Pastor, The cattr, Vanderkruit, Zandperl, 59 anonymous edits

Dance squad *Source*: http://en.wikipedia.org/w/index.php?title=Dance_squad *Contributors*: Achangeisasgoodasa, Animal cookie, CG124, Clarenceville Trojan, Darth Mike, Dfrg.msc, Elmo5159, Ewlyahoocom, Fanficgurl, Guyforsports, Jademushroom, Joe21, Kmonin, Lambtron, Libertywr, Meke13, MsDivagin, NawlinWiki, Nihonjoe, Od Mishehu, Skoban, Stifle, Tarheelz123, Yamla, 43 anonymous edits

Dancing with the Stars *Source*: http://en.wikipedia.org/w/index.php?title=Dancing_with_the_Stars *Contributors*: 23skidoo, A Nobody, Aakashoza, AaronWK, Adabow, Aiyda, Ajaysreedharan, Alan Liefting, Alansohn, Alex.muller, AllKellyMonaco, Allissonn, Altenmann, Altzinn, Alyssa kat13, Anaghabhat, Anonymous Dissident, Anthony Dean, Anung Mwka, AriGold, Arpingstone, Art LaPella, Atlasvan, Aussietv, AxG, Azumanga1, B.s.n.R.N., B1mbo, Baby Luigi, Back2the50s, Bartledan, Beccariota, Benzy19, Bgnkid, Big Bird, Biruitorul, BleuDXXXIV, Bluap, Bonalaw, Bookandcoffee, Boyau, Brandenburg, Burliegh, CASE, Cacau Toledo, Camo1992, Can't sleep, clown will eat me, Carolus2006, Catgut, CeeGee, Ceyockey, Chandler, ChicosBailBonds, Chivista, Ckatz, Closedmouth, Cnwb, Colonies Chris, Conn, Kit, Cooliocheck1, Cristybepfan1, Cromag, DONOVAN, Dale Arnett, Dancter, DannyZ, Danski14, Danzigland, Dario1250, DarkFireYoshi, Darz Mol, DeadEyeArrow, Deanb, Deinaked, DeltaGoodremFan, Derek Ross, Dessysaurus, Devlin adl, Discospinster, Domino theory, Dondfan998, Dramatic, Dreadstar, Drork, Dsreyn, Dudesleeper, Dunaszerdahely, DutchTreat, Dycedarg, E. Ripley, Eagle2ch, Edward321, El estudiante, Elmo1, Enpitsu, Everyguy, Evil Monkey, ExRat, Ezeu, Facu 25del10, Fakus Edition 2008, FamousDance, Ferdinand h2, Ferpunk, FireInMySoul, FordPrefect42, FredFix, Gaius Cornelius, Galaxiaad, Gary King, Gianluca91, Giornada, Gleba, Gman814, Gottago, Gpie944, Gragox, Gregoryhelen77, Harland1, Hello4321, Hermione1980, HexaChord, Hookoo, Hu12, Ian Pitchford, Ianblair23, Insanity Incarnate, Irishguy, JaGa, Jacobandkyra, JamesB3, JamesMLane, JamesTeterenko, Jezorn, JimmB, Joaq0, John wesley, Jonohill, Jorgebarrios, Jw21, Jxan3000, KF, Kanabekobaton, Kanthony39us, Kappa, Karl Smart, Kay444, King of Hearts, Kirev, Kiteinthewind, Kman543210, Knightfan2000, Knowledgeman800, Korg, Krisblank, Kurt Shaped Box, LOL, Laca, Lakeyboy, Lambertman, Lancini87, Latka, Latka1, Leebo, Lefferage, Legitimate, Lemonflash, Lenci10, Lightmouse, Lilac Soul, Ling.Nut, Lizg, Lochok, Loft, Longhair, Lpoggi, LukaP, Lumos3, Luwilt, M-le-mot-dit, M.R.Forrester, M.nelson, MASWJ, Maahn, Maltmomma, Manderr, Manscher, Marianin, Marvin Monroe, Marybdn, Mattbrundage, Matthew kokai, Maxamegalon2000, Mb731, Mccain.blogging, Meno25, Mhking, Michfreak, MilanRuffian, MissIzzy, Mitsukai, Moondyne, Mpr1234, MrFinland, Mrschimpf, Muéro, Mxcatania, NYC2TLV, Nakon, Nazarian1, Ndenison, Neelix, Netkinetic, Nholling, Nicklachey472, Nn123645, Nording, Northgrove, Ntsimp, Nukualofa, Nv8200p, Nynurse, Nz26, ONEder Boy, Obli, Ohmyn0, Ohthelameness, Oobopshark, Oohoui1123, OrangeDog, Ospinad, Otto4711, Pafcool2, Palazov, Pardy, Pascal.Tesson, PatrikR, Paul Erik, PaulHanson, Paxik, Permafrost, Peter McGinley, Philip Stevens, Pimlottc, Piranna, Pmsyyz, Porfitron, PowerCS, Przepla, Quintote, R7604, RMM77, Rama's Arrow, Raymond Cruise, Recurring dreams, Reinthal, Revth, Rich Farmbrough, Rionescu13, Rmhermen, Robinepowell, Rodrigosama, Roke, RonGrail, Rsrikanth05, Sanfranciscotreat, Shaizakopf, Sharon105, Silver Edge, Sing66, Skierpage, Slawojarek, Slj, Slumgum, SoWhy, Soczewa, Sohollywood, Spiky Sharkie, Spring12, Strangnet, Straps, Strum that guitar, Syrthiss, Szyslak, T, TKLM, TPIRFanSteve, Tbone, The emm, TheTruthiness, Thobiah, Tigerfur, Tinlinkin, Tkynerd, Tntnnbltn, TommieDrash, Tony164, Transity, Triping, TseiTsei, Turnstep, Unclemikejb, Veggiehead, Violetriga, Vizcarra, W guice, WLU, Wahkeenah, WaldoChump, Walther, Wasted Time R, WereSpielChequers, WestlifeWoman, WikHead, WikipedianMarlith, Willgunton, William Avery, Woohookitty, World Indexer, Wrc666, Wtshymanski, Wwfanz, Xavier Martín, Xcentaur, Xiabravery, XinJeisan, YUL89YYZ, Yakudza, YellowMonkey, Zanimum, Zarevak, Zingostar, Zloblewoble, Zouhi, 1169 anonymous edits

Image Sources, Licenses and Contributors

Image:Two dancers.jpg *Source*: http://en.wikipedia.org/w/index.php?title=File:Two_dancers.jpg *License*: Creative Commons Attribution 2.0 *Contributors*: Barry Goyette from San Luis Obispo, USA
File:Il Ballo2.jpg *Source*: http://en.wikipedia.org/w/index.php?title=File:Il_Ballo2.jpg *License*: unknown *Contributors*: Giuseppe Piattoli
Image:Phenakistoscope 3g07690b.gif *Source*: http://en.wikipedia.org/w/index.php?title=File:Phenakistoscope_3g07690b.gif *License*: unknown *Contributors*: Origamiemensch, Selket, Trialsanderrors, 1 anonymous edits
Image:Pierre-Auguste Renoir 146.jpg *Source*: http://en.wikipedia.org/w/index.php?title=File:Pierre-Auguste_Renoir_146.jpg *License*: Public Domain *Contributors*: AndreasPraefcke, Infrogmation, Irish Pearl, Mattes, Olivier2, Ribberlin, Tangopaso
Image:MIT 2006 Standard Prechamp Final 2.jpg *Source*: http://en.wikipedia.org/w/index.php?title=File:MIT_2006_Standard_Prechamp_Final_2.jpg *License*: unknown *Contributors*: Nathaniel C. Sheetz
Image:HavanaDancers2.jpg *Source*: http://en.wikipedia.org/w/index.php?title=File:HavanaDancers2.jpg *License*: Public Domain *Contributors*: User:Jongleur100
Image:nonkudri.jpg *Source*: http://en.wikipedia.org/w/index.php?title=File:Nonkudri.jpg *License*: Public Domain *Contributors*: Kumarrajendran
Image:morris.dancing.at.wells.arp.jpg *Source*: http://en.wikipedia.org/w/index.php?title=File:Morris.dancing.at.wells.arp.jpg *License*: Public Domain *Contributors*: Arpingstone, ClemRutter, Man vyi, 1 anonymous edits
File:Harlekin Columbine Tivoli Denmark.jpg *Source*: http://en.wikipedia.org/w/index.php?title=File:Harlekin_Columbine_Tivoli_Denmark.jpg *License*: unknown *Contributors*: AndreasPraefcke, DionysosProteus, Editor at Large, Goldfritha, Hebster, Lucarelli, Malene, Mattes, Wst
Image:Westlake Center Dancers.jpg *Source*: http://en.wikipedia.org/w/index.php?title=File:Westlake_Center_Dancers.jpg *License*: unknown *Contributors*: User:Rootology
Image:Leaving Yongsan Station.jpg *Source*: http://en.wikipedia.org/w/index.php?title=File:Leaving_Yongsan_Station.jpg *License*: unknown *Contributors*: Danleo, FREEZA, J o, LERK, 아§, 1 anonymous edits
File:Kanyewestdec2008.jpg *Source*: http://en.wikipedia.org/w/index.php?title=File:Kanyewestdec2008.jpg *License*: GNU Free Documentation License *Contributors*: User:Mfield
Image:Phil Stacey (cropped, full shot) - 071118-N-1644C-007.jpg *Source*: http://en.wikipedia.org/w/index.php?title=File:Phil_Stacey_(cropped,_full_shot)_-_071118-N-1644C-007.jpg *License*: Public Domain *Contributors*: Anthony Casullo
Image:Accordion Bass.jpg *Source*: http://en.wikipedia.org/w/index.php?title=File:Accordion_Bass.jpg *License*: Creative Commons Attribution 2.0 *Contributors*: Ellmist, JoJan, Strangerer
File:Veiled dancer Louvre Myr660.jpg *Source*: http://en.wikipedia.org/w/index.php?title=File:Veiled_dancer_Louvre_Myr660.jpg *License*: Public Domain *Contributors*: User:Jastrow
Image:Raghs-isfahan.jpg *Source*: http://en.wikipedia.org/w/index.php?title=File:Raghs-isfahan.jpg *License*: Public Domain *Contributors*: Mick Knapton, Zereshk
Image:Pietro Longhi 060.jpg *Source*: http://en.wikipedia.org/w/index.php?title=File:Pietro_Longhi_060.jpg *License*: Public Domain *Contributors*: AndreasPraefcke, Diomede, GeeAlice, Irish Pearl, Mattes, Warburg
Image:Yamini Reddy kuchipudi.jpg *Source*: http://en.wikipedia.org/w/index.php?title=File:Yamini_Reddy_kuchipudi.jpg *License*: Creative Commons Attribution 2.0 *Contributors*: Ramesh Lalwani
Image:Classical_indian_dance_11.jpg *Source*: http://en.wikipedia.org/w/index.php?title=File:Classical_indian_dance_11.jpg *License*: GNU Free Documentation License *Contributors*: Indian Dance, Jmabel, Pieter Kuiper
Image:Bolywood.jpg *Source*: http://en.wikipedia.org/w/index.php?title=File:Bolywood.jpg *License*: Creative Commons Attribution-Sharealike 2.0 *Contributors*: Ekabhishek, FlickreviewR, Indianhilbilly, Martin H., Mattes, Ranveig, Varunbhandanker
Image:Edgar Germain Hilaire Degas 005.jpg *Source*: http://en.wikipedia.org/w/index.php?title=File:Edgar_Germain_Hilaire_Degas_005.jpg *License*: Public Domain *Contributors*: Alter Mandarine, AndreasPraefcke, Emijrp, 1 anonymous edits
Image:New York State Theater by David Shankbone.jpg *Source*: http://en.wikipedia.org/w/index.php?title=File:New_York_State_Theater_by_David_Shankbone.jpg *License*: unknown *Contributors*: David Shankbone
Image:Wiener Staatsoper Schwanensee Szene Akt4.jpg *Source*: http://en.wikipedia.org/w/index.php?title=File:Wiener_Staatsoper_Schwanensee_Szene_Akt4.jpg *License*: GNU Free Documentation License *Contributors*: User:PeterGerstbach on de.wikipedia
Image:Ballet-dancer 01.jpg *Source*: http://en.wikipedia.org/w/index.php?title=File:Ballet-dancer_01.jpg *License*: Creative Commons Attribution 2.5 *Contributors*: Stano Novak
Image:Pas de deux 01.jpg *Source*: http://en.wikipedia.org/w/index.php?title=File:Pas_de_deux_01.jpg *License*: Creative Commons Attribution 2.0 *Contributors*: FlickreviewR, Man vyi, 555
Image:wikisource-logo.svg *Source*: http://en.wikipedia.org/w/index.php?title=File:Wikisource-logo.svg *License*: logo *Contributors*: Nicholas Moreau
Image:20th-century-concert-dance.png *Source*: http://en.wikipedia.org/w/index.php?title=File:20th-century-concert-dance.png *License*: unknown *Contributors*: Original uploader was Ohkaat en.wikipedia
Image:AmericaAfrica.svg *Source*: http://en.wikipedia.org/w/index.php?title=File:AmericaAfrica.svg *License*: GNU Free Documentation License *Contributors*: User:Fibonacci, User:Interiot
Image:Vernon and Irene Castle2.jpg *Source*: http://en.wikipedia.org/w/index.php?title=File:Vernon_and_Irene_Castle2.jpg *License*: Public Domain *Contributors*: Johnston, Frances Benjamin, 1864-1952, photographer.
Image:Gaskellball02282006.JPG *Source*: http://en.wikipedia.org/w/index.php?title=File:Gaskellball02282006.JPG *License*: unknown *Contributors*: User:Miskatonic
Image:Galliard.jpg *Source*: http://en.wikipedia.org/w/index.php?title=File:Galliard.jpg *License*: Public Domain *Contributors*: Original uploader was Primetime at en.wikipedia
Image:fredginger.jpg *Source*: http://en.wikipedia.org/w/index.php?title=File:Fredginger.jpg *License*: unknown *Contributors*: D7240, PrinceCharming, Rossrs, TheDarkArchon, 4 anonymous edits
Image:Rumba_2005_nationals_champ_latin.jpg *Source*: http://en.wikipedia.org/w/index.php?title=File:Rumba_2005_nationals_champ_latin.jpg *License*: GNU Free Documentation License *Contributors*: User:Tendancer
Image:2005 ballroom dance championships.JPG *Source*: http://en.wikipedia.org/w/index.php?title=File:2005_ballroom_dance_championships.JPG *License*: unknown *Contributors*: Porfitron
Image:MIT 2006 Latin Intermediate.jpg *Source*: http://en.wikipedia.org/w/index.php?title=File:MIT_2006_Latin_Intermediate.jpg *License*: unknown *Contributors*: Nathaniel C. Sheetz
Image:120843583 e22b153125 o.jpg *Source*: http://en.wikipedia.org/w/index.php?title=File:120843583_e22b153125_o.jpg *License*: Creative Commons Attribution-Sharealike 2.0 *Contributors*: Tashiya Mirando from Sheffield, United Kingdom
Image:Downrock.jpg *Source*: http://en.wikipedia.org/w/index.php?title=File:Downrock.jpg *License*: Creative Commons Attribution 2.0 *Contributors*: FlickreviewR, Gbern3, Malo
File:Corro Bboying Battle.jpg *Source*: http://en.wikipedia.org/w/index.php?title=File:Corro_Bboying_Battle.jpg *License*: Public Domain *Contributors*: User:Ventobb
File:GrillaStep-Krump.jpg *Source*: http://en.wikipedia.org/w/index.php?title=File:GrillaStep-Krump.jpg *License*: Creative Commons Attribution 2.0 *Contributors*: Andrew Braithwaite from Melbourne, Australia
File:Sri Lanka traditional drum.jpg *Source*: http://en.wikipedia.org/w/index.php?title=File:Sri_Lanka_traditional_drum.jpg *License*: Creative Commons Attribution 2.0 *Contributors*: Steve Evans from India and USA
Image:As31.jpg *Source*: http://en.wikipedia.org/w/index.php?title=File:As31.jpg *License*: Public Domain *Contributors*: AtulaSiriwardane
Image:Kandyan-Drummer.jpg *Source*: http://en.wikipedia.org/w/index.php?title=File:Kandyan-Drummer.jpg *License*: Public Domain *Contributors*: AtulaSiriwardane
Image:Nilame-Kandy-pagent1.jpg *Source*: http://en.wikipedia.org/w/index.php?title=File:Nilame-Kandy-pagent1.jpg *License*: Public Domain *Contributors*: AtulaSiriwardane
Image:Kandy-peraharaTN.jpg *Source*: http://en.wikipedia.org/w/index.php?title=File:Kandy-peraharaTN.jpg *License*: Public Domain *Contributors*: Atula Siriwardane
Image:DSCN0044_irishdancers_e.jpg *Source*: http://en.wikipedia.org/w/index.php?title=File:DSCN0044_irishdancers_e.jpg *License*: GNU Free Documentation License *Contributors*: User:Decumanus
Image:Shramore Set.jpg *Source*: http://en.wikipedia.org/w/index.php?title=File:Shramore_Set.jpg *License*: unknown *Contributors*: Cuchullain10
Image:Irish 138.jpg *Source*: http://en.wikipedia.org/w/index.php?title=File:Irish_138.jpg *License*: Public Domain *Contributors*: Deeptrivia, Nikesrunner, 2 anonymous edits
Image:Bharatanatyam 44.jpg *Source*: http://en.wikipedia.org/w/index.php?title=File:Bharatanatyam_44.jpg *License*: GNU Free Documentation License *Contributors*: User:Siebrand
Image:Indian-dance.png *Source*: http://en.wikipedia.org/w/index.php?title=File:Indian-dance.png *License*: GNU Free Documentation License *Contributors*: Sri Devi Nrithyalaya

Image Sources, Licenses and Contributors

File:Two dancers.jpg *Source*: http://en.wikipedia.org/w/index.php?title=File:Two_dancers.jpg *License*: Creative Commons Attribution 2.0 *Contributors*: Barry Goyette from San Luis Obispo, USA

Image:Batsheva Dance Company by David Shankbone.jpg *Source*: http://en.wikipedia.org/w/index.php?title=File:Batsheva_Dance_Company_by_David_Shankbone.jpg *License*: unknown *Contributors*: David Shankbone (attribution required)

Image:Resistance modern dance andrew parodi.jpg *Source*: http://en.wikipedia.org/w/index.php?title=File:Resistance_modern_dance_andrew_parodi.jpg *License*: GNU Free Documentation License *Contributors*: User:Andrew Parodi, User:Riceflan

File:Rocknroll-dancing-somersault-worldgames2005.jpg *Source*: http://en.wikipedia.org/w/index.php?title=File:Rocknroll-dancing-somersault-worldgames2005.jpg *License*: unknown *Contributors*: User:sleske

File:Rocknroll-dancing-swan.jpg *Source*: http://en.wikipedia.org/w/index.php?title=File:Rocknroll-dancing-swan.jpg *License*: unknown *Contributors*: User:sleske

File:Dancing With the stars world map3.png *Source*: http://en.wikipedia.org/w/index.php?title=File:Dancing_With_the_stars_world_map3.png *License*: Public Domain *Contributors*: User:ArturM

File:Flag of Mexico.svg *Source*: http://en.wikipedia.org/w/index.php?title=File:Flag_of_Mexico.svg *License*: Public Domain *Contributors*: User:Nightstallion

File:Flag of Romania.svg *Source*: http://en.wikipedia.org/w/index.php?title=File:Flag_of_Romania.svg *License*: Public Domain *Contributors*: AdiJapan

File:Flag of Argentina.svg *Source*: http://en.wikipedia.org/w/index.php?title=File:Flag_of_Argentina.svg *License*: Public Domain *Contributors*: User:Dbenbenn

VDM publishing house ltd.

Scientific Publishing House

offers

free of charge publication

of current academic research papers, Bachelor's Theses, Master's Theses, Dissertations or Scientific Monographs

If you have written a thesis which satisfies high content as well as formal demands, and you are interested in a remunerated publication of your work, please send an e-mail with some initial information about yourself and your work to *info@vdm-publishing-house.com*.

Our editorial office will get in touch with you shortly.

VDM Publishing House Ltd.
Meldrum Court 17.
Beau Bassin
Mauritius
www.vdm-publishing-house.com

GNU Free Documentation License Version 1.2, November 2002

Copyright (C) 2000,2001,2002 Free Software Foundation, Inc. 59 Temple Place, Suite 330, Boston, MA 02111-1307 USA Everyone is permitted to copy and distribute verbatim copies of this license document, but changing it is not allowed.

0. PREAMBLE

The purpose of this License is to make a manual, textbook, or other functional and useful document "free" in the sense of freedom: to assure everyone the effective freedom to copy and redistribute it, with or without modifying it, either commercially or noncommercially. Secondarily, this License preserves for the author and publisher a way to get credit for their work, while not being considered responsible for modifications made by others.

This License is a kind of "copyleft", which means that derivative works of the document must themselves be free in the same sense. It complements the GNU General Public License, which is a copyleft license designed for free software. We have designed this License in order to use it for manuals for free software, because free software needs free documentation: a free program should come with manuals providing the same freedoms that the software does. But this License is not limited to software manuals; it can be used for any textual work, regardless of subject matter or whether it is published as a printed book. We recommend this License principally for works whose purpose is instruction or reference.

1. APPLICABILITY AND DEFINITIONS

This License applies to any manual or other work, in any medium, that contains a notice placed by the copyright holder saying it can be distributed under the terms of this License. Such a notice grants a world-wide, royalty-free license, unlimited in duration, to use that work under the conditions stated herein. The "Document", below, refers to any such manual or work. Any member of the public is a licensee, and is addressed as "you". You accept the license if you copy, modify or distribute the work in a way requiring permission under copyright law. A "Modified Version" of the Document means any work containing the Document or a portion of it, either copied verbatim, or with modifications and/or translated into another language. A "Secondary Section" is a named appendix or a front-matter section of the Document that deals exclusively with the relationship of the publishers or authors of the Document to the Document's overall subject (or to related matters) and contains nothing that could fall directly within that overall subject. (Thus, if the Document is in part a textbook of mathematics, a Secondary Section may not explain any mathematics.) The relationship could be a matter of historical connection with the subject or with related matters, or of legal, commercial, philosophical, ethical or political position regarding them. The "Invariant Sections" are certain Secondary Sections whose titles are designated, as being those of Invariant Sections, in the notice that says that the Document is released under this License. If a section does not fit the above definition of Secondary then it is not allowed to be designated as Invariant. The Document may contain zero Invariant Sections. If the Document does not identify any Invariant Sections then there are none. The "Cover Texts" are certain short passages of text that are listed, as Front-Cover Texts or Back-Cover Texts, in the notice that says that the Document is released under this License. A Front-Cover Text may be at most 5 words, and a Back-Cover Text may be at most 25 words. A "Transparent" copy of the Document means a machine-readable copy, represented in a format whose specification is available to the general public, that is suitable for revising the document straightforwardly with generic text editors or (for images composed of pixels) generic paint programs or (for drawings) some widely available drawing editor, and that is suitable for input to text formatters or for automatic translation to a variety of formats suitable for input to text formatters. A copy made in an otherwise Transparent file format whose markup, or absence of markup, has been arranged to thwart or discourage subsequent modification by readers is not Transparent. An image format is not Transparent if used for any substantial amount of text. A copy that is not "Transparent" is called "Opaque". Examples of suitable formats for Transparent copies include plain ASCII without markup, Texinfo input format, LaTeX input format, SGML or XML using a publicly available DTD, and standard-conforming simple HTML, PostScript or PDF designed for human modification. Examples of transparent image formats include PNG, XCF and JPG. Opaque formats include proprietary formats that can be read and edited only by proprietary word processors, SGML or XML for which the DTD and/or processing tools are not generally available, and the machine-generated HTML, PostScript or PDF produced by some word processors for output purposes only. The "Title Page" means, for a printed book, the title page itself, plus such following pages as are needed to hold, legibly, the material this License requires to appear in the title page. For works in formats which do not have any title page as such, "Title Page" means the text near the most prominent appearance of the work's title, preceding the beginning of the body of the text. A section "Entitled XYZ" means a named subunit of the Document whose title either is precisely XYZ or contains XYZ in parentheses following text that translates XYZ in another language. (Here XYZ stands for a specific section name mentioned below, such as "Acknowledgements", "Dedications", "Endorsements", or "History".) To "Preserve the Title" of such a section when you modify the Document means that it remains a section "Entitled XYZ" according to this definition. The Document may include Warranty Disclaimers next to the notice which states that this License applies to the Document. These Warranty Disclaimers are considered to be included by reference in this License, but only as regards disclaiming warranties: any other implication that these Warranty Disclaimers may have is void and has no effect on the meaning of this License.

2. VERBATIM COPYING

You may copy and distribute the Document in any medium, either commercially or noncommercially, provided that this License, the copyright notices, and the license notice saying this License applies to the Document are reproduced in all copies, and that you add no other conditions whatsoever to those of this License. You may not use technical measures to obstruct or control the reading or further copying of the copies you make or distribute. However, you may accept compensation in exchange for copies. If you distribute a large enough number of copies you must also follow the conditions in section 3. You may also lend copies, under the same conditions stated above, and you may publicly display copies.

3. COPYING IN QUANTITY

If you publish printed copies (or copies in media that commonly have printed covers) of the Document, numbering more than 100, and the Document's license notice requires Cover Texts, you must enclose the copies in covers that carry, clearly and legibly, all these Cover Texts: Front-Cover Texts on the front cover, and Back-Cover Texts on the back cover. Both covers must also clearly and legibly identify you as the publisher of these copies. The front cover must present the full title with all words of the title equally prominent and visible. You may add other material on the covers in addition. Copying with changes limited to the covers, as long as they preserve the title of the Document and satisfy these conditions, can be treated as verbatim copying in other respects. If the required texts for either cover are too voluminous to fit legibly, you should put the first ones listed (as many as fit reasonably) on the actual cover, and continue the rest onto adjacent pages. If you publish or distribute Opaque copies of the Document numbering more than 100, you must either include a machine-readable Transparent copy along with each Opaque copy, or state in or with each Opaque copy a computer-network location from which the general network-using public has access to download using public-standard network protocols a complete Transparent copy of the Document, free of added material. If you use the latter option, you must take reasonably prudent steps, when you begin distribution of Opaque copies in quantity, to ensure that this Transparent copy will remain thus accessible at the stated location until at least one year after the last time you distribute an Opaque copy (directly or through your agents or retailers) of that edition to the public. It is requested, but not required, that you contact the authors of the Document well before redistributing any large number of copies, to give them a chance to provide you with an updated version of the Document.

4. MODIFICATIONS

You may copy and distribute a Modified Version of the Document under the conditions of sections 2 and 3 above, provided that you release the Modified Version under precisely this License, with the Modified Version filling the role of the Document, thus licensing distribution and modification of the Modified Version to whoever possesses a copy of it. In addition, you must do these things in the Modified Version: A. Use in the Title Page (and on the covers, if any) a title distinct from that of the Document, and from those of previous versions (which should, if there were any, be listed in the History section of the Document). You may use the same title as a previous version if the original publisher of that version gives permission. B. List on the Title Page, as authors, one or more persons or entities responsible for authorship of the modifications in the Modified Version, together with at least five of the principal authors of the Document (all of its principal authors, if it has fewer than five), unless they release you from this requirement. C. State on the Title page the name of the publisher of the Modified Version, as the publisher. D. Preserve all the copyright notices of the Document. E. Add an appropriate copyright notice for your modifications adjacent to the other copyright notices. F. Include, immediately after the copyright notices, a license notice giving the public permission to use the Modified Version under the terms of this License, in the form shown in the Addendum below. G. Preserve in that license notice the full lists of Invariant Sections and required Cover Texts given in the Document's license notice. H. Include an unaltered copy of this License. I. Preserve the section Entitled "History", Preserve its Title, and add to it an item stating at least the title, year, new authors, and publisher of the Modified Version as given on the Title Page. If there is no section "Entitled "History" in the Document, create one stating the title, year, authors, and publisher of the Document as given on its Title Page, then add an item describing the Modified Version as stated in the previous sentence. J. Preserve the network location, if any, given in the Document for public access to a Transparent copy of the Document, and likewise the network locations given in the Document for previous versions it was based on. These may be placed in the "History" section. You may omit a network location for a work that was published at least four years before the Document itself, or if the original publisher of the version it refers to gives permission. K. For any section Entitled "Acknowledgements" or "Dedications", Preserve the Title of the section, and preserve in the section all the substance and tone of each of the contributor acknowledgements and/or dedications given therein. L. Preserve all the Invariant Sections of the Document, unaltered in their text and in their titles. Section numbers or the equivalent are not considered part of the section titles. M. Delete any section Entitled "Endorsements". Such a section may not be included in the Modified Version. N. Do not retitle any existing section to be Entitled "Endorsements" or to conflict in title with any Invariant Section. O. Preserve any Warranty Disclaimers. If the Modified Version includes new front-matter sections or appendices that qualify as Secondary Sections and contain no material copied from the Document, you may at your option designate some or all of these sections as invariant. To do this, add their titles to the list of Invariant Sections in the Modified Version's license notice. These titles must be distinct from any other section titles. You may add a section Entitled "Endorsements", provided it contains nothing but endorsements of your Modified Version by various parties--for example, statements of peer review or that the text has been approved by an organization as the authoritative definition of a standard. You may add a passage of up to five words as a Front-Cover Text, and a passage of up to 25 words as a Back-Cover Text, to the end of the list of Cover Texts in the Modified Version. Only one passage of Front-Cover Text and one of Back-Cover Text may be added by (or through arrangements made by) any one entity. If the Document already includes a cover text for the same cover, previously added by you or by arrangement made by the same entity you are acting on behalf of, you may not add another; but you may replace the old one, on explicit permission from the previous publisher that added the old one. The author(s) and publisher(s) of the Document do not by this License give permission to use their names for publicity for or to assert or imply endorsement of any Modified Version.

5. COMBINING DOCUMENTS

You may combine the Document with other documents released under this License, under the terms defined in section 4 above for modified versions, provided that you include in the combination all of the Invariant Sections of all of the original documents, unmodified, and list them all as Invariant Sections of your combined work in its license notice, and that you preserve all their Warranty Disclaimers. The combined work need only contain one copy of this License, and multiple identical Invariant Sections may be replaced with a single copy. If there are multiple Invariant Sections with the same name but different contents, make the title of each such section unique by adding at the end of it, in parentheses, the name of the original author or publisher of that section if known, or else a unique number. Make the same adjustment to the section titles in the list of Invariant Sections in the license notice of the combined work. In the combination, you must combine any sections Entitled "History" in the various original documents, forming one section Entitled "History"; likewise combine any sections Entitled "Acknowledgements", and any sections Entitled "Dedications". You must delete all sections Entitled "Endorsements".

6. COLLECTIONS OF DOCUMENTS

You may make a collection consisting of the Document and other documents released under this License, and replace the individual copies of this License in the various documents with a single copy that is included in the collection, provided that you follow the rules of this License for verbatim copying of each of the documents in all other respects. You may extract a single document from such a collection, and distribute it individually under this License, provided you insert a copy of this License into the extracted document, and follow this License in all other respects regarding verbatim copying of that document.

7. AGGREGATION WITH INDEPENDENT WORKS

A compilation of the Document or its derivatives with other separate and independent documents or works, in or on a volume of a storage or distribution medium, is called an "aggregate" if the copyright resulting from the compilation is not used to limit the legal rights of the compilation's users beyond what the individual works permit. When the Document is included in an aggregate, this License does not apply to the other works in the aggregate which are not themselves derivative works of the Document. If the Cover Text requirement of section 3 is applicable to these copies of the Document, then if the Document is less than one half of the entire aggregate, the Document's Cover Texts may be placed on covers that bracket the Document within the aggregate, or the electronic equivalent of covers if the Document is in electronic form. Otherwise they must appear on printed covers that bracket the whole aggregate.

8. TRANSLATION

Translation is considered a kind of modification, so you may distribute translations of the Document under the terms of section 4. Replacing Invariant Sections with translations requires special permission from their copyright holders, but you may include translations of some or all Invariant Sections in addition to the original versions of these Invariant Sections. You may include a translation of this License, and all the license notices in the Document, and any Warranty Disclaimers, provided that you also include the original English version of this License and the original versions of those notices and disclaimers. In case of a disagreement between the translation and the original version of this License or a notice or disclaimer, the original version will prevail. If a section in the Document is Entitled "Acknowledgements", "Dedications", or "History", the requirement (section 4) to Preserve its Title (section 1) will typically require changing the actual title.

9. TERMINATION

You may not copy, modify, sublicense, or distribute the Document except as expressly provided for under this License. Any other attempt to copy, modify, sublicense or distribute the Document is void, and will automatically terminate your rights under this License. However, parties who have received copies, or rights, from you under this License will not have their licenses terminated so long as such parties remain in full compliance.

10. FUTURE REVISIONS OF THIS LICENSE

The Free Software Foundation may publish new, revised versions of the GNU Free Documentation License from time to time. Such new versions will be similar in spirit to the present version, but may differ in detail to address new problems or concerns. See http://www.gnu.org/copyleft/. Each version of the License is given a distinguishing version number. If the Document specifies that a particular numbered version of this License "or any later version" applies to it, you have the option of following the terms and conditions either of that specified version or of any later version that has been published (not as a draft) by the Free Software Foundation. If the Document does not specify a version number of this License, you may choose any version ever published (not as a draft) by the Free Software Foundation ADDENDUM: How to use this License for your documents To use this License in a document you have written, include a copy of the License in the document and put the following copyright and license notices just after the title page: Copyright (c) YEAR YOUR NAME. Permission is granted to copy, distribute and/or modify this document under the terms of the GNU Free Documentation License, Version 1.2 or any later version published by the Free Software Foundation; with no Invariant Sections, no Front-Cover Texts, and no Back-Cover Texts. A copy of the license is included in the section entitled "GNU Free Documentation License". If you have Invariant Sections, Front-Cover Texts and Back-Cover Texts, replace the "with...Texts." line with this: with the Invariant Sections being LIST THEIR TITLES, with the Front-Cover Texts being LIST, and with the Back-Cover Texts being LIST. If you have Invariant Sections without Cover Texts, or some other combination of the three, merge those two alternatives to suit the situation. If your document contains nontrivial examples of program code, we recommend releasing these examples in parallel under your choice of free software license, such as the GNU General Public License, to permit their use in free software.

Lightning Source UK Ltd.
Milton Keynes UK
UKOW04f0727010715

254408UK00001B/53/P